Lone Star Vistas

Bridwell Texas History Series

Lone Star Vistas

Travel Writing on Texas, 1821–1861

Astrid Haas

University of Texas Press ⟁ Austin

Requests for permission to reproduce material from this work should be sent to:
Permissions
University of Texas Press
P.O. Box 7819
Austin, TX 78713–7819
utpress.utexas.edu/rp-form

♾ The paper used in this book meets the minimum requirements of ANSI/NISO Z39.48–1992 (R1997) (Permanence of Paper).

Library of Congress Cataloging-in-Publication Data

Names: Haas, Astrid, author.
Title: Lone Star Vistas : Travel Writing on Texas, 1821–1861 / Astrid Haas.
Other titles: Bridwell Texas history series.
Description: First edition. | Austin : University of Texas Press, 2021. | Series: Bridwell Texas history series | Includes bibliographical references and index.
Identifiers: LCCN 2020034107
        ISBN 978-1-4773-2260-4 (cloth)
        ISBN 978-1-4773-2261-1 (library ebook)
        ISBN 978-1-4773-2262-8 (non-library ebook)
Subjects: LCSH: Travel writing—Texas—History—19th century—Case studies. | Travelers' writings, American—Texas. | Travelers' writings, Mexican—Texas. | Travelers' writings, German—Texas. | Texas—Description and travel—History—19th century—Case studies.
Classification: LCC F386 .H275 2021 | DDC 917.64/05—dc23
LC record available at https://lccn.loc.gov/2020034107

doi:10.7560/322604

Contents

Lone Star Vistas

Introduction

[Texas is] the most deserted part of a sparsely populated province.
... The climate is scorching, the soil ... very fertile. ... The coast is
bad, without a known port, full of shallows and dotted with small
islands inhabited by independent Indians. ... The part that Your
Excellency claims does not include any towns except for the miserable, small San Antonio de Bexar. ... This is a virgin land and uninhabited. The Spaniards of Mexico ... have not had any reason to
spread there. ... The Indians, on the contrary, have withdrawn to the
North, where they live like Arab shepherds and ... Bedouin thieves.

ALEXANDER VON HUMBOLDT TO THOMAS JEFFERSON, 1804

All the country to the west of the Mississippi, from the Ox River
to the Rio Colorado of Texas is uninhabited. These steppes, partly
marshy, present obstacles ... which the industry of new colonists
will soon penetrate. In the United States the population ... flowed
first towards the Ohio and the Tennessee [Rivers], and then towards
Louisiana. A part of this fluctuating population will soon move
farther to the westward.

ALEXANDER VON HUMBOLDT, *POLITICAL ESSAY ON THE
KINGDOM OF NEW SPAIN* (1811)

In June 1804, US president Thomas Jefferson asked Alexander von Humboldt to
furnish him with information on Texas (Humboldt, *Briefe*, 296).[1] Drawing on
material he had collected during his recent stay in Mexico, the German scientist
responded with a brief account of the population groups and economic potential
of the region. Seven years later, he predicted in his *Political Essay on the Kingdom
of New Spain* (1811) the process of United States territorialization, that is, of
Anglo-American settlement and appropriation of the land (Doolen 6, 8–10).
Although Humboldt never set foot on Texas soil, these passages capture the
ambivalent elements that were soon to profoundly inform the experiences of visitors and immigrants to the region. Unhealthy, infertile marshlands and conflicts
with Amerindian nations troubled many travelers. Simultaneously, abundant

productive soil and access to the sea promised opportunities for farmers and traders, whereas the wilderness lured adventurers and naturalists. As a result, Texas underwent a profound demographic, economic, and sociocultural transformation during the second quarter of the nineteenth century. Between 1821 and 1861, the region turned from a sparsely settled Mexican province overlapping with the areas of residence of several Native nations into an Anglo-dominated slave state of the United States with a growing European immigrant community and a shrinking indigenous presence.

The Native nations were "full-fledged historical actors who played a formative role in the making of early America" (Hämäläinen 6). Yet the three population groups whose text production most profoundly shaped public perceptions and representations of Texas were Mexicans, Anglo-Americans, and Europeans, particularly Germans. The United States and Mexico were the two nations that claimed the territory, and Germans formed the largest group of European immigrants to the region. They also penned the largest body of travel and migration literature about Texas, after the Anglo-Americans (Sibley 167). As Mike Crang argues, "Most people's knowledge of most places comes through media of various sorts, so that for most people the representation comes before the 'reality'" and "literature . . . plays a central role in shaping people's geographical imaginations" (44). Thus, written texts create "literary landscapes" (Crang 7) or "imaginative geographies" (Said, *Orientalism*, 55, 71) that powerfully inform perceptions and representations of places—and the people associated with them. In nineteenth-century North America, "the invention of a continental imaginary was an essential element in the process of territorialization," Andy Doolen observes. "Travelers, novelists, politicians, newspapermen, explorers, poets, merchants, and many others . . . collectively authored the spatial logic of an enlarged [US or Mexican] republic" whose claims to the contested terrain they sought to legitimize (10–11).

TRAVEL, EXPLORATION, AND COLONIZATION

The present study analyzes narrative constructions of Texas from 1821 to 1861 in selected works of travel writing by representatives of these three groups of visitors. Among the genres of writing, written journey accounts have often played a prominent role in informing conceptualizations of geographies and identities (Clifford 3). Travel writing is a hybrid genre. Integrating elements of a variety of text types, including scientific reports, diaries, memoirs, letters, and works of fiction, it frequently blurs the boundaries of factual and fictional writing and appeals to readers, since it provides them with knowledge about unfamiliar places and peoples based on travelers' supposedly authentic, individual experiences

(Blanton 2–29; Ette 25–31). But journey accounts are always culturally prefigured. Writers' backgrounds, previously available information on journeys and destinations, and literary canons of textual depiction inform practices of traveling and writing. Many journey narratives are compiled from authors' travel notes, retrospectively structured and shaped into a coherent narrative. Writers further select and present pieces of information from external sources to support the traveler-narrators' voices and the authority of their own accounts. As a result, travelogues offer models of journeying, observing, and representing places and people, and these models inform both subsequent travels and writing conventions (Ette 24–25, 29–41; Nünning 12–22, 25).

In its broadest sense, the term "travel writing" can refer to all kinds of journey narratives, including fictional accounts. Narrow definitions, in contrast, tend to limit the term to narratives of actual travels penned for publication and written with a subjective "literary purpose" (Blanton 4–5). Although Texas became the subject of a large body of travel accounts during the mid-nineteenth century (Callahan; Doughty; Ritzenhofen; Sibley), the region attracted neither professional travel writers nor leisure travelers at the time (Sibley 4–6, 10). Therefore, the present study analyzes texts written for private circulation or for publication that claim to narrate facts observed on actual journeys undertaken by their authors for a variety of purposes. Thus, the study builds on and develops Magnus Mörner's division of nineteenth-century travel narratives into text types. In addition to the text production by literary travelers and tourists, Mörner distinguishes among scientific exploration accounts, travelogues that either promote or warn against migration, and narratives of itinerant professionals. The last text corpus includes accounts by soldiers, governmental agents, missionaries, traders, sailors, adventurers, and wives of officers or merchants (Mörner 96–97). Connected with some of the major pillars of society—the state, the military, private investors, the churches, and the press—most of these text categories articulate perspectives of deep societal impact: the type and purpose of the journeys undertaken most profoundly informed functions and target audiences of the narratives recording these trips. The travelers' ethnic and national vantage points shaped the concerns and perspective of their journey accounts, as did their gender, social class, religious affiliation, and political bent. Finally, the political, economic, and social development of Texas from 1821 to 1861 influenced visitors' perceptions of the region.

This last point is particularly relevant, since the major contribution of travel writing to public discourse is its engagement with geographic and sociocultural differences. Traveler-narrators usually address audiences from their own sociocultural and linguistic backgrounds (Ette 18–19, 29; Nünning 16). To render unknown places and people comprehensible to wide audiences, their texts engage in strategies that "both familiarize and distance the foreign" (Blanton 5). Travelers commonly provide comparisons and contrasts between the territories and societies they encountered during their journeys and those they share with their target audiences. Moreover, Western travelogues frequently make cultural and intertextual references—most prominently to mythology, scripture, works of literature, history, and travel writing—to underline notions of topographical or cultural similarity or difference. Simultaneously, they position themselves and their texts in the Western intellectual tradition and its canon of journey narratives (Blanton 1–2; Ette 18, 24). While some travelers use portrayals of sociocultural otherness to scrutinize their home cultures, most authors not only affirm the perspectives and interests of their sponsors and target readers but also posit the superiority of their civilizations over others (Ette 24; Nünning 16).

As Edward Said reminds us, social power relations determine topics and modes of representation (*Culture and Imperialism*, 80). By conveying certain images of places and people while suppressing alternative representations, narrative texts have prominently contributed to discourses of colonization (xii–xiii). Applying a postcolonial studies perspective is particularly fruitful for the study of Texas in the second quarter of the nineteenth century. Scholars have pointed out that a postcolonial condition does not necessitate anticolonial consciousness and that the United States during the late eighteenth century and throughout the nineteenth was "both postrevolutionary and colonizing" at the same time (Mackenthun 12; see also Doolen 15 and Mignolo 54, 94, 97). In both Mexico and the United States, the settler descendants of European colonizers, not the indigenous or enslaved Black populations, formed their nations' postindependence elites (Mignolo 137–139). Unsurprisingly, they upheld unequal power structures that privileged populations of European descent over all others, based on their presumed racial superiority and exclusive association with modernity, rationality, and civilization (Mignolo 22–23, 30–31; Quijano 170–174).

Although both the United States and Mexico engaged in the rhetoric of anticolonial commitment during the nineteenth century, they simultaneously pursued a discourse that justified white settlement and Amerindian subjugation within their territories (Hernández; Rifkin). The United States further upheld African American slavery in the South and oppressed its Hispanic minorities (Mackenthun 4, 11–18, 22–26; McDougall 57–98; Rifkin). As a region claimed by both Mexico and the United States, Texas between 1821 and 1861 provides a unique case. Here, United States expansionism was met with Mexican and Amerindian resistance to the growing Anglo hegemony. Both US and Mexican public discourses about the region framed it as an outpost of civilization whose socioeconomic development required further colonization and government by their populations. This line of reasoning strongly resonated with political players and intellectuals in Europe. Most prominently, Germany witnessed both a large migration wave to the Americas, especially to the United States, and a vivid public debate about German overseas settlement. Driven by the popular desire for stronger national unity, greater international influence, and domestic economic relief, one line of discourse advocated establishing German settler colonies in rather sparsely populated and uncultivated regions such as Texas. Its purposes were twofold: open new markets for German businesses and financial investments, and reduce the risk of poverty-induced political unrest in Germany by encouraging the country's poor to relocate overseas (Fenske).

With its focus on Anglo-American, Mexican, and German travelogues of Texas from 1821 to 1861, my study is steeped in the research paradigms of borderlands studies (Hämäläinen and Truett; Mignolo), Inter-American studies (Bauer; Fox and Sadowski-Smith), and Atlantic studies (Cañizares-Esguerra and Breen; Gabbaccia). In its Inter-American dimension, it foregrounds the political, economic, and sociocultural conflicts and connections between Latin and Anglo-American nineteenth-century Texans, and it draws on scholarship from both the United States and Mexico. The book is further indebted to the approach of the new western history and its understanding of the frontier—the contested contact zone between Euro-American colonists and resident indigenous nations, an area whose "geographic and cultural borders were not clearly defined" (Adelman and Aron 815). Following Pekka Hämäläinen, I view the North American frontier as "a socially charged space where Indians and invaders competed for resources and land but also shared skills, foods, fashions, customs, languages, and beliefs" (7). Similarly, my study treats Texas from 1821 to 1861 as a borderland region, that is, as an "ambitious and often-unstable [realm] where boundaries are also crossroads, peripheries are also central places, homelands are also passing-through places, and the end points of empire are also forks in the road" (Hämäläinen and Truett 338).

Moreover, while existing scholarship on the US-Mexico border region has largely focused on Anglo-Mexican or white-Amerindian relations, my comparative approach enlarges this perspective to include other major participants in the formation of nineteenth-century Texas cultures as they manifested themselves in the eyes of travel writers. These actors include a large number of German immigrants whose presence in the region provided another connection with the Atlantic world. I read Texas in the second quarter of the nineteenth century as an example of what Nathaniel Millett calls the "Atlantic Borderlands"—areas that belonged to the Atlantic world and were characterized by "borderlands conditions" (273–277). Texas in this period was a much-contested borderland region between the United States, Mexico, and several Native nations; a potential British and French pawn against US territorial expansion; a destination for European migration and colonization endeavors; and a part of indigenous and colonial Inter-American and Atlantic trade networks.

TRAVELING TERMS

Writing about the Americas and a contested borderland region of Anglo, Native, and Latin America such as nineteenth-century Texas requires some clarification about the terminology used to denote places and people. I am aware that the terms "America" and "American" refer to the entire Americas and not merely to the United States. But for reasons of readability and a lack of useful alternatives, I follow the convention of employing these terms as references to the United States and US Americans. While US Americans of European descent are commonly not identified by their ethnicities, I use the terms "Euro-American" and "Anglo-American" to denote white American populations of, respectively, European and British descent. Although Germany did not exist as a nation-state until 1871, I use "Germany" as an umbrella term for the thirty-nine states joined in the German Confederation (1815–1866), and "Germans" for their hegemonic populations. While I employ "Mexican" to denote ethnically Mexican populations, I also refer to the Mexicans of Texas by the already widespread self-designation "Tejanas/os." Similarly, I use the terms "Black" and "African American" to denote the African-descendant population of Texas, the clear majority of which at the time studied here were brought to the region as slaves from the United States. "Amerindians" and "Natives," along with the descriptor "indigenous," are the umbrella terms I employ interchangeably for the aboriginal populations and civilizations of North America, except for established terms. When speaking about specific Amerindian peoples, I use their individual nations' names, following conventional English spelling for reasons of familiarity. Because national borders were drawn and redrawn across many Native nations' territories of residence, and because neither the indigenous populations identified with the new nation-states nor the states themselves recognized Amerindians as citizens of the newly formed polities, using terms such as "Native Americans" or "Native Mexicans" seems inadequate.

I use "North American West" to denote those regions that today belong to the United States but formerly (in part) also to Britain, France, Spain, or Mexico and that lay beyond the—always vaguely defined and constantly moving—Anglo-American line of settlement. To refer to locations in Texas, I use the currently employed names. In the case of major towns and rivers, such as San Antonio, Goliad, or the Rio Grande, which were alternatively, and often primarily, known by their (usually earlier) Spanish names from the 1820s through the 1850s, I add the Spanish name in parentheses when mentioning a location for the first time. Finally, although some scholars distinguish among terms such as "travelogue," "travel narrative," and "journey account," depending on particular types of travel texts, I use these and related terms interchangeably. I do this to avoid tedious repetitions and to sidestep a hierarchization of travel texts based on presumed differences in the cultural "value" associated with their aesthetic qualities, social contexts, or political agendas.

RESEARCHING TEXAS TRAVELS

Although a comprehensive body of research exists on both European and American travelogues of the United States, including Texas (Birkle 198), Latin American journey narratives about the United States have received little attention to date (Haas, "Monroe Doctrine"; Carballo). Further, no single study currently offers a comparative in-depth analysis of selected American, Mexican, and German (or any other nation's) travelogues about Texas throughout its Mexican, independent, and antebellum US periods. Both Sister Generosa Callahan's unpublished dissertation, "The Literature of Travel in Texas, 1803–1846" (1945), and Marilyn McAdams Sibley's *Travelers in Texas, 1761–1860* (1967) study nineteenth-century travel narratives of Texas. Although they performed pioneering work in assembling a large number and generic variety of texts, the two volumes remain rather descriptive and offer little in-depth analysis of the material. Similarly, Del Weniger's two-volume *The Explorers' Texas* (1984, 1997) discusses journey accounts from the seventeenth century to the mid-nineteenth as sources for reconstructing the nature and wildlife of the region and does not interrogate their textual constructions of places and people. In contrast, Andrea Kökény's essay "Travellers and Settlers in Mexican Texas" (2002) focuses on travelogues of Texas, but deals with only a single ethnic group and a very short period. And although it addresses American and European travelogues, Robin Doughty's *At Home in Texas: Early Views of the Land* (1987) also draws on a host of other text types, such as memoirs or novels, from the 1820s to the early twentieth century.

Several scholarly works on specific types of travelogues of the North American West address nineteenth-century Texas journey accounts. Samuel Geiser's *Naturalists of the Frontier* (1937; 2nd ed., 1948), Eric Sundquist's "Exploration and Empire" (1995), and William Goetzmann's *Exploration and Empire: The Explorer and the Scientist in the Winning of the American West* (1966; rpt., 2003) and his *New Lands, New Men: America and the Second Great Age of Discovery* (1986/1995) analyze scientific expedition accounts of the region. John Miller Morris's *El Llano Estacado: Exploration and Imagination on the High Plains of Texas and New Mexico, 1536–1860* (1999) focuses on such journey accounts of the Texas–New Mexico border region. Goetzmann's *Army Exploration in the American West, 1803–1863* (1959;rev. ed., 1991) and Vincent Ponko's "The Military Explorers of the American West, 1838–1860" (1997) analyze American military exploration of the North American West. This text corpus is discussed alongside soldiers' memoirs in Sherry Lynn Smith's *The View from Officers' Row: Army Perceptions of Western Indians* (1990) and Michael Tate's *The Frontier Army in the Settlement of the West* (1999).

Narratives by nineteenth-century American women travelers and settlers in the North American West have recently received greater attention. Among this body of scholarship, Nina Baym's *Women Writers of the American West, 1833–1927* (2011) covers a broad range of text types and literary subject matters. Sandra Myres's *Westering Women and the Frontier Experience, 1800–1915* (1982; rev. ed., 1993), Annette Kolodny's *The Land before Her: Fantasy and Experience of the American Frontiers, 1630–1860* (1984), Brigitte Georgi-Findlay's *The Frontiers of Women's Writing: Women's Narratives and the Rhetoric of Westward Expansion* (1996), and Adrienne Caughfield's *True Women and Westward Expansion* (2005) study women's narratives of western overland travels. But only a few of the works analyzed in these studies touch on Texas. In contrast, Myres's "Army Women's Narratives as Documents of Social History: Some Examples from the Western Frontier" (1990) and "Women and the Texas Military Experience: The Nineteenth Century" (1995), Robin Dell Campbell's *Mistresses of the Transient Hearth: American Army Officers' Wives and Material Culture, 1840–1880* (2005), and Smith's *The View from Officers' Row* discuss travelogues of Texas. Yet they also study other text genres, such as letters and memoirs of US officers' wives about their sojourns at army posts in the North American West.

While there is substantial scholarship on nineteenth-century German travelogues of North America and the period's German writing about the region, only a few of the analyses address journey accounts of Texas. Peter Brenner's *Reisen in die "Neue Welt": Die Erfahrung Nordamerikas in deutschen Reise- und Auswanderberichten des 19. Jahrhunderts* (1991), Stephan Görisch's *Information zwischen Werbung und Warnung: Die Rolle der Amerikaliteratur in der Auswanderung des 18. und 19. Jahrhunderts* (1991), and Wolfgang Helbich's "Land der unbegrenzten Möglichkeiten? Das Amerika-Bild der deutschen Auswanderer im 19. Jahrhundert" (1993) treat travelogues of Texas rather marginally. This leaves Ute Ritzenhofen's *Amerikas Italien: Deutsche Texasbilder des neunzehnten Jahrhunderts* (1997) as the only study to date that deals exclusively with German travelers to Texas in the period covered by this volume. Ritzenhofen also addresses fictional journey narratives as well as emigration guides not based on the writers' trips, alongside travel narratives based on firsthand observations, and hence she addresses a wider range of primary texts and their genre-related thematic concerns than I do.

Research on Mexican journeys to Texas in the first half of the nineteenth century is scarce. Mexican visitors to the region at the time rarely wrote accounts of their journeys (Weber 383–385), and Mexicans who traveled to the United States usually bypassed Texas. Thus, scholarship on these bodies of texts hence rarely addresses the region (Haas, "Monroe Doctrine" 30–32). In a similar vein, only a few studies of the period's Mexican discourse on the "Texas question" discuss Mexican journey accounts of the region. Moisés González Navarro's *Los extranjeros en México y los mexicanos en el extranjero, 1821–1970* (1993), Emmanuel Carballo's *¿Qué país es este? Los Estados Unidos y los gringos vistos por escritores mexicanos de los siglos XIX y XX* (1996), and Enrique Rajchenberg and Catherine Héau-Lambert's "La frontera en la comunidad imaginada del siglo XIX" (2007) and "*¿Wilderness* vs. desierto? Representaciones del septentrión mexicano en el siglo XIX" (2009) analyze a variety of text types, most of which address Mexican journeys to the United States or the Mexican North. Nettie Lee Benson's "Texas as Viewed from Mexico, 1820–1834" (1987) and my "Mexican Travelers and the 'Texas Question,' 1821–1836" (2016) focus on Texas but draw on text types besides journey accounts. Since no Mexican-written travel account of Mexican journeys to the Lone Star State from 1836 to 1861 is known, these studies limit themselves to analyzing journeys to Mexican Texas.

Against this backdrop, I undertook the first comparative study of narrative constructions of Texas from 1821 to 1861 in journey accounts penned by members of the three largest nonnative ethnic groups that traveled to and settled in the region during the period. Since Anglo-Americans authored the largest and most formally diverse body of travelogues about Texas during the second quarter of the nineteenth century, most of the texts studied here belong to this corpus. My discussion excludes reports about coerced journeys, especially Indian captivity narratives (Sibley 8, 80–82, 186), since their purposes and concerns significantly differed from those of the text types I focus on (Sayre). For the same reason, I do not include African American slave narratives here. All known Texas slave narratives are oral histories collected during the 1930s and thus fall beyond the time frame of my study (Baker and Baker; Tyler and Murphy). Moreover, no Texas travelogue by a free African American from the time is known, and the single known Amerindian journey account about the region during the era offers few descriptions of the land and its resident populations (Oo-Chee-Ah). Consequently, no texts by Black or Native authors are discussed here.

In contrast, European travelers and immigrants, particularly from Ireland, France, Austria-Hungary, and the Nordic countries, produced a sizable body of journey accounts during the time, and they have been addressed in single-nation studies (Davis; Lagarde; Machann and Mendl; Scott). Their observations, experiences, and representations of the region at least partially overlap with the perception of their German counterparts. Therefore, and to avoid a lack of focus by discussing texts from too many national backgrounds, I limited my analysis of European travelogues to German texts. While they relate to the situation of nineteenth-century German lands, they simultaneously voice attitudes and experiences shared by many other European travelers and immigrants to Texas at the time. I therefore read them as representative of a European perspective in addition to a specifically German one.

CONTENTS OF THE BOOK

The core of this book includes a textual analysis of works of travel writing based on a theory-informed close reading of the journey accounts in their sociocultural contexts and as contributions to discourses that targeted particular audiences. Rather than examining an exhaustive number of texts, I discuss a series of paradigmatic case studies of travelogues that represent types of journey narratives and their poetic specificities. Because of the large number of potential sources, all the narratives analyzed in the following chapters focus exclusively on Texas and its immediate surroundings, including the area between the Nueces River and the Rio Grande, which did not belong to the region before 1848. This book examines how Texas travelogues by representatives of these groups contributed to conceptualizations of "Texas" as a geographic and social space against the backdrop of the authors' national public discourses, on the one hand, and of the journeys undertaken, on the other. Owing to the entangled social discourses of nature and cultures, my analysis integrates the texts' representations of Texas landscapes and their depictions of the region's different population groups. I particularly interrogate how descriptions and characterizations of places and peoples interact, inform one another, and thereby establish argumentative links between territories and societies to justify ideological agendas. I argue that these texts construct notions of Texas's nature and cultures to affirm their writers' self-identifications and value systems, and that they are thereby implicated in discourses or policies of colonization and settlement, territorial expansion, economic exploitation, and ideological appropriation.

In part I of my study, "Military-Scientific Exploration," chapter 1 examines official reports and private accounts documenting the military-scientific tours of inspection in which the Mexican Comisión de Límites of 1828–1829 and the Mexican Army colonel Juan Nepomuceno Almonte in 1834 assessed conditions on the then-Mexican province. Its second chapter discusses the accounts of two military-scientific expeditions led by US Army captain Randolph B. Marcy to survey North Texas and locate land on which to set up the first Indian reservations in the 1850s. In part II, "Colonization and Settlement," chapter 3 turns to the

discussion of Anglo-American colonization in the travelogues of the colonization agent Stephen F. Austin and his cousin Mary Austin Holley, as well as the
report that Joshua James and Alexander MacRae penned about the region for the
Wilmington Emigration Society. The fourth and fifth chapters are dedicated to
five German journey narratives addressing German migration to Texas. While
the merchant Detlef Dunt, the emigration agent Carl of Solms-Braunfels, and
the geologist Ferdinand Roemer sought to entice Germans to settle in the region,
the narratives of the German migrants Eduard Ludecus and Jakob Thran warn
against such endeavors. Part III, "Professional Journeys," looks at travelogues
by writers who journeyed through or temporarily settled in Texas as part of
their professions or as accompanying spouses. Chapter 6 examines how the
Anglo-Protestant missionaries Orceneth Fisher and Melinda Rankin sought to
mobilize Catholics and the unchurched for their brands of faith through their
accounts of missionary labor. The seventh chapter studies the accounts that
two US Army officers' wives, Teresa Griffin Vielé and Eliza Griffin Johnston,
penned about their Texas sojourns with their husbands' regiments. Chapter
8 analyzes how two journalists, Jane McManus Cazneau and Frederick Law
Olmsted, reported on the Lone Star State for American audiences concerned
with the impact of westward expansion and Black slavery on the nation. Since
no texts by Mexican or German missionaries or military wives are known, nor
are any Mexican journalistic accounts, and since German journalists reporting
about Texas were resident immigrants rather than temporary travelers, this part
remains limited to the perspectives of Anglo-Americans.

PART I

Military-Scientific Exploration

During the colonial period, the Spanish Crown deployed military and civilian explorers to the North American West to survey and claim the land (R. B. Campbell, *Gone to Texas* 24–37, 45–61, 64–71; Goetzmann, *Exploration and Empire* 15–16, 38–41, 68–70). Americans followed them after the Louisiana Purchase of 1803. Throughout the nineteenth century, the US government sent a series of military-scientific expeditions to reconnoiter both the newly acquired territory and the remaining continent west of the US border (Goetzmann, *Army Exploration*; Goetzmann, *Exploration and Empire* 41–64, 146–159, 231–312; Ponko). Their stated goals were "to expand American political and economic influence and control ... and to learn about the resource base of the continental interior ... for the long-range objectives of an expanding agricultural and industrial civilization" (Ponko 332–333). Mexico, in contrast, did not advance such a politics of territorial gain. Yet, concerned with maintaining the country's territorial integrity in the face of growing domestic separatism and increasing American expansionism, the Mexican government, too, deployed several military-scientific expeditions to obtain information about the country's northern provinces. Moreover, the unknown West resonated with scientists in Europe. Throughout the nineteenth century, several European naturalists, sometimes sponsored by a learned society such as Britain's Royal Society or the Berlin Academy of Sciences, explored the nature and indigenous civilizations of the region (Goetzmann, *Exploration and Empire* 76–77, 159–168, 181–198; Greenfield 11, 21–22).

In addition to collecting and classifying plant and animal specimens, rock samples, and Amerindian cultural artifacts, civilian and military scientists from Europe and North America claimed authority, significance, and legitimacy by publicizing their observations in written travel accounts (Greenfield 18–19, 24–27, 78–80). These texts

1

crucially "rationalized the extension of state power into contested border zones" (Doolen 56). They formed part of a larger body of exploration writing on the West penned by trappers, traders, adventurers, soldiers, and professional authors and encompassing diverse formats, including private diaries, travelogues, newspaper reports, and narrative fiction (Goetzmann, *Exploration and Empire* 17–35, 64–68, 70–76, 105–145; Bryan). Besides showing similarities with other travel texts, exploration accounts reached out to audiences beyond the realm of those interested in the sciences (Greenfield 17). Since the military and civilian scientists who participated in such expeditions were overwhelmingly white men from the upper and middle classes, their texts tend to articulate and cater to the political, economic, strategic, and scientific concerns of these hegemonic social groups (Pratt 34–35, 55).

Brad Hume convincingly argues that neither the "Romantic imagination," which framed exploration as a heroic journey, nor the "scientific imagination," which emphasized the production of scientific knowledge, characterizes the scientific exploration accounts of the first half of the nineteenth century, which instead exhibit a blend of both approaches (302–314). At the time, this subgenre of the travelogue developed into a structured report, often following the model of Alexander von Humboldt's travel narratives (Brenner 77, 234–235, 237; Pratt 109–137) in their organization and approach to their subject matter. These works sought to provide audiences with hitherto little-known facts about places and people that would satisfy curiosity, follow standards of scientific observation and description, and serve the political and economic interests of their authors (Brenner 193, 197–198, 203–238, 240, 243). Consequently, Bruce Robert Greenfield observes, the writers "restricted themselves to reporting on what they . . . actually saw and experienced; they told their stories from the observer's point of view; they focused on regions that were 'unknown' to their readers; . . . and they held out the advancement of scientific knowledge as a concern transcending their more immediate practical goals" (71).

To underline their claims to factual objectivity, explorers commonly integrated tables, maps, statistics, and references to the writings of other scientists or travelers into their journey narratives. Using comparisons with familiar equivalents, the exploration accounts render unknown natural phenomena and cultural practices comprehensible to their target audiences. Illustrations provided not only visual documentation but also alluring images that inspired readers' imaginations about the newly explored areas. Many reports of expeditions further complement or replace chronological narratives with a systematic overview of the explorers' findings, usually divided into disciplinary categories such as geography, geology, climate, agriculture, trade, history, and population groups (Brenner 223–228; Goetzmann, *Exploration and Empire* 312–329; Hume 305–308, 311).

Most of the American and European civilian scientists who explored Texas during the second quarter of the nineteenth century published accounts largely concerned with scientific matters (Geiser; Lawson 1–5, 24, 79; Sibley 5–6, 9–10, 179, 192). The only notable exceptions include several posthumously published travelogues. The naturalist Gideon Lincecum's "Journal of Lincecum's Travels in Texas, 1835," not published until 1949, resulted from his first trip to the region, whereas accounts of his later travels appeared in 1994 in a collection of autobiographical texts, *Adventures of a Frontier Naturalist: The Life and Times of Dr. Gideon Lincecum* (Haas, "Nature"). Similarly, the ornithologist John James Audubon published a report of his trip to the Galveston area in 1837 in his memoir, *The Life of John James Audubon, the Naturalist* (1870). The chapters in this section focus exclusively on accounts resulting from military scientific expeditions.

The dominance of military exploration of the North American West placed written accounts of these journeys at the forefront of shaping public knowledge of and opinion about the region. Many reports of expeditions praise western landscapes as unrivaled sublime spectacles and proudly assert the geological age of North America, countering the widespread European belief that the continent was a rather recent geological formation. Simultaneously, they present the region as suitable for white settlement and promote its economic exploitation (Greenfield 82–88; Hume 306, 309–310). The military expedition accounts further differ from the narratives of civilians in their articulating the function and authority of the expeditions as official representatives of their national governments (Greenfield 77–82). They thus embody what John Miller Morris calls "scientific imperialism": the use of science and scientific discourse to legitimize colonial agendas (251). These included the westward expansion of the United States, with its attendant Amerindian displacement and spread of Black slavery; the Mexican subjugation of indigenous populations; Mexico's attempts to ward off American encroachments on its territory; and European projects of large-scale overseas migration and settlement.

Despite the writers' entanglement in colonial policies, nineteenth-century military-scientific exploration accounts often engage in a discourse of "anti-conquest" (Pratt 8–9). According to Mary Louise Pratt, the term designates "a Utopian, innocent version of European" or Euro–North American "global authority" that voices "a great longing for a way of taking possession without subjugation and violence" (38, 56). This view particularly manifests itself in the expedition reports' depictions of nature. Although the visitors' active gaze commanded the vistas around them, many present themselves as passive onlookers rather than conquerors. Moreover, their narratives often aestheticize the terrain to be claimed by applying the categories of visual art as a way to provide structure to the surveyed spaces and to convey the travelers' sensual responses. Panoramic views from elevated vantage points engendered a sense of entitlement to the land, a gesture that Pratt labels the "monarch of all I survey" trope. Framing the land overviewed as empty and therefore "calling" for human intervention to put it to use is a common strategy for claiming possession. Such views of landscapes often entail a vision of such future use by populations of European descent (Pratt 201; Doolen 154; Spurr 96, 99). In addition to aesthetic experiences, exploration accounts foreground the scientific value and economic potential of a given terrain for settlement, mineral exploration, overland travel, or trade (Hume 209; Spurr 28–29). "This scientization of the landscape," Morris argues, "was . . . a discourse of power, a path to both dominance and affection over the new land" (339).

This sense of entitlement to not only view but also possess the lands of the North American West is embedded in Eurocentric and Americentric notions of civilization, modernity, and rationality (Quijano 168, 171–174). This sense also provides the backdrop for the ways the American, Mexican, and European exploration accounts of the West portray the region's resident Amerindian nations. Based on individual experiences with Natives and on notions of them as "inferior" races and cultures (Quijano 171), Mexican and American military-scientific exploration accounts depict this populace as a hindrance to white settlement and progress. The texts tended to both endorse and contribute to the two countries' policies of subjugating or relocating the Amerindians. Despite this, several US Army officers' narratives of the 1850s acknowledge that contact with white settlers, traders, soldiers, and governmental agents brought harm to the Natives, which the government should compensate for by assisting the indigenous nations in assimilating to Anglo-American society (S. Smith 20–27, 93–125).

Like other travelogues of the North American West, military-scientific exploration accounts commonly adopted the hierarchical classification of the indigenous population introduced by British and Spanish colonizers (Spurr 73–74). Depending on their perceived way of life and relations with whites, especially their readiness to adopt Christianity, pursue agriculture, and submit to colonial rule, Native nations were categorized as either "friendly" or "warlike/barbarous" (Berkhofer 10–12; Rifkin 111–112, 126–138; Velasco Ávila 441–450, 453). This approach included using—and, at times, revising—indigenous stereotypes such as the innocent, precontact "noble savage," the nomadic "wild savage," who resisted civilization, and the postcontact "degraded Indian," who had adopted the vices of whites but not their virtues (Berkhofer 28–30, 72–80; S. Smith 12, 20, 27, 30–31, 56–57; Spurr 125–126, 132, 159).

At the same time, the narratives homogenize the Amerindians by treating their physical appearance, "character," cultural practices, and individual behavior as generic expressions of their shared "Indian race." In particular, they use exotic images of "savage" Otherness to emphasize how indigenous tribes differ ethnically and culturally from the travelers (Berkhofer 25–28; Brenner 199–218; Spurr 62, 65–66, 76, 98–99). As Richard Francaviglia points out, many Americans journeying to the West (and the same was true of many Europeans) made sense of the region's unfamiliar places and peoples by comparing them with popular images of the Orient—which encompassed North Africa, the Middle East, and Central Asia in most people's views—known to American and European readers from fiction, travelogues, and the Bible. In reports from military-scientific expeditions, especially in depictions of indigenous gender roles and warfare, stereotypes of "Oriental" cruelty and masculine sexual license frequently recur (*Go East* 37–39, 42, 56, 59–62, 130–132). Moreover, the texts often treat Natives as an integral part of nature whose "primitive" stage of development and mobile way of life disqualified them from claiming either autonomy or territory. Through this Natives-as-nature trope, exploration accounts contributed to the colonial discourses and policies of Native subjugation and white territorial expansion (Brenner 213–216; Doolen 154–155; Spurr 69–70, 86, 99, 156–164). "The anti-conquest," Mary Louise Pratt concludes, thus "'underwrite[s]' colonial appropriation, even as it rejects the rhetoric ... of conquest and subjugation" (52).

The Mexican public showed little interest in Texas, viewing Mexico's Far North primarily as a sparsely settled, hostile wilderness. Although the Spanish colonial government had repeatedly deployed military and scientific expeditions to Texas (Sibley 4, 32, 173), the only Mexican travelogues about Texas after Mexican independence include reports from two expeditions the Mexican government deployed to inspect the province in the late 1820s and early 1830s. These accounts, the earliest scientific exploration narratives of Mexican Texas, are discussed in chapter 1. The French naturalist Jean Louis Berlandier took part in the Mexican Comisión de Límites (boundary commission) and wrote its official report. In addition to this *Diario de viaje de la Comisión de Límites* (1832), he recorded his observations from that journey and subsequent scientific travels through Texas in the travelogue *Journey to Mexico during the Years 1826 to 1834*. Both volumes provide the most comprehensive scientific accounts of Texas during its Mexican era and are further distinguished among nineteenth-century travelogues about the region for their complex depiction of the Texas Natives. The private travel journals of two officers of the Comisión de Límites, the commanding general's "Fragmento del diario de Manuel de Mier y Terán" and Lieutenant José María Sánchez's *Viaje a Texas en 1828–1829*, valuably complement Berlandier's writings. They cover a part of the commission's journey not depicted in the French scientist's accounts and put greater emphasis on strategic matters than Berlandier's travelogues. Five years after the boundary commission, the Mexican government sent Colonel

Juan Nepomuceno Almonte on a tour of military-scientific assessment through Texas. In addition to capturing the state of the region on the brink of the Texas Revolution, this officer's two travelogues are significant for their distinct political agendas. The official statistical account, *Noticia estadística sobre Texas* (1834), was published to entice Mexican migration to the province and thereby counter the influx of Anglo immigrants, whereas the secret report submitted to the government, "Informe secreto sobre la presente situación de Texas, 1834," views sociopolitical conditions in the province much more critically and calls for Mexican political and military intervention to prevent the region's secession.

In contrast to Mexicans, Americans were curious about the landscapes and resident peoples of the North American West. Thus, while the Mexican government's interest in the exploration of Texas waned after the loss of the province in 1836, US public attention to the region grew after that time, especially after the annexation of Texas to the Union in 1845. In connection with this public interest, the second chapter analyzes the reports of two military explorations commanded by Captain Randolph Barnes Marcy in 1852 and 1854. These journeys through the North Texas–Oklahoma border region stand out among the scientific expeditions the US government deployed to the Lone Star State, since they led the white explorers into a part of the state that at the time was known almost exclusively to resident indigenous nations. Moreover, akin to Berlandier's travelogues, the journey accounts that Marcy submitted to the adjutant general of the US Army, *Adventure on Red River* (1854) and *Report of an Expedition to the Sources of the Brazos and Big Witchita Rivers* (1856), offer a complex portrayal of several Amerindian nations, based on close contact. Complementing the captain's official accounts and their military-scientific vantage point is the narrative of a civilian traveler attached to the second expedition, William B. Parker's *Through Unexplored Texas* (1856). Published for a general audience, this travelogue tends to foreground the exotic over the scientific; yet its ethnographic observations provide readers with rare insights into Native cultures and army life on the US frontier.

ONE

Assessing El Norte

Mexican Government Expedition Accounts

After Mexico gained its independence from Spain in 1821, Texas formed part of the Mexican Republic. To develop the sparsely populated region, the Mexican government passed a liberal colonization law in 1824, followed by a similar law on the provincial level a year later, which permitted foreign settlement and land ownership in Mexico. The laws regulated the influx of immigrants, which had been growing since 1815, through a system of land grants given to empresarios (colonization agents), who committed themselves to settle a certain number of families (R. B. Campbell, *Gone to Texas* 99–110; Moyano Pahissa 27–28, 39–41, 51–62; Reséndez 25–29, 37–38, 64–68; Vázquez y Vera 49–54). But Mexican authorities began to worry, since US American colonists not only soon outnumbered the Mexican population but also gained significant economic power in Texas and increasingly refused to assimilate to Mexican society. Many of these settlers, moreover, were white southerners who supported Black slavery and were biased against Mexicans on ethnic-religious grounds (R. B. Campbell, *Empire for Slavery* 2–3, 10–27, 32–33; Moyano Pahissa 27–28, 30–32, 71–77, 80–82; Reséndez 21–22, 105, 161–163, 233–234; Vázquez y Vera 55–57, 60–64). The large and diverse Amerindian population of Texas posed another challenge to both Anglos and Tejanos (Mexican Texans), whose land hunger increasingly jeopardized Native farming and hunting grounds and consequently triggered frequent indigenous raids on white settlements (LaVere 167–168). The Mexican government attempted to negotiate peace with and assimilate these tribes as well as the region's sedentary indigenous nations through land grants or enforced resettlement (DeLay 19–20, 35–41, 50–56, 61–64, 68–70; Hernández 299, 307–309, 316; Reséndez 46–52, 163–164).

JEAN LOUIS BERLANDIER'S *DIARIO DE VIAJE* AND *JOURNEY TO MEXICO*

In early 1828, the United States and Mexico signed a boundary treaty that confirmed the border laid down in the Adams-Onís Treaty of 1819 and required both nations to create a boundary commission to map and mark the exact borderline (Moyano Pahissa 97–100; Reséndez 19–20). As early as September 1827, the

Mexican government had formed a military-scientific commission to investigate the geography and demography of the East Texas border region, demarcate the international boundary line between the United States and Mexico, elaborate plans for establishing a series of garrisons, and make recommendations for a future Mexican border policy (Jackson, introduction 1–2; Vázquez Salguero 12–13). This Comisión de Límites was headed by General Manuel de Mier y Terán, one of Mexico's most prominent military leaders. The commission's scientific staff included two civilian naturalists, the mineralogist Rafael Chovell and the French botanist Jean Louis Berlandier (Lawson xviii; Vázquez Salguero 12–13). The commission left Mexico City on November 10, 1827, and crossed the Rio Grande (Rio Bravo or Rio Bravo del Norte in Mexican usage) on February 1, 1828. After spending eighteen days in Laredo, it traveled to San Antonio and San Felipe (originally San Felipe de Austin). Owing to illnesses and transportation problems, most members of the commission returned to San Antonio (then called San Antonio de Béxar or simply Béxar) on May 29. Except for several shorter excursions, they stayed there through July 14, 1829. Only General Terán and the commission's cartographer and illustrator, Lieutenant Sánchez, followed along the planned itinerary, arriving in Nacogdoches on June 3, 1828. From there, they undertook two expeditions to the Sabine and Red Rivers between October 1828 and January 1829. Political turmoil in Mexico demanded Terán's attention, so the general departed from Nacogdoches shortly afterward, reaching Matamoros in the neighboring state of Tamaulipas on March 7, where he was joined by the rest of the boundary commission in August (Jackson, introduction 3–5, 10; Lawson 49–126).

The Comisión de Límites publicized its scientific observations of Texas in an official expedition account written mainly by Berlandier, with contributions by Chovell. Born in France and trained in Geneva, Berlandier (c. 1805–1851) had come to Mexico in 1826 to serve as a naturalist on the boundary commission as well as to collect native plants and write a natural history of the country. He never returned to Europe, settling in Matamoros after his journey with the commission (Lawson; Vázquez Salguero 13–16, 20, 30–35). The botanist's expedition account, which retained the diary format of his travel journal, was originally published as "Diario del viaje de Luis Berlandier" in 1831, probably as part of a governmental campaign to promote Mexican settlement in Texas (Benson 281). It first appeared in book form under joint authorship with Chovell, titled *Diario de viaje de la Comisión de Límites que puso el Gobierno de la República* (1850).[1] The volume reports the journey of the Comisión de Límites until it reached San Antonio in March 1828, as well as its return trip to Matamoros in July and August 1829 (Vázquez Salguero 16–20, 37–38). In 1834, Berlandier undertook a second journey to Texas to further map the region and collect plant specimens. Departing from Matamoros on April 18, 1834, he stayed in La Bahía (today Goliad) and San Antonio. After an excursion to the Medina River, he returned to Matamoros on June 28 (Lawson 155–163). Once again recording his observations in a private diary, Berlandier subsequently revised the manuscripts of his two Texas journeys as well as several other journals about his travels through northern Mexico for a larger book publication. This work appeared posthumously as *Journey to Mexico during the Years 1826 to 1834* (1980).[2]

As Russell Lawson observes, "Berlandier's greatest significance was as a scientific explorer, the first such naturalist to make extensive journeys and commensurate observations in northern Mexico and Gulf Coast Texas" (xxi). In largely chronological order, the botanist's *Diario de viaje* and *Journey to Mexico* describe the settlements, population groups, and economic development of Texas as well as the region's geography, flora, fauna, and climate. As several scholars note, Berlandier's encyclopedic approach and writing style were informed by his admiration for Alexander von Humboldt and his desire to follow in the German's footsteps (Lawson 25, 27, 44, 46, 146, 167, 170; Muller xxix). Like his role model, he sought to correct factual errors about the territories he journeyed through, particularly concerning their topography and wildlife (Berlandier, *Diario* 140, 144, 286; Berlandier, *Journey* 271, 275). Moreover, like Humboldt and myriad other travel writers, Berlandier used comparisons to render unknown places and cultures meaningful to his readers (Lawson 55, 65). For instance, the vegetation between Laredo and San Antonio "offered...that pleasant springlike verdure of the southern regions of Europe," and near the Medina River, "the naturalist observes the same vegetation found in South Carolina and eastern Florida." Elsewhere in his text, he likens the architecture of American settler cabins in Central Texas to "the chalets of Switzerland" and describes the clothes of Kickapoo Natives as recalling "the fashion of poor Scottish Highlanders" (*Journey* 272, 414, 305, 334; see also *Diario* 122, 140, 164–166).

Berlandier's *Diario de viaje* praises the potential of Texas to become the "agricultural garden of the [Mexican] Republic" (157). Although uncommon in Mexican writing of the time (Rajchenberg and Héau-Lambert, "Wilderness" 28), the garden was a popular trope in European and American letters and was applied widely in descriptions of North America to express the landscape ideal of a tamed and fertile nature (Marx; H. Smith). Combining aesthetic pleasure and horticultural use, the garden legitimizes human intervention in nature. Berlandier implies that Texas could become an earthly paradise if Mexico fostered Mexican migration to the region, assisted newcomers in cultivating the land, and better equipped the province's garrisons to protect settlers against Amerindian raids (*Diario* 157–159). In a similar vein, the narrator takes up the metaphor, used in

American discourses of colonization, of the untouched, empty terrain waiting to be seized by white settlers. In *Journey to Mexico*, Berlandier remarks, "The beauty of the countryside was so constant that even the road itself was covered with flowers.... Everything signals that these virgin lands are calling the laborer to cultivate them" (304). Following up on this line of reasoning, several passages assert the suitability of Texas for Mexican colonization and suggest measures to improve the cultivation of the land (286, 298–300, 319–321, 555).

While the *Diario de viaje* and *Journey to Mexico* advocate Mexican settlement in Texas, both texts portray the Mexicans already residing in the region rather critically. According to the *Journey*, the Mexican Texans were lazy and ignorant. As Marilyn McAdams Sibley points out, laziness or indolence was a common reproach made in nineteenth-century travelogues of Texas about people who showed no inclination to cultivate the land to earn their living, to plant vegetable gardens to enrich their diet, or to improve their dwellings for greater comfort (98). Berlandier particularly targets the Tejano dream of easy wealth. In San Antonio, "one rarely hears talk about a well-cultivated field or a splendid harvest, but rather hears it said that here or there . . . is a gold or silver mine," the traveler complains (*Journey* 300). Both of his accounts primarily attribute this trait to the social background of the Mexican Texans. Rarely of farming stock, they lacked the knowledge and the will to work the land for profit. "The inhabitants are gay and not very hardworking," the narrator remarks about San Antonio residents. "Most of the families are linked to the military." Likewise, the civilians would rather risk exposure to Amerindian attacks on the town than "take the trouble of watering their fields," and so they "contented themselves with living wretchedly, waiting from day to day for money to be distributed to the [military] companies" (*Journey* 300, 290–291, 375; see also *Diario* 135, 161–163). The text similarly scrutinizes the largely Mexican settler colony of Martín de León, this time blaming the despotism, greed, and dishonesty of the empresario for the failure of the settlement to prosper (*Journey* 383–384). Only upon returning to Texas in 1834 did Berlandier note, with approval, the emergence of a Mexican farmer culture in the province: "Various newly built ranchos proved that the inhabitants of Texas are beginning to learn that agricultural products are the wealth which Nature has reserved for them" (556).

The naturalist's focus on the state of the Tejano economy closely relates to his concern for the political future of Texas. *Journey to Mexico* characterizes the political situation as a natural consequence of Mexico admitting many Anglo-American colonists, "whose customs and interest[s] were so different" from those of Mexicans (318). This difference was perceived to be particularly perilous, since the Mexican elite viewed the country's northern provinces and their Hispanic residents as topographically and culturally distinct from—and inferior to—the rest of the country (Rajchenberg and Héau-Lambert, "La frontera" 39–40, 43–45; Rajchenberg and Héau-Lambert, "Wilderness" 24–26). In Berlandier's account, the distinction of the Mexican Texans resulted primarily from their embracing Anglo-American culture: "Trade with the Anglo-Americans and the blending in to some degree of their customs make the inhabitants of Texas a little different from the Mexicans of the interior, whom those in Texas call foreigners and whom they scarcely like because of the superiority . . . they recognize in them. In their gatherings the women prefer to dress in the fashion of Louisiana, and by so doing they participate both in the customs of the neighboring nation and of their own" (*Journey* 291). Perceiving the Tejanos as neither fully Mexican nor able to adopt the work ethic and agricultural expertise required to develop the region, Berlandier's *Journey to Mexico* voices the anxiety, widespread among Mexican political observers in the late 1820s and early 1830s, of losing Texas to an overpowering Anglo economy. "Unfortunately for the creoles of Texas," the text points out, "the agricultural industry which they have shown in our times is so wretched that a monopoly over them by the American colonies founded in this department is to be feared" (297). Although his use of the term "creoles" refers to the *criollo* class, the social elite of Mexican-born descendants of Spanish colonizers, the context of the naturalist's complaint suggests that he feared cultural creolization had rendered Mexican Texan society inferior, and hence vulnerable, to Anglo civilization.

While the *Diario de viaje* rarely mentions the Anglo colonists in Texas, *Journey to Mexico* gives ample reasons for their economic success, emphasizing their diligence, persistence, and professional skills (305–306, 314, 318–319). The latter travelogue further refers to the widespread Anglo practice of Black slavery yet does this only in passing and with a sense of understanding for the slaveholders' legal maneuverings to uphold the institution (320, 323–324). In so doing, the volume aligns itself with the widespread Tejano tolerance of slavery, which was at odds with mainstream Mexican views (R. B. Campbell, *Empire for Slavery* 17–21, 25–26; Torget 71–72, 79–80, 94–95, 140–141). But Berlandier's *Journey to Mexico* also looks critically at the Anglo settlers. They counted adventurers and criminals in their midst, but worse, they flouted the rules of hospitality to strangers, an essential cultural practice in sparsely settled regions (305–306, 300, 318). With retrospective insight (the manuscript was revised after the independence of Texas), the narrator targets the growing political and economic influence of white Texans, which allowed them to defy Mexican rule in the province. He accuses them of being "ingrates, who, at first received as colonists, soon wished to dictate laws to those who should be dictating [the laws] to them." In particular, the first Anglo empresario, Stephen Austin, "always knew how to conduct himself to lull the authorities to sleep," and the largely Anglo-driven Texas Revolution and war of independence appear in the travelogue as "these catastrophes" (180, 321, 377).

Reversing the Anglo-American discourses of Texas at the time, Berlandier presents the region as a legitimate Mexican homeland into which the Anglo immigrants had intruded, in as "savage" a manner as the nomadic indigenous nations raided white settlements in the region.

Amerindian raids were, indeed, a major concern of both settlers and travelers in early nineteenth-century Texas, and many journey narratives, Berlandier's included (*Diario* 162, 302; *Journey* 298, 553), voice concern over the impact of these incursions on the development of the region. But the French botanist stood out among travel writers "through his focused and learned curiosity about indigenous peoples" (DeLay 21), which transcended the prevailing European or Mexican views of his time. Although he occasionally denotes them as "savages," he much more frequently calls the Natives "tribes," "Indians," "indigenes," or by the names of their nations. Berlandier also wrote several ethnographic studies of Texas Natives (Lawson 90–98; Vázquez Salguero 31, 34). His *Diario de viaje* and *Journey to Mexico* point out the distinctions among nomadic nations. The texts depict the Comanches as numerically dominant, yet timid and unable to guard their camps (*Diario* 290–293; *Journey* 269, 346–347, 349). The Lipan Apaches, in contrast, appear as more courageous and capable of acquiring "civilization," being as "suited to agriculture as to a nomadic life" (*Journey* 353). At the same time, Berlandier's travelogues frame the Lipans as utterly depraved. Not only did this once-proud warrior nation depend on Mexican protection against the Comanches (*Diario* 135, 287; *Journey* 262, 347), but "everything about them had an aspect at once barbarous and nomadic," Berlandier writes: "Most of its members are corrupt and inclined to drunkenness. This in turn gives rise to disputes, and I myself have seen them stab their comrades and then flee" (*Journey* 269). While such encounters with the Lipans diminished his respect for the tribe, his contacts with the Comanches made him revise his notions of "Indian character." After joining a Comanche hunting party near San Antonio, he noted the contrast between urbanized and range Indians: "We had already begun to observe a great difference in the character of the indigenes who accompanied us. In the towns and the villages, they are more suspicious, more taciturn ... and never manifest that gay and open nature which they have in the wilds. ... During the entire time ... they were always moderate" (344–345).

The civility of the Comanches undermines the strict hierarchical distinctions in Eurocentric thought between the "civilized" societies of European descent and "savage" Others, on the one hand, and between the "peaceful" sedentary indigenous nations and the "hostile" nomadic ones, on the other. In line with this subversion, Berlandier's *Diario de viaje* and *Journey to Mexico* characterize the sedentary Carrizos and Garzas of the Rio Grande Valley as "thieves and lazy," who have partially lost their original languages through assimilation. Nonetheless, the narrator notes approvingly that the two nations posed little threat to white settlers, since they were "mission Indians" (*Diario* 135; *Journey* 24, 263). This term denotes Natives who lived in one of the missions that Franciscan friars had established during the Spanish colonial period, and who had converted to Spanish Catholicism and somewhat adapted to Tejano culture (R. B. Campbell, *Gone to Texas* 36–37, 49–60, 64–71; Velasco Ávila 441–442; Weber 43, 46–47). Elsewhere in his *Journey to Mexico*, though tellingly not in the account published for the Comisión de Límites, the naturalist scrutinizes the mission system: "Clergy ... frequently abus[ed] the powers which had been accorded to them. Their conduct towards the indigenes was inhumane. ... Those [Natives] who escaped from the bayonets of the soldiers ... were taken to the missions under the pretext of ... saving their souls, which a just God had condemned to eternal suffering for not having received the waters of baptism or absolution from men just as sinful as they" (285). The passage particularly targets the hypocrisy of the missionaries. Rather than "saving" fellow humans, whose sinfulness they shared, they joined the Spanish colonial army in treating the indigenous population like wild animals. In so doing, the missionary friars played an active role in the destruction of Amerindian cultures.

Berlandier's *Diario de viaje* as well as other passages of his *Journey to Mexico*, however, contradict this critique, presenting the work of the Spanish missionaries as a model for the Mexican state to emulate in order to "civilize" its Amerindian populace. The two texts repeatedly treat the missions in Texas as symbols of the state of political affairs in the province. Even though "in 1829 the missions were abandoned and daily falling into decay," their example endured: "But their standing walls yet proved the activity, the hardiness, the good taste, and above all, the devotion of the missionaries" (*Journey* 378; *Diario* 161). In the same vein, the narrator of the *Journey to Mexico* observes, "In the time of the Spanish government ... the countryside [near San Antonio] was dotted at intervals with small ranchos, and covered with immense herds belonging to the inhabitants of the region or to the missions. Nowadays, without any guarantees in these wilds, the laborer does not dare to venture far from the presidios, and often he is not sheltered from danger even there" (390). Evoking the European romanticist trope of a lost arcadia, this passage engages with competing discourses about "culture" and "civilization." On the one hand, it juxtaposes an idealized image of safety and prosperity under Spanish colonial rule with a dystopian view of insecurity and poverty after Mexican independence in order to emphasize Mexico's inability to either "civilize" the Texas Natives or subjugate them through military force. On the other hand, despite his worries about Anglo dominance in Texas, Berlandier puts up the US practice of Amerindian subjugation as a legitimate model for Mexico: "The neighboring republic has sufficiently demonstrated to us what philanthropy, consistency, and ... a firm resolve have been able to do with the tribes who arrived at the frontiers of Texas. Today, enlightened and hardworking, the Cherokees, Alabam[a]s, Delawares, etc., do honor to the nation which has made them take a great stride towards a civilization in which they can be of use to their fellowmen" (*Journey* 258).

In another scene in the *Journey to Mexico*, Berlandier praises the Spanish missionaries he criticized earlier, commending them for "preparing . . . the first elements of civilization among inimical and often ferocious hordes" (377). Most prominently, the text applauds the Spaniards for having "inspired a great horror" of cannibalism among the Karankawas, who once "had spread terror" for eating their captives "with pleasure, and amidst dances" (380). By depicting the Karankawas as former cannibals, the travelogue follows a widespread Spanish, Mexican, and Anglo-American discourse that justified and naturalized the physical and spiritual subjugation of this native nation (LaVere 62, 178). What these and other passages do not address, however, is the enforced relocation and subjugation of the indigenous nations, which provided political continuity in the North American West from European colonial rule to the postcolonial nation-states of the continent. While Berlandier correctly warned against the growing influence of Anglo-Americans in Mexican Texas, his travelogues simultaneously contributed to the politics of white colonization of indigenous lands, which both Mexico and the United States engaged in.

MANUEL DE MIER Y TERÁN'S AND JOSÉ MARÍA SÁNCHEZ'S TEXAS DIARIES

While Berlandier's travelogues cover the first half of the journey of the Comisión de Límites, the private journals of two military officers provide accounts of the second part of this trip. The diary of the commanding general was published, posthumously and incompletely, as "Fragmentos del diario de Manuel de Mier y Terán" (1988), followed by an English translation of the complete manuscript, "Texas by Terán, His Journey, 1828" (2000). A graduate in engineering from the College of Mines in Mexico, Mier y Terán (1789–1832), who is usually referred to only as Terán, fought for the insurgent forces in the Mexican War of Independence and subsequently served as a military commander, congressman, and secretary of war and of the navy under different administrations during the 1820s (Jackson, introduction 3, 10; Morton). His Texas travel journal covers the commission's itinerary from the moment he and Sánchez left San Antonio in April 1828 to their arrival in Matamoros in March 1829.[3] The text records the topography, climate, wild animals, population groups, roads, and settlements of the province, along with the general's assessment of the region's agricultural, mineralogical, and commercial potential. According to Jack Jackson, it "give[s] us a sense of how Terán's ideas about Texas changed after direct contact with the land and its people, of how his opinions were formed concerning the course of action necessary to preserve Texas and keep it attached to the Mexican nation" (introduction, 11).

Articulating social-class prejudice, the general's diary acknowledges that the Mexican settlers of Martín de León's empresario colony were "well-behaved people from the decent laboring class" in search of economic opportunities. The text agrees with Berlandier's observation, though, that the colonists lacked the economic knowledge and farming skills, the ambition and diligence, considered necessary to succeed (Mier y Terán, "Texas" 149–150). Paired with his critical attitude to the ill-functioning Mexican administration of Texas, Terán's class bias may explain his praise for the Anglo-Texan cotton economy as well as his rather cursory and defensive remarks about Black slavery and Anglo lobbying to maintain the slave trade (56–57, 73, 151–152). For instance, his journal paints a rather benign picture of Texas's largest slaveholder, Jared E. Groce, pointing out his seemingly decent treatment of his slaves: "Nowhere around the house are there cages, prisons, or any other sign that force is necessary to subordinate so many slaves. Furthermore, the latter appear well dressed, with indications that they enjoy abundance" (145). This example ties in with the text's complaint that the African American population was a source of crime and conflict in Texas. Even though he acknowledges the impact of their suffering on their conduct, Terán, in line with the racialist thought of his time, ultimately blames the slaves for their misery: "The blacks are generally very badly treated, and it is necessary that they be so [treated] because it is their lot to have such immoral owners" (79). This depiction contrasts with his official letters and reports to the Mexican government, which adduce slavery, Anglo land seizures, and settlers' disrespect for Mexican laws as sources of the conflict between Texas and Mexico (Mier y Terán, "Texas" 31–39, 95–111, 177–179; Mier y Terán, *Reflexiones* xiv–xxiv).

In addition to discussing Anglo and Mexican settlers, Terán's journal deals at length with the Amerindian nations of Texas, noting their distinct cultures but also their conflicts with one another and with the nonnative populations. Like Berlandier, the general wrote several reports about the Texas Natives (Molina 129–144). His travelogue calls the Natives "savages," "tribes," "Indians," "indigenous [people]," and by the names of individual nations. The diary, like Sánchez's journal (Sánchez, "Trip" 285), remarks that the Amerindians "call themselves red men" owing to their practice of applying reddish colors to their faces ("Texas" 77). But Terán's conclusion that the Natives thereby "creat[ed] in this color a race, like that of the whites and of the blacks" (77) simultaneously reveals and undermines a Eurocentric conception of race. On the one hand, the general's comment reveals his Eurocentric notion of race as an unchangeable biological essence, rendered visible in people's skin tone. On the other hand, his words subvert the biological essentialism of this racial ascription and, instead, grant the Natives the agency of choosing and creating their race through the performative act of temporary facial painting.

"Accustomed to the Hispanicized Native Americans of central Mexico," Andrés Reséndez observes, Terán "was ill prepared to cope with a constant stream of native visitors who arrived at his improvised quarters ... in the hopes of obtaining official recognition for their lands in Texas" (48). Although the general's journal gives accounts of the origins, movements, and territorial claims of a host of these Amerindian nations, he fails to see the strategy behind the tribes' diplomatic rhetoric ("Texas" 59, 61, 78, 80). Instead, he takes the behavior of the Natives at face value. "They swear that they respect property and claim to be humble and ignorant people to whom *the being on high* has not given the knowledge of reading and writing as to the whites," the general notes about the indigenous emissaries he received. "They repeat this point so often that they must have a vehement desire to achieve this degree of civilization" (77, original emphasis). As the last sentence makes clear, Terán's assessment of the situation is, once again, marred by his Eurocentric thinking, in this case, his belief in the superiority of writing-based civilizations of European descent over the mostly oral Amerindian cultures (Greenblatt 10–12; Spurr 102–103). Accordingly, his journal praises the Cherokees for having a constitution and a written language ("Texas" 59), even though he claims that the Natives "would scarcely survive without trading with cultivated nations" (52). Ironically, what Terán identifies as the worst habit of the Cherokees, their regular "drunkenness," most likely resulted from contact with "civilized" white traders, who introduced alcohol to many Amerindian nations (59).

While the diarist fails to grasp the detrimental impact of contacts with whites on Amerindians' health, he correctly identifies whites' insatiable land hunger for causing repeated Native relocations from ancestral territories, especially in the United States. For instance, the Cherokees "have moved in constant retreat from the North American population toward the Mexican border," the journal states (59). Thus "placed in the borderlands," both they and other indigenous nations "spread into Mexican territory that they find empty" (61). Although the general echoes Berlandier in criticizing the Spanish endeavor to assimilate the Natives through military force rather than inspiration (136), his journal simultaneously rejects the idea that all "works of missionaries are useless or fanatical," and gives examples of how missionary kindness saved indigenous lives (152). His diary particularly stresses the fact that American Protestant missionaries "are obliged to respect the independence, habits, and customs of the savages" (122–123). This appears in his text like a Protestant continuation of the Spanish colonial missionary effort. Thus, like Berlandier, Terán hoped to buttress the Mexican character of Texas on two pillars: curtailing Anglo-American influence in the region and subjugating the Natives through political and missionary efforts.

Like the general's journal, the private diary kept by José María Sánchez y Tapia (1801–1835), a lieutenant of artillery, during his travels with the Comisión de Límites covers the journey of the commission until Sánchez and the general reached Nacogdoches. Born in Querétaro, Sánchez had fought for Mexican independence in 1821 and subsequently held administrative positions within the military. After Terán died in 1832, Sánchez remained a functionary of the boundary commission and preserved the general's extensive records of it; Sánchez's death brought them into the hands of Berlandier, who added them to his own scientific materials (Jackson, introduction 13). His Texas journal was first published in an English translation as "A Trip to Texas in 1828" (1926) and later appeared in its Spanish original, *Viaje a Texas en 1828–1829* (1939). Although Sánchez's descriptions of the settlements, population groups, climate, and nature of Texas lack the natural-science observations that abound in Terán's text, they share the latter's concern with the massive Anglo-American colonization of Texas (Jackson, introduction 5).[4]

"Romantic sentimentalism" infuses Sánchez's depiction of Texas, Eduardo Castañeda remarks (112). According to Marissa López, Mexican romanticism sought to establish a Mexican national identity by forging an essentialist connection between territory and society. Writers commonly achieved this through expressions of emotional attachment to the land, either by re-creating a lost indigenous world or by documenting contemporary social reality (López 388–392). In contrast to Berlandier and Terán, Sánchez rarely points out the role of topography and climate in the settling of Texas (Sánchez, "Trip" 251, 259, 267). In line with early Mexican romanticism, López argues, "Sánchez's observations . . . ground . . . a national morality in the relations between landscape and the individual" (388). His diary reiterates the widespread Mexican view, also voiced in Berlandier's travelogues, that the region north of the Rio Grande represented an "alien" land, even though it formally belonged to Mexico. For instance, the lieutenant casts the prospect of leaving the Mexican mountains, some hundred miles before reaching Laredo, as parting with his native country and entering another one, for which he felt no affection (Sánchez, *Viaje* 15; see also Rajchenberg and Héau-Lambert, "Wilderness" 26). Nonetheless, he claims that Texas belongs to Mexico, because it strongly affects his senses (López 388). He rapturously describes the area near the settlement of Gonzales: "The meadows . . . present to the eye of the imaginative traveler all the beauty of wild nature. When one sees the herds of deer fleeing, inhales the perfume of numerous flowers, and listens to the singing of the birds, the soul seems to revel in an unknown joy; and those who have a romantic heart seem to be transported to an enchanted country, or to be living in the illusionary Arcadia" ("Trip" 267). Appropriating the European concept of arcadia—an idyllic pastoral landscape—for a description of Mexican territory, the passage aligns with other scenes in the diary that frame the sensual experience of nature according to the aesthetic concepts of the beautiful, the picturesque, and the sublime, which cause sensations of joy or terror (Hyde 14–15, 17–18; Trott). While Sánchez characterizes the varied and fertile landscape of La Parrita Creek as "beautiful" in his journal, and the woods of fruit trees and blackberry bushes surrounding Nacogdoches as "picturesque," the vast night sky elicits feelings of sublime awe ("Trip" 255, 282, 253). To convey his deep impressions of nature, he resorts to metaphors from architecture, furnishing, or clothing (Callahan 80). Thus, the Rio Grande was "lying like a silver thread upon the immense plains," the countryside near San Antonio was decked with "delicately tinted tapestries of living flowers," and the sky formed an "immense dome" ("Trip" 250, 257, 253).

In contrast to Sánchez's deeply affectionate portrayals of nature, his depiction of the population of Texas is rather sober and critical. In line with the Mexican intellectual discourse of his time, which represented Americans as materialistic, aggressive, fraudulent, and arrogant (Moyano Pahissa 42), the lieutenant paints a wholly negative picture of the Anglo colonists of Texas. He blames the settlers' lack of agricultural inclination on their indolence; this contradicts Berlandier's perception of the Anglo-Americans as skilled and industrious farmers. For instance, Sánchez's journal characterizes the Anglo residents of San Felipe as "lazy people of vicious character" who accepted the harsh conditions of frontier life and showed little concern for the rules of courtesy and the comforts of home ("Trip" 271). Moreover, their national pride made them unwilling to adopt Mexican laws, culture, and customs (283). Third, the diary condemns their practice of slavery and severe treatment of their human property (271). All these negative traits come together in Sánchez's portrayal of the Anglo planter Jared Groce:

> [Groce and his friends] did not deign to offer us shelter. . . . Later they asked us in the house for the sole purpose of showing us the wealth of Mr. Groce and to introduce us to three dogs called Ferdinand VII, Napoleon, and Bolívar. . . . Groce . . . came from the United States . . . to avoid the numerous creditors that were suing him. He brought with him 116 slaves of both sexes, most of which were stolen. These wretched slaves are the ones who cultivate the corn and cotton, both of which yield copious crops to Mr. Groce . . . [who] treats his slaves with great cruelty. ("Trip" 274)[5]

This example of Anglo ruthlessness supports Sánchez's fear of the growing Anglo dominance in Texas. Reminiscent of Berlandier's writings, other passages in Sánchez's journal complain about a massive, unauthorized influx of Anglos to the region and their ambitious pursuit of their interests: "The Americans from the

North have taken possession of practically all the eastern part of Texas, in most cases without the permission of the authorities. They immigrate constantly... and take possession of the [site] that best suits them without either asking leave or going through any formality" (260). Even legal settlements are not exempt from this critique. On the contrary, the diplomatic skills of Stephen F. Austin and the success of his colony jeopardized the Mexican Republic in the eyes of the diarist. Accordingly, he concludes that "the spark that will start the conflagration that will deprive [Mexico] of Texas, will start from this colony" (271).

As much as the cunning of Anglo colonists, the diarist blames Mexican ineptness for a situation that he views as posing an imminent danger of losing Texas to the United States. On the one hand, he targets political inefficiency and corruption (López 388, 392–394). Sánchez's journal attributes the Anglo-Americans' "ill opinion of all Mexicans" to the poor administration of Texas ("Trip" 283). Similarly, "the vigilance of the highest [Mexican] authorities has been dulled while our enemies of the North do not lose a single opportunity of advancing... their treacherous design," the narrator claims (261). On the other hand, once again drawing on the Mexican belief in Norteño cultural differences and in the virtues of farming, Sánchez's journal finds fault with the largely working-class Tejano population, which fails to conform to his middle-class values, education, and way of life (Callahan 190, 196). Accordingly, the lieutenant's diary characterizes the Mexican Texans as carefree and lazy, fond of luxury and leisure, and inclined to immorality ("Trip" 250–251, 258). Laredo provides an example of squalor: "The houses have no conveniences. A desolate air envelops the entire city, and... food is extremely scarce" (251). Sánchez saw Mexican culture as being under siege by an uneducated Tejano populace living in an Anglo-dominated environment: "Accustomed to the continued trade with the North Americans, they have adopted [Anglo] customs and habits, and one may say that truly they are not Mexicans except by birth, for they even speak Spanish with marked incorrectness" (283). In line with the Western understanding of language as a carrier of culture and an instrument of power (Greenblatt 24, 82–83, 104, 145), the flawed Spanish of the Mexicans in Nacogdoches strongly signified their presumed lack of Mexicanness, which rendered them vulnerable to Anglo-Americanization—and thereby jeopardized the Mexican character and possession of Texas.

Sánchez's perception of contemporary Tejano life strikingly contrasts with his view of colonial Spanish culture. For the lieutenant, arriving at the Mission San Francisco de la Espada near San Antonio was like a "deliverance from [the] wilderness" (Jackson, introduction 15). A bond of religious-cultural identity made the diarist feel connected with the place. "The view of this temple and the few small houses that surround it," Sánchez admits, "brought forcefully to my mind the fact that I was still living among my fellowmen" ("Trip" 257). Like Berlandier and General Terán, he acknowledges the spiritual and physical labor of the Spanish missionaries. Even more, whereas Berlandier addresses the exploitation of the mission Indians and points out the poverty of the Mexican Texans, who settled there after secularization (*Journey* 285, 293), Sánchez sees only Norteño greed and indolence replacing Spanish industry. Normally "persons of [good] judgment," Tejano "property owners...abolished the missions and divided among themselves the lands they have not known how to cultivate and which they have left in a sad state of neglect," his journal laments ("Trip" 259).

Like his fellow boundary commissioners and like most other Mexicans of his time, the lieutenant not only considered Norteños to lack Mexicanness but also never regarded any indigenous nation as "Mexican." In so doing, he did not belong to the strain of Mexican romanticism that would come to regard the Amerindians as the seed of the nation (López 393). Echoing Berlandier and Terán, Sánchez usually refers to the indigenous population in his diary as "tribes" or "nations," or by their names, rather than calling them "Indians" or "savages." Nonetheless, his depiction of the Amerindians follows the Western tradition of establishing a hierarchy of Native societies according to their ways of life, their relations with people of European descent, and their resemblance to those populations. His journal approvingly describes the Cherokees and the Shawnees as peaceful farmers and traders in East Texas seeking to align themselves with their Mexican "brothers" and "fathers" ("Trip" 287–288). Like General Terán, Sánchez further fails to recognize the Natives as independent political actors professing loyalty as a diplomatic strategy. Instead, he praises the Cherokees by pointing out their ethnic and cultural similarities to Hispanic Mexicans: "The greater part of these Indians are fair, and one does not see shell or feather ornaments among them as among the others, though they are all alike in their filth. They wear no paint on their faces, they hold no dances . . . in the settlements of the Mexicans. . . . They trade with skins and fruits, are good workmen, and are the best of all the Indians I have known" (288).

Apart from Shawnees and Cherokees, Sánchez disapproves of Texas Natives. This dislike manifests itself in his targeting the apparent low status of women in Amerindian societies as a sign of indigenous depravity; he employs imagery reminiscent of his critique of Black slavery among the Anglo colonists. For example, the women of the Comanches "are real slaves to their men," one of Sánchez's journal entries reads, and another passage notes that Amerindian men in Nacogdoches "were in the greatest inaction, while the women worked the fields with the greatest fatigue in this burning climate to maintain their tyrants" (262, 282). In so judging the Natives, Sánchez prefigures the widespread view among American and European travelers in the mid-nineteenth-century North American West that "women were to be cloistered and protected" and that indigenous gender roles thereby signified Native "savagery" (Hämäläinen 249).

Even more than their gender roles, the migration of Amerindian nations from US territories to Texas, where they struggled for limited land and hunting grounds, worried Sánchez ("Trip" 261–262). As Marissa López argues, the diarist draws a parallel between these Natives and the Anglo colonists as ethnic groups whose immigration to Mexico had been tolerated but whose growing number increasingly jeopardized the cultural and territorial integrity of the country (394). Sánchez particularly rejects the nomadic life of the Comanches and Lipan Apaches, which his text characterizes as a major obstacle to the well-being of Texas. Above all, his depiction of these nations blends notions of cultural and geographic Otherness into an image of predation and purposeless mobility with no entitlement to land or liberty. The journal, for example, denigrates the Lipans: "[They] differ from other tribes in their cruel, deceitful, and sly character and in their inclination to steal. . . . It is said that they came from regions north of Texas and . . . that they were the last ones to give up eating human flesh" ("Trip" 252). In a similar vein, the diary calls the Comanches "barbarians who are useless with their present customs and habits" and who stand out for their "vengeance, pride, and excessive laziness" (265, 262). The lieutenant admits that the Comanches originated in Texas, but as López points out (394), he frames their residence in the region in the terms he employs to criticize Anglo-American land seizures. Sánchez writes that the Comanches had "occupied" their territory ("Trip" 261). Unsurprisingly, he explicitly recommends eliminating both indigenous nations (252, 265). In so doing, he joins Berlandier and Terán in advocating a Mexicanized settler economy in Texas as a guarantee of the region's political and economic development as a Mexican province.

JUAN NEPOMUCENO ALMONTE'S STATISTICAL AND SECRET REPORTS ON TEXAS

Although none of the accounts of the Comisión de Límites proposed to end immigration from the United States, General Terán's letters and report to the Mexican government, in which he summarized the observations first penned in his journal, became the basis for a stricter Mexican colonization law in 1830, whose intent was to curtail Anglo dominance in the region. Among other provisions, this law prohibited the sale of land to American citizens, restricted slavery, and sought to entice Mexicans and Europeans to migrate to Texas. It added fuel to the growing discontent of the Anglo colonists as well as that of many Tejanos disgusted with the ill-functioning administration, weak military protection against Native raids, and lack of political representation in the province (R. B. Campbell, *Gone to Texas* 116–127; Moyano Pahissa 66–71, 83–94, 111–138; Reséndez 22–29, 117–123; Vázquez y Vera 66–79). The ensuing conflict between insurgent Texans and an uncompromising Mexican government culminated in an armed uprising, the Texas Revolution of 1835—the Texas Rebellion or First War of Texas in Mexican terminology (Jackson, *Almonte's Texas* vii). When Anglo and Mexican Texan militias defeated the Mexican Army in the spring of 1836, Texas obtained its independence from Mexico (R. B. Campbell, *Gone to Texas* 128–158; Moyano Pahissa 138–160; Reséndez 149–170; Vázquez y Vera 79–93).

On the eve of the Texas Revolution, governmental concern over the rising conflicts with American colonists and Amerindian nations moved Mexican vice president Valentín Gómez Farías to deploy another military-scientific mission to the state of Coahuila y Texas. Colonel José María Noriega was sent to Coahuila, and his peer in rank Juan Nepomuceno Almonte was appointed director of colonization and dispatched to inspect Texas. On his mission, Almonte spent six months in the region gathering relevant geographic, demographic, and military information (Gutiérrez Ibarra 59–60; Jackson, *Almonte's Texas* 31–33, 36–38, 55). According to his official instructions, the colonel was to hear colonists' complaints, reconcile their interests with those of the Mexican state, and promise the possible separation of Texas from Coahuila. Confidential instructions, however, ordered him to collect demographic data, identify potential troublemakers and places of unrest, and hamstring any insurgence movements in Texas (Jackson, *Almonte's Texas* 38–47).

A child soldier on the Republican side in the Mexican War of Independence, Almonte (1803–1869) spent several years in New Orleans before fighting against Royalist troops in Texas between 1822 and 1824 and then serving his country as a diplomat and congressman (Campos-Farfán 11–17; Jackson, *Almonte's Texas* 12–28). Appointed to his Texas inspection mission on January 17, 1834, Almonte took a ship from Veracruz to New Orleans in February and continued to Nacogdoches, which he reached on April 26. In early July, he left for San Felipe de Austin. From that town, he also visited Brazoria, Velasco, Harrisburg, Matagorda, and possibly Galveston Bay. Leaving from San Felipe in mid-August, Almonte stayed in San Antonio, crossed the Rio Grande on September 10, and returned to Mexico City in October (Jackson, *Almonte's Texas* 56–66, 89–117, 131–144, 149–158, 173–176). Almonte penned two reports on his Texas journey. The statistical report *Noticia estadística sobre Texas* (1835)—published in English as "Statistical Report on Texas" (1925)—addressed a general audience and appeared shortly after the colonel's return. The secret account, "Informe secreto sobre la presente situación de Texas, 1834," which he submitted to the government on November 25, 1834, was not published until 1987, and it appeared in translation as "Secret Report on the Present Situation in Texas 1834" in 2003 (Jackson, *Almonte's Texas* 4–6, 493). Two years after his tour of inspection, Almonte returned to Texas as an officer in Mexican president and general Antonio López de Santa

Anna's military campaign to prevent the independence of the region. His diary of this sojourn, however, focuses exclusively on military action (Jackson, *Almonte's Texas* 360–374, 390–407).

Almonte's published account "has long been acknowledged as the most detailed statistical report of the era about Texas," Jack Jackson observes (*Almonte's Texas* 308), even though some scholars have criticized it as conveying a too optimistic impression. It results primarily from Almonte's findings, buttressed at times by material that Colonel Noriega collected in Coahuila (206). The "Statistical Report" provides a survey of the province's topography, climate, vegetation, animals, and natural resources; its population groups, settlements, and infrastructure; and its agriculture and commerce. Partly informed by General Terán's earlier findings, Almonte's "Informe secreto," in Jackson's words, "is a comprehensive blueprint for managing Texas and keeping it under Mexican control" (7). The piece not only contains all the data of the statistical report but also integrates military strategic information as well as Almonte's political observations and recommendations. To bolster his arguments, the colonel reprinted local government publications, newspaper clippings, letters, maps, and statistical tables in his account (González Navarro 141; Gutiérrez Ibarra 63–64).

While the "Secret Report" begins by explaining Almonte's true mission in Texas (Almonte, "Secret" 208–211), this information is never provided in the "Statistical Report." Instead, except for his critique of land speculation in the region, Jackson points out, "Almonte used [his text] to praise the fertility of Texas to his fellow Mexicans" (*Almonte's Texas* 309). In his introduction and conclusion, the colonel justifies his publication by referring to the widespread public interest in Mexican settlement in Texas as well as his goal of promoting it (Almonte, "Statistical" 178–180, 216). The almost identical statistical sections of the two texts focus on the suitability of Texas towns and regions for settlement, agriculture, and commerce, indicating, among other things, their topography, vegetation, wild animals, climate, and likelihood of Amerindian raids ("Statistical" 201, 205, 212–213, 221; "Secret" 240–241, 251, 258, 274–275). Like Berlandier's writings as well as the American and German travelogues following in the 1830s to the 1850s, Almonte's reports constantly use a language of fecundity to describe the agricultural and mineralogical riches of Texas. "Pasturage and water are abundant throughout the department and of good quality even in drought," the narrator states about the Brazos River watershed, and elsewhere in his text he adds that "whatever is produced in one part of Texas can be produced in any other part in more or less abundance" ("Statistical" 206, 284; "Secret" 252). The "Secret Report" connects this assertion with Almonte's political task, namely, "giving the Supreme Government an idea of the current situation in that most fertile and important country" (232). The "Statistical Report," in contrast, only hints at the political goal of keeping Texas within Mexico. One telling passage predicts: "If the immense development which industry has enjoyed there is considered; and if its advantageous geographic position, its ports, its navigable rivers . . . , its products . . . , its soil, its climate, etc., are taken into account, one must admit that Texas is soon destined to be the most flourishing section of this republic" (178).

Randolph Campbell remarks, "Although his statistics demonstrated the ever-increasing control of Anglos, Almonte found the political situation generally quiet and suggested that stability in the government of Mexico would maintain calm in Texas" (*Gone to Texas* 126). As David Weber points out, this calm was relative, since the colonel had expected to find the province in open upheaval (247). Unlike the writings of the Comisión de Límites, Almonte's "Statistical Report" paints a largely benign picture of American colonists in Texas, assuring its readers of their usefulness for the Mexican state. The Anglo settlers dominating the East Texas town of Tanaha, the account notes, "are peaceful now, and are dedicated to the raising of cotton, corn, and other products" ("Statistical" 210). Elsewhere the text attributes the growing trade in Texas to "the increasing consumption of goods due to the continued emigration from the United States" (213). The "Secret Report," in contrast, depicts the American presence in Texas with greater complexity. On the one hand, Almonte admits that he "admires the foreigners for their industry, activity, etc." ("Secret" 223). He understands their attachment to their native country and emphasizes that only a small group of them had openly rebelled against Mexico (214, 216–217, 223–224). On the other hand, the report warns of the growing discontent and disregard for Mexican laws among the Americans, which could cause even loyal Anglo colonists to be "carried along by the revolutionary torrent" (217). Moreover, the text alerts readers to the settlers' resistance to Mexicanization. While some of the well-established Texas Anglos "wish to unite with the Mexicans," the colonel's argument continues, "the first thing [newcomers] will do is to think of new practices and become involved in interests which are totally contrary to our own" (223).

These "practices" and "interests" allude to the cotton economy that the American colonists had established in Texas and to the institution of slavery, which they considered indispensable for cotton production (Torget 7–8, 122–124, 139–141, 154–159). Almonte's journey accounts reject slavery; yet the "Statistical Report," written to attract Mexican colonists, treats the issue rather leniently. Thus, both texts provide statistical data on the slaves in Texas and criticize their importation as an "abuse" ("Statistical" 198, 204; "Secret" 245, 250, 253).[6] But Almonte qualifies his remarks in the "Statistical Report" by pointing out that "the slave trade [is being] carried on by a few adventurers that enter Texas" (204). In so doing, he downplays the size of the trafficking and locates its culprits outside the state's borders. Similarly, both of his reports blame the spread of slavery in Texas exclusively on "backward" Anglos from the American South rather than pointing to the support it enjoyed among the entire Anglo-Texan population: "The first settlers that emigrated from the United States to Texas, being from the southern states of that republic, who are considered there as the least advanced in civilization, introduced customs that were somewhat crude ... [and] not compatible with the manners practiced by persons of good breeding. Lately, however, very honorable and highly cultured families have begun to establish themselves in Texas" ("Statistical" 211; "Secret" 257). In contrast to the "Statistical Report," the "Secret Report" explicitly targets the extent and illegality of Texas slavery. Likely speaking of the slaveholder Jared Groce (Jackson, *Almonte's Texas* 245n33), the narrator states, "I know an individual who owns more than 140 of these wretches, as I am told, in violation of the literal tenor of our laws ("Secret" 245). He continues to warn that if the Mexican government did not intervene quickly, "it will be difficult to [do so] later without causing a revolution of far-reaching consequences" (253). In several letters to the secretary of foreign relations, Almonte suggests military and administrative measures to curb slavery in Texas (Jackson, *Almonte's Texas* 138–139, 184–185).

Unlike the Anglo colonists, the Tejano population appears in both the statistical report and the secret report as likely victims of the adverse conditions of frontier life. Both texts imply that poverty and land speculation seriously had hampered the well-being of Mexican Texan settlers and thus might further impair Mexico's future claim to Texas ("Statistical" 208–209; "Secret" 255). Almonte particularly appeals to the patriotism and political anxieties of his Mexican readers to incite popular concern and governmental action. He writes that rather than fulfilling their contracts, certain Mexican and Anglo empresarios engaged in "pernicious stock-jobbing ... with the lands of the nation" ("Statistical" 207; "Secret" 253–254). In the "Statistical Report," he further urges his government to issue land titles to Mexican colonists who had illegally settled on disputed lands. Since these settlers were "ignorant whether they [were] under the jurisdiction of the United States of America or of Mexico," such a step would secure their ties to their homeland (207).

Tejano culture further served as a litmus test for the state of the province (Callahan 191–192). Articulating the common Mexican perception, also visible in the accounts of the Comisión de Límites, that the Mexican North was culturally backward, the narrator of both of Almonte's texts asks, "What fate can there be in store for those unfortunate Mexicans who now live amidst barbarians without a hope of civilization?" ("Statistical" 193; "Secret" 241). Simultaneously, the two reports blame the Mexican Texans for that very condition, since they claim that the Texas Natives "will never make any progress in civilization if the Mexicans themselves living in those regions are lacking in it" ("Statistical" 194; "Secret" 242).

The travel accounts particularly target the Tejanos' presumed lack of interest in preserving their culture through education. "Those settlers who have the means prefer to send their children to the United States for an education, while those who do not have the means care little about educating their children" ("Statistical" 205; "Secret" 252). Sharing, with Sánchez, the Western view of language as a tool of power, Almonte fears Mexico's loss of Texas if the Mexican population there did not maintain its culture. "Texas needs a good public school where Spanish may be taught," he argues in a passage about the eastern part of the region. "Otherwise this language will disappear. Almost nothing but English is spoken in that part of the republic" ("Statistical" 210; "Secret" 256, 34). While this repeats observations that Almonte included in several letters to Mexican governmental representatives during his journey, it contradicts his concurrent advice to the governor of Coahuila y Texas, enclosed with the secret report, to establish English at least temporarily as a second official language in Texas (Jackson, *Almonte's Texas* 185).

In addition to greedy empresarios and Anglo colonists, the Native population appears as a major threat to Mexican Texas in the "Secret Report." In their descriptions of the Amerindians, Almonte's texts follow the common distinction between nomadic and sedentary nations, frequently calling the former "wild Indians" or "hostile tribes" and the latter "peaceful" or "friendly Indians." Both reports argue that the more powerful Comanches and Tawakonis jeopardized the development of Texas and therefore outline plans to eliminate the two nations by military force ("Statistical" 195, 205; "Secret" 225–226, 242–243, 252; see also Gutiérrez Ibarra 65–67). The "Secret Report" particularly foregrounds the menace that bellicose Amerindians represented for the Mexican Texan population. It strategically evokes the specter of American expansionism to induce Mexican governmental intervention in this matter: having "no more than a weak defense" against the Natives might "force" the Tejanos "to cooperate with the [Anglo] colonists with the aim of uniting with the United States of America" (214). In contrast to this text, the Mexican-settlement-promoting "Statistical Report" assures its readers that "the wild Indians are not as fierce as some travelers describe them" and that "a Mexican is equal to five of them" (184, 195). The "Secret Report" further identifies the steady influx of Amerindians from the United States as another source of conflict in Texas. Although peaceful, these tribes represented a political, cultural, and economic burden. Almonte adds, however, that he preferred Native to Anglo migration: "The Indians are more loyal to [Mexico] . . . and . . . less fearsome than the Americans, should the case arise, because—though they are valiant—they cannot yet combine their movements. Besides that, they do not understand intrigue to the degree that the Americans of the North do" (221). In the colonel's eyes, the Natives' alleged lack of "civilization" rendered them more "desirable" immigrants than the Americans. Underlying this perception was a dualistic view of "civilization" as not only signifying cultural, technological, and intellectual advancement but also entailing the perils of corruption and manipulation.

Both of Almonte's journey accounts repeatedly emphasize the potential usefulness of the peaceful Texas Natives for the Mexican state and downplay their possible threat. They belong to the few non-Native-written texts of the period to question the widespread stereotype of Karankawa anthropophagy. For instance, the narrator of the "Statistical Report" remarks: "[Karankawas] are excellent fishermen and good swimmers. . . . I believe they could be advantageously used in the navy. . . . They have been accused of being cannibals, but I believe this is merely a fable" (194). But like the writings of the Comisión de Límites as well as American and European travelogues, the colonel's texts reserve their highest praise for the sedentary native nations of East Texas, on the grounds of their agrarian lifestyle and political loyalty. "They plant, raise cattle, and are fairly well civilized. In general, they are attached to the Mexican government" ("Statistical" 215). The two reports also support a petition for federal land grants that these nations had filed with the Mexican government as a reward for their political allegiance and cultural assimilation ("Statistical" 215; "Secret" 221, 227, 260; Rajchenberg and Héau-Lambert, "Frontera" 50). The "Secret Report" goes further, suggesting that the tribes could serve as a regional residential barrier against further Anglo immigration to Texas and pointing out their suitability as military allies. Having been "stripped of their lands" by the United States, the text argues, "these Indians are the natural enemies of the Anglo Americans" (221). To render these potential partners more acceptable to his readers, Almonte, like the Comisión de Límites, follows the Western notions of writing and sedentary life as signs of civilization. He thus stresses the Natives' possession of a written language, their knowledge of English, and their willingness to live in houses as evidence of their higher development (221).

In line with other Mexican intellectuals of his time (Weber 284), Almonte considered Mexican governmental action the only solution to the problems he identified in Texas. Both the "Statistical Report" and the "Secret Report" primarily call for the federal administration to promote and financially back Mexican settlement in Texas, invest in infrastructure, modify laws to facilitate commerce, and provide security against warlike Natives ("Statistical" 181, 192–193, 203–204, 207–209; "Secret" 213–214, 233). The "Secret Report" even speaks out against any foreign immigration to Texas. Instead, it argues for a class-based selection of Mexican settlers: "Mexicans of the farming class are just as industrious as any foreigner" (224). This assertion shows how the journey informed Almonte's opinions. In a letter sent from New Orleans in March 1834 to the secretary of foreign relations, he advocated governmental sponsorship of European immigration to Texas (Jackson, *Almonte's Texas* 63–64). In the same vein, both of the colonel's travel accounts seek to prod the Mexican government into enforcing its military presence in Texas: "sending there a competent military force to punish the savages" would make "Mexicans . . . fly to settle those fertile lands that are inviting the settler to work" ("Statistical" 190; "Secret" 224, 237). The "Secret Report" further alerts the government to the larger problem of Mexico's poor border defense, a "disaster, which continually has threatened . . . and continues to threaten" the country (217). The text, accordingly, calls for reinforcing Mexican troops in Texas not only to subdue the Natives and attract Mexican migration but also to fight US expansionism, insurgent Anglo colonists, land-speculating empresarios, and illicit trade, all of which jeopardized Mexican authority and, thereby, its claim to the region (213–215, 217–220, 231, 254; see also Gutiérrez Ibarra 61–62, 65–67). With their focus on seeking to attract Mexican settlers, on the one hand, and making policy recommendations to secure the Mexican status of Texas, on the other, Almonte's reports reveal the dual struggle—and ultimate failure, as the following chapters show—of the Mexican Republic to maintain control over Texas.

As Generosa Callahan observes, the Mexican explorers of Texas "saw the beauty of nature, the undeveloped wealth, and the commercial possibilities; they realized the danger of losing this wealth to the Americans and [they] warned the proper officials" (101). In particular, the skyrocketing number of Anglo immigrants in East Texas, who refused to adapt to the culture of their host country, "blurred the boundary with Louisiana" and thus undermined the idea of the border as a geographic boundary line separating ethnically, culturally, and politically distinct nations (Reséndez 22). Coming from the higher social strata of Mexican society, the travel writers were further appalled by the ignorance and cultural "backwardness" of Tejano society (Callahan 188–189). Similarly, the large number of Amerindians in Texas and their acting as independent nations worried the Mexican visitors. The writers shared their government's view that a large Mexicanized white population would provide a bulwark not only against US territorial expansion but also against indigenous resistance to white settlement in the region. Accordingly, the reports of the Comisión de Límites crucially informed the passing of Mexico's Law of April 6, 1830, which curtailed US immigration to Texas. Reporting favorably about the province for a general Mexican audience while simultaneously compiling a critique for the government, Colonel Almonte "aspired to do what General Terán had labored in vain to accomplish: lure Mexican settlers to Texas in order to preserve its territorial integrity in the face of uncontrolled Anglo-American immigration" (Jackson, *Almonte's Texas* 309). But since the government never took the actions Almonte recommended, his work, like that of the Boundary Commission, failed to help preserve the territorial integrity of Mexico in its boundaries of 1821.

TWO

Charting the Land

Reports of Anglo-American Explorations of Texas

After breaking away from Mexico, Texas became an independent republic and would remain so until the United States permitted its annexation to the Union in 1845 (R. B. Campbell, *Gone to Texas* 159–186; Moyano Pahissa 164, 189–192). Offering generous land grants to white colonists and permitting Black slavery, the Texas Republic attracted Anglo-American settlers from the United States and Europe (R. B. Campbell, *Empire for Slavery* 4, 50–66; Torget 182–183, 194–197, 202–203). Two lines of conflict ensued from their growing number. On the one hand, Amerindian raids continued throughout the region, provoked by ongoing white encroachments on Native lands. Texan troops employed violence to quench indigenous uprisings and forced many Natives to relocate to the periphery of the state, to allocated reservations, or to the adjacent Indian Territory (DeLay 74–85, 194–198, 207–208, 212–217; LaVere 170–176, 180–181, 184–189, 194–201). On the other hand, Anglo-Tejano relations deteriorated, and the border with Mexico remained a further cause of disagreement. Many Mexican Texans found themselves marginalized and even stripped of land titles and citizens' rights, a development that intensified after the annexation of Texas to the United States in 1845 (Gonzales 74, 83–85, 106–112; Montejano 5, 26–29, 82–85). Moreover, the Texas Republic claimed to stretch as far south as the Rio Grande, while Mexico insisted on the original boundary line, which was farther north along the Nueces River (R. B. Campbell, *Gone to Texas* 163–164; Montejano 16–19). When the Mexican government refused to recognize the Rio Grande as the border with its northern neighbor, the United States declared war on Mexico in early 1846. After winning decisively, the Americans forced Mexico to cede all its northern territory, from Texas to Alta California, in the Treaty of Guadalupe Hidalgo in 1848 (R. B. Campbell, *Gone to Texas* 187–189; Vázquez y Vera 118–133).

Although several US military-scientific expeditions had ventured into and through Texas since the early 1800s, the systematic American exploration of the region began only after 1848. At that time, the US Army designated Texas as its Eighth Military Department, deployed nearly 1,500 soldiers there, and erected several lines of fortified military posts to control the Native and Mexican contact zones. I employ the term "contact zones" here to denote "social spaces where disparate cultures meet, clash, and grapple with each other, often in highly asymmetrical relations of dominance and subordination—like colonialism, slavery, or their aftermaths" (Pratt 7). The largest American military-scientific exploration to Texas was the joint US-Mexico boundary commission established to determine and map the exact border between the two countries. The army further deployed a series of local expeditions to survey and prepare suitable lands for white settlement, Native reservations, overland roads, and a transcontinental railroad. For instance, Brevet Lieutenant Colonel Joseph E. Johnston penned his "Reports of... Reconnaissances of Routes from San Antonio to El Paso ... and from Fort Smith to Santa Fe" in 1850. Five years later, Lieutenant John G. Parke and Captain John Pope followed with their "Report on the Exploration of a Route for the Pacific Railroad ... from the Red River to the Rio Grande" (R. B. Campbell, *Gone to Texas* 194–200; Goetzmann, *Army* 211–218, 225–239, 262–266, 289–292; Tate 48–51, 55–57, 72–73).

RANDOLPH B. MARCY'S EXPLORATION ACCOUNTS OF THE RED AND BRAZOS RIVERS

The explorers deployed to the southern and western parts of Texas could rely on earlier American expedition accounts of the region, such as the journalist and soldier George Wilkins Kendall's *Narrative of an Expedition across the Great South-Western Prairies, from Texas to Santa Fé* (1845) or the Santa Fe trader Josiah Gregg's memoir *Commerce of the Prairies* (1844). In contrast, only resident Amerindian nations knew the North Texas–Indian Territory border region. Although several American expeditions, as well as trading or adventuring parties, had explored the lower part of the Red River, they never succeeded in venturing to its upper half (Goetzmann, *Army* 36–38, 41–44; Goetzmann, *Exploration* 42, 46–47, 53–55, 60–61). This state of affairs changed in 1852 when the government commissioned army captain Randolph B. Marcy (1812–1887) to explore and map the headwaters of the Red River (Ward xi). Born and raised in Massachusetts, Marcy had graduated from West Point in 1832 and was immediately assigned to the Fifth Infantry. After fighting in the war with Mexico, he served at army posts in the American Southwest until the late 1850s. From there, he carried out several expeditions through North Texas, New Mexico, and the southern Rocky Mountains (Fehr 2–15; Foreman v–xii; Hollon 3–125).

Pointing out the lack of information about the Red River region to the adjutant general of the US Army in 1852, Marcy offered to lead a military-scientific expedition to the area (Fehr 15; Foreman xii–xiii; Hollon 123–124). In March, he received orders "to make an examination of the Red river, and the country bordering upon it, from the mouth of Cache Creek to its sources" (Marcy and McClellan, *Adventure* 3). His instructions specifically asked him to "collect and report everything that may be useful or interesting in relation to [the region's] resources, soil, climate, natural history, and geography." His duties further included assessing the possibility of settling the area's nomadic indigenous nations and threatening them with military force if they continued to attack Texas settlements (Foreman xiii–xiv; Hollon 133). Setting out from Fort Belknap near the mouth of the Wichita River on May 2, the company traveled to the headwaters of the North Fork of the Red River in mid-June. It subsequently journeyed south toward the stream's South Fork. A small group explored its main branch, and when it reached a spring at the base of the Llano Estacado—most likely in Tule Canyon (Morris 271, 274, 277)—Marcy proclaimed it the source of the South Fork. The entire company returned along the Red River and via the Wichita Mountains, which run parallel to it, reaching Fort Arbuckle in Indian Territory on July 28 (Fehr 15–16; Hollon 130–153). The expedition had been widely publicized even before the explorers returned, because of media rumors that Comanches had murdered the party (Foreman xix–xx; Hollon 150–151, 153–157). In March 1853, Marcy gave a well-received lecture about his journey before the American Statistical and Geographical Society in New York, and during the 1853–1854 session, Congress printed his expedition report, written with his assistant, George B. McClellan. Owing to the ongoing popular interest in the expedition, the War Department published it in book form as *Exploration of the Red River of Louisiana in the Year 1852* (1854) and afterward as *Adventure on Red River* (Foreman xiv, xvii–xix; Hollon 145–146, 164–166). Marcy also integrated parts of this report in his memoirs *Thirty Years of Army Life on the Border* (1866) and *Border Reminiscences* (1872).

The captain returned to North Texas less than two years after his journey to the Red River. In response to ongoing Amerindian raids of settlements on the Texas frontier, the Texas Legislature approved a measure on February 6, 1854, to provide "eighteen leagues of unlocated lands to form a reserve for the settlement of all Indians within the State's borders" (Hollon 169). In April, the army ordered Marcy to command a military-scientific expedition to explore the sources of the Brazos and Wichita Rivers, with instructions similar to those for his Red River journey; that exploration would complement the task of identifying suitable land for the planned reservation. The captain's company set out from Fort Smith, Arkansas, on June 1 and arrived at Fort Belknap six weeks later. The group continued to the Little Wichita River and then followed the Wichita (also called the Big Wichita) to its source. From there, they traveled south, crossing the source branches of the Brazos River, and then east to explore the region between the Salt Fork and Clear Fork of the Brazos. After examining a land tract for an Indian reservation on the Clear Fork, Marcy's party held councils with several indigenous nations in the area and at Fort Belknap, where the company had returned by September 7. After the consultations, they surveyed a tract for a second reservation near the fort before heading east in October. In 1855, Marcy submitted his official expedition report to the adjutant general, and Congress published it in the following year as *Report of an Expedition to the Sources of the Brazos and Big Witchita Rivers, During the Summer of 1854* (Fehr 17; Hollon 169–187).

Marcy's reports of his two North Texas expeditions have a similar structure. A chronological section, based on the captain's travel journal and retaining its diary format, charts the itinerary of each journey. Upon this follows a thematically organized part that strongly articulates the writer's scientific agenda. In a largely sober tone and employing Linnaean terminology (Morris 266–267, 340), these sections describe and evaluate the topography, geology, plant and animal life, weather conditions, and resident indigenous nations of the explored territories. A topographical map accompanying each narrative charts the explorers' routes, marks notable geological formations, and identifies Amerindian dwelling places.[1] In *Adventure on Red River*, references to earlier American expedition accounts of the Lower Red River and neighboring regions further reveal Marcy's concern to complement his observations with those of others in order to increase the accuracy of his report (5–10, 95, 153). To underline the scholarly character of the expedition, the volume provides information on the military and civilian scientists who took part in the exploration and analyzed the collected specimens (xxix–xxxi; see also Hollon 133–135). In the same vein, the report on the Brazos and Wichita Rivers integrates the comments by two renowned scientists that confirm Marcy's assessments of the natural-science value of the expedition (Marcy, *Report* 24–28, 46–47). Of greatest interest to Marcy's sponsors, *Adventure on Red River* discusses potential routes for a transcontinental railroad (vi, 178). This was a subject of heated debate in American politics at the time, since states were competing for the prospective railway line to run through their territories (Hollon 167). The *Report of an Expedition*, on the other hand, identifies those stretches of land that Marcy had located for the first two Indian reservations in Texas. To justify this endeavor, Marcy explicitly stresses the agreement of several Native nations to settle there (2–3, 22–23).

In the Brazos River report, Marcy paints a largely differentiated picture of a host of indigenous nations living in North Texas (2–3, 8–9, 17–22, 28–41). Both here and in his other North Texas exploration account, he occasionally refers to Amerindians as "savage(s)." More often, however, he calls them "Indians," "tribes," or "nations," or uses their names. In characterizing indigenous peoples as a group, *Adventure on Red River* and the *Report of an Expedition* follow both Mexican and American observers' writings in relying on cultural stereotypes, denying the nations the status of "civilizations" and providing generalizing moral judgments about Natives according to their way of life and behavior toward whites. Yet in contrast to the many US Army officers who utterly mistrusted the loyalty of their Native scouts (S. Smith 164–166, 172–175), Marcy's writings reveal his deep attachment to the Shawnee and Delaware guides and hunters employed on his expeditions. Both journey accounts call these men "our" Indians, or by their names, and praise them not only for their professional skills in shooting and horseback riding but also for their bravery, loyalty, and obedience (*Adventure* 46–47, 54–56, 121–124; *Report* 18, 39–40; see also Hollon 127–128, 149–150). The truly "good Indians," the Red River exploration report, in particular, implies, used their cultural background to help the very Anglo-American society that had earlier harmed their nation to now advance against other Amerindians. This positive view of local tribes becomes most obvious in Marcy's recommendation that US troops in the Indian contact zones hire such guides: "Their knowledge of Indian character and habits, and their wonderful powers of judging of country . . . [would] enable us to operate to much greater advantage against the prairie tribes" (*Adventure* 56).

In addition to the Natives directly serving Anglo-Americans, *Adventure on Red River* and the *Report of an Expedition* favor those indigenous nations whose way of life came closest to Euro-American cultural norms and particularly the ideal of the industrious yeoman farmer. For instance, Marcy notes approvingly of the Choctaws: "[They had] abandoned the precarious and uncertain life of the hunter for the more quiet avocation of the husbandman. They look upon the wild Indian in much the same light as we do" (*Adventure* 120). The only semi-sedentary Wichitas and Wacos appear in a more ambivalent light in the captain's books. Although they cultivated fertile lands, the narrator argues in the Red River expedition report that the two nations' lack of foresight profoundly marred their agriculture: "The prolific soil gives them bountiful returns; and were it not for their improvident natures, they might, with little labor, have sufficient for the whole year. Instead of this, they only care for the present, and from the time the corn is fit for roasting, are continually eating and feasting until it is gone. They are then obliged to depend on the precarious results of the chase during the remainder of the year" (24–25). In a similar vein, the travelogue acknowledges the legitimacy of the Wichitas' concern about white encroachments on their ancestral lands (30–31, 68, 112). Yet the text simultaneously denounces the tribe members as infamous beggars and "the most notorious and inveterate horse-thieves upon the borders" (112).

Like many of his peers, Marcy paints a more differentiated picture of individual Natives with whom he established a relationship (S. Smith 29, 42). In addition to his Delaware and Shawnee scouts, this favorable view takes in some of the Comanche chiefs with whom he negotiated their tribe's settlement on a reservation, and whose humanity and intelligence the captain acknowledges (*Report* 17, 20–22; see also Hämäläinen 308–309). In contrast, the Comanche Nation appears in his North Texas narratives as the epitome of a warlike nomadic Plains

Indians tribe, even though *Adventure on Red River* recognizes the socioeconomic function of raids as a means for young men to obtain status, wealth, and marriage opportunities (156, 159; see also Hämäläinen 266–269). In many other respects, the book sketches a rather homogenous image of the Comanches (141–143, 154–168), whereas the *Report of an Expedition* acknowledges distinctions within the nation. Although no Comanche band lived a fully nomadic life year-round (Hämäläinen 283–290), the text establishes a clear hierarchy of value among different branches of the Comanches, depending on their perceived degree of nomadism and the character traits Marcy attached to it. This becomes particularly evident in the language of the travelogue. Thus, the Southern Comanches, who showed readiness to become fully sedentary, were "lead[ing] a predatory and pastoral life, roving from place to place" (*Report* 28). The Northern Comanches, in contrast, "range[d] the plains upon the trail of the buffaloes, with that wild spirit of adventure," and their "savage instincts elevate[d] them little above the level of the brute" (30, 34).

Both of Marcy's exploration accounts frame not only the Comanches but also other Plains Indians, with their equestrian hunter cultures, nomadic way of life, and independence from white dominance, as opposites of both Anglo civilization and the sedentary Native nations of the eastern United States. For example, the journey narrative to the Red River characterizes the generic Plains Indian as "free as the boundless plains over which he roams," adding that "he sighs not for the titles and distinctions which occupy the thoughts and engage the energies of civilized man" (*Adventure* 155–156). A yearning to abandon the social constraints of Anglo civilization resonates in these lines, as it does in utterances by other US Army officers (S. Smith 134). But this passage nonetheless asserts Native inferiority to Anglo culture in order to discredit indigenous land claims and to justify the US colonial policy of westward expansion and Amerindian removal. To strengthen this line of reasoning further, *Adventure on Red River* conveys the Otherness of the Plains Indians by likening them to Oriental nomads. Drawing on a common analogy in European and American writings about the North American West, the narrator frames both groups as simultaneously noble and abject: "The Arabs of the desert, the Tartar tribes, and the aboriginal occupants of the prairies, are alike wanderers, having no permanent abiding-places. . . . Their government is patriarchal. . . . They are insensible to the wants and comforts of civilization. . . . Theirs is a happy state of equality, which knows not the perplexities of ambition nor the crimes of avarice. They never cultivate the soil but subsist altogether upon game and [upon] what they can steal" (157–158). Marcy does not explicitly extend the Orientalist analogy to these areas of discourse. Yet his depictions of indigenous gender roles and raids on white settlements resort to Orientalist stereotypes of male cruelty and sexual license. The captain's North Texas travelogues point out the practice of polygyny among the Comanches (*Adventure* 157, 165, 169; *Report* 32) and compare Native women's status to that of African American slaves in the US South: "The distance of rank and consideration which exists between the black slave and his master is not greater than between the Comanche warrior and his wife" (*Adventure* 167; see also *Report* 32). Like many other American military officers, Marcy viewed the Amerindian nations' treatment of women—as seen through the lens of Anglo-American gender roles—as a key indicator of their degree of "civility" (S. Smith 57–60, 67–72). Accordingly, the captain admits, in a mixture of admiration and unease, not only that Native women excelled on horseback and appeared content with their lives, but also that some Anglo women captives of the tribe had chosen to adopt Comanche life rather than return to white society (*Adventure* 128, 156, 167; see also Sibley 81–82).

Even more than their defiance of Anglo gender norms, the Comanches' violation of the racialized slave code aroused Marcy's scrutiny (Hämäläinen 250–259). Although his texts do not explicitly endorse the "peculiar institution" of the South—African American slavery—neither of the North Texas travelogues takes much issue with it, certainly not to the degree that they condemn women's status in Native societies and Plains Indians' raiding of Texas settlements (*Adventure* 128–129, 160, 169; *Report* 9, 13–14, 17, 30–31). Marcy's rejection of such raids becomes particularly obvious in his calling the Plains Indians "freebooters" (*Adventure* 159; *Report* 37, 40). Widely feared for their naval mobility, cruelty, and abducting of white voyagers, the pirates of the Caribbean and the Barbary Coast had been subdued by British and US forces only a few decades earlier. Through the reference to piracy, Marcy supports his claim, quite typical of a US Army officer in the Indian contact zones (S. Smith 97–102, 106–109), that a strong American military presence close to Native regions was needed in order to subjugate the Amerindians and settle them on reservations (*Adventure* 142–145; *Report* 34–35, 40–41). In so arguing, the captain contributed to the US colonial policy of opening and securing the entire West for white settlement.

Marcy's rejection of nomadism was not limited to indigenous nations but, in line with the views of other US Army officers, also extended to the white population of the North American West (S. Smith 21–22, 27, 114–130). *Adventure on Red River* and the *Report of an Expedition* show disdain for "semi-civilized" and "unprincipled" white traders and settlers. "Preferring a life of dangerous adventure and solitude to personal security and the comforts and enjoyments of society," these men, the texts claim, formed "a lawless border population, which does not hesitate to take the life of an Indian upon the slightest provocation" (*Adventure* 5, 155; *Report* 33). The volumes further alert readers to the harm that both white frontier dwellers and government agents had done to the Amerindians by decimating the key component of their livelihoods, the buffalo; by introducing them to a range of vices; and by treating them unfairly in the whites' greed for land (*Adventure* 171–172, 176–177; *Report* 28–29, 34). In so arguing, the two books delegitimize those groups of whites that rivaled the military's claim to power in the Amerindian contact zone while simultaneously endorsing the American colonization of the North American West. In line with other US Army officers' writings (S. Smith 107), both volumes call for governmental intervention to protect Natives from white land hunger and to help them assimilate to Anglo culture (*Adventure* 173–175; *Report* 35–36). In his Red River exploration account, Marcy goes even further:

> While our benevolent and philanthropic citizens are making such efforts to ameliorate the conditions of savages in other countries, should we not do something for the benefit of these wild men of the prairies? Those dingy noblemen of nature . . . have been despoiled, supplanted, and robbed of their just and legitimate heritage, by the avaricious and rapid encroachments of the white man. . . . It is now in our power to . . . introduc[e] among them the light of Christianity and the blessings of civilization, with their attendant benefits of agriculture and the arts. (*Adventure* 176)

Strikingly, the narrator falls victim to his colonial discourse. On the one hand, he scrutinizes the irony inherent in American missionaries' spreading Christianity across the globe while ignoring the indigenous population of the United States. On the other hand, his call to Christianize the Plains Indians as compensation for their suffering at the hands of whites fails to grasp the role that evangelization had played in the country's postcolonial policy of territorial expansion and indigenous genocide.

Moreover, in line with other military-scientific exploration accounts of the West, this and other passages in *Adventure on Red River* inextricably connect the Amerindian nations of Texas with the landscapes they reside in. One of these scenes imbues the topography of the Cross Timbers, a stretch of land forming part of the transition ecoregion between the eastern forests and the Great Plains, with a civilizing aura. For Marcy, as for many of his contemporaries, the area signified "a natural barrier between civilized man and the savage" (139; see also Francaviglia, *Cast Iron* 80–81, 84, 106). Without mentioning the subject of settlement, *Adventure on Red River* presents the woodland bordering the Cross Timbers to the east as a picturesque and fertile area that invites the farmer: "There are numerous spring-brooks flowing over a highly prolific soil . . . , teeming with the delightful perfume of flowers of the most brilliant hues . . . [and] the most beautiful natural meadows that can be imagined" (139). In contrast, and similarly echoing other travelers' accounts, the captain's text portrays the Great Plains stretching westward from the Cross Timbers as an utterly hostile space: "barren and desolate wastes" whose "few small streams . . . are soon swallowed up by the thirsty sands over which they flow" (139; see also Francaviglia, *Cast Iron* 78, 92). Elsewhere, Marcy's travelogues describe indigenous peoples and wild beasts as (almost) interchangeable parts of nature. For instance, the reports depict the Plains Indians as freely "roam[ing]," "roving," or "rang[ing]" across the region (*Adventure* 154; *Report* 28, 30). *Adventure on Red River* remarks, in similar phrasing, that the buffalo once enjoyed its "free range from one end of the continent to another" (171).

Like the Mexican scientific-military expedition accounts of Texas in the late 1820s and early 1830s, Marcy's travel reports blend scientific observations and a utilitarian discourse of the land with "florid prose" (Morris 273) and a romanticist aesthetic imaginary. Owing to the different conditions of the regions traveled through, the captain's two expedition accounts strikingly differ in their assessment of the territories. The *Report of an Expedition* comments on both arable and infertile lands (5–11, 15–16, 18–20, 23–24). Near the confluence of the Wichita River's headstreams, the narrator encountered "a barren and parsimonious soil" whose vegetation of cacti and scarcity of wood or potable water made "even the Indians shun this country" (11). Later, he cites the counterexample of a white settler whose farm thrived with little effort, to demonstrate that his journey had been worthwhile, since part of the explored territory was suited to establishing Indian reservations (19). In contrast, the pastoral imagery of a usually "fertile" or "productive" soil dominates *Adventure on Red River*. Settlements would flourish easily near the Upper Red River because water, timber, fruit, and game were "abundant" there, and both wild and stock animals would prosper on "luxuriant" pasturage (24, 33, 105–106, 119). In addition to this rhetoric of plenitude, Marcy engages in a discourse of pleasure, integrating vivid depictions of several hunting expeditions, which promised relief from toil (19–20, 46–47, 82–83, 114–115).

In a similar vein, both *Adventure on Red River* and the *Report of an Expedition* take note whenever a landscape provided the traveler with an emotional experience according to the romanticist categories of the beautiful, the picturesque, and the sublime. For example, the Wichita Mountains offer the traveler "beautiful and majestic scenery . . . , with the charming glades lying between [the mountains], clothed with a luxuriant sward up the very bases of the almost perpendicular and rugged sides" (*Adventure* 39). This and several other vistas in the two texts were observed from an elevated vantage point that, as noted earlier, implies a traveler's sense of entitlement to claim the land thus overviewed (*Adventure* 36–37, 39, 90–92, 114; *Report* 4, 10, 15). This rhetoric of aesthetic pleasure available for the taking complements the claim to agricultural value. Both arguments present many areas in North Texas as suited for either white settlers or Indian reservations, thereby toning down governmental concerns about the hardships of subjugating the Natives and economically developing the region. In so doing, Marcy's travel reports contributed to the American colonial discourse of westward expansion that framed the North American West as an economic and spiritual promise. The nation could thus justify appropriating the land, promoting white settlement there, and removing the resident Amerindian populations.

In addition to emphasizing the aesthetic appeal of a given area, *Adventure on Red River* and the *Report of an Expedition* seek to render the North Texas landscape comprehensible to their target readers in the eastern United States by comparing the plains and mountains to those in Europe or the Orient. This was a common strategy in nineteenth-century travel writing about the North American West, since many educated Americans were familiar with these reference landscapes from other texts or works of visual art (Francaviglia, *Go East* 15–17, 25–33, 48–49, 75–80; Morris 251, 263, 335, 341). For instance, John Miller Morris observes that Marcy's account depicts the entrance into Tule Canyon as "a landscape analogous to Scottish mountain highlands" (273; see Marcy, *Adventure* 87). An even more striking example is the captain's depiction of the Llano Estacado, the "staked plains" plateau in the Texas Panhandle. *Adventure on Red River* frames the Llano as the opposite of the fertile and pleasant Red River valley: "These towering and majestic cliffs ... rise almost perpendicularly from the undulating swells of the prairie at the base ... and terminate at the summit in a plateau ..., which spreads out to the south and west like the steppes of Central Asia, in an apparently illimitable desert" (81). In thus describing the Llano, the captain follows the popular representation of the Great Plains in earlier travelogues as the "Great American Desert," akin to the Sahara or the Asian steppe (Francaviglia, *Go East* 32–33; H. Smith 175–180), which discouraged white settlement in the region (LeMenager 24–25, 45–46).

This passage further illustrates another common feature of romanticist aesthetic discourse that Marcy employs in his reports. As Robin Doughty observes, the captain's texts "treated landscape as a spectacle for wonder and contemplation" (49). *Adventure on Red River* in particular conveys the travelers' emotional and intellectual responses to nature rather than describing its appearance. For instance, the narrator expresses the group's awe at encountering what they considered the headwaters of the Red River's South Fork, a place presumably unknown to white travelers: "We all, with one accord, stopped and gazed with wonder and admiration upon a panorama, which was now for the first time exhibited to the eyes of civilized men" (91). In a similar vein, Marcy views the nature of Tule Canyon through the cultural lens of a romanticist European-landscape aesthetic, particularly the Gothic sublime, with its fondness for chiaroscuro effects, rugged shapes, and ancient European architecture (Morris 274): "The stupendous escarpments of solid rock ... [had] the most fantastic forms. ... Occasionally might be seen a good representation of the towering walls of a castle of the feudal ages, with its giddy battlements pierced with loopholes, and its projecting watch-towers.... All here was crude nature, as it sprang into existence at the fiat of the Almighty architect of the universe, still preserving its primeval type, its unreclaimed sublimity and wildness" (*Adventure* 91). According to Robin Doughty, invoking the divine creator of this landscape and establishing "such analogies to man-made structures placed the observer above nature and in a superior position to it," despite his insignificance in relation to its vastness and longevity (49). Hence, in addition to providing an analogy that rendered the "wild" western nature familiar to Eastern audiences, the architectural comparison endowed it with cultural value. The analogy stands in the tradition of an American nature discourse that sought to compensate for the short history of white civilization on the continent by emphasizing the age, splendor, and size of the territory (Hyde 13, 16–19). Such passages once again exemplify how Marcy's reports contributed to US policy, and the US Army's role in it, of Anglo-Americanizing its newly obtained territories in the North American West through enforced Amerindian removal and the establishment of white settlements.

WILLIAM B. PARKER'S *THROUGH UNEXPLORED TEXAS*

In 1854, Marcy invited William Brown Parker (c. 1818–1862), a civilian journalist and friend, to accompany him on his expedition to the Brazos and Wichita Rivers. A graduate of Dickinson College in Pennsylvania, Parker had worked in the iron business in New York for several years, and from 1850 to 1853 he edited *Parker's Journal* (Parker 10–11; Ward xi–xii). Two years after the journey with Marcy, he published his travel diary as *Through Unexplored Texas: Notes Taken during the Expedition Commanded by Capt. R. B. Marcy, U.S.A., in the Summer and Fall of 1854*. In a chronological narrative that retains the format of the private diary, the volume charts the itinerary of the expedition, with an emphasis on describing the land and characterizing its indigenous inhabitants. The final chapter further provides a thematic survey of the Native nations he encountered. In contrast to Marcy's reports, which express a military officer's point of view and target political and military readers, Parker's travelogue articulates the perspective of a civilian novice to the West for a general American audience. In his preface, the writer justifies his work through a *figura modestiae*, a rhetorical gesture of modesty. He argues that his friends persuaded him to publicize his reminiscences, and he expresses his wish to simultaneously educate and entertain his readers (Parker 7–8). The title of the narrative sets the tone for the way the volume frames North Texas as a terra incognita and the expedition as a dangerous errand into this wilderness: "a country entirely unknown to white men, except as a retiring spot of numerous predatory bands of Indians" (143). To underline its claim to scholarly value and authority, the text refers to the scientific expertise and activities of the party's leading officers. Moreover, the title page of the book explicitly states that the author was "attached to the expedition" (n.p.).

Parker's intention to entertain his readers becomes obvious in his writing style. Interspersing descriptions of the journey with numerous anecdotes about places and people, "Parker's narrative runs from the comic to the tragic, the ridiculous to the sublime" (Ward xiii). *Through Unexplored Texas* employs cultural references to the Bible, classical mythology, and European and American geography to make unfamiliar experiences and vistas comprehensible and vivid to educated readers seeking armchair adventures. For instance, the book gently ridicules the expedition's enlisted soldiers by calling these rough men "gallant sons of Mars," and it likens a passage through difficult terrain to "descending the Alps" (Parker 70, 144). Elsewhere the text describes the simultaneous occurrence of a prairie fire and a thunderstorm by alluding to the biblical image of "a pillar of fire and a pillar of cloud" (88; see Exod. 13:21–22). The most striking references of this kind are the analogies between the Panhandle Plains and an Oriental desert or steppe, and between the original residents of these landscapes, the Plains Indians, and the Arab and Tartar nomads (62, 143, 239). These Orientalist references form a key element of Parker's writing. Although he admits in his text that not all the incidents in his book stem from his experiences (8), the writer rarely acknowledges his sources. Parker paraphrased or copied many of the descriptions and observations in *Through Unexplored Texas*, including the Oriental references, from Marcy's accounts of his four expeditions through North Texas and Indian Territory, without giving the captain credit for his writings.

Like Marcy and other US Army officers deployed to the North American West, Parker depicts the Amerindian nations of Texas in a blend of stereotypes and differentiation. The book praises the loyalty and scouting abilities of the expedition's Delaware and Shawnee guides (83–84, 144–145, 212, 221–228), but depicts the Wacos, Tawakonis, and Wichitas as culturally degraded beggars and horse thieves. The Comanches are warlike "Lords of the Plains" whose ongoing defiance of Anglo-Americanization would doom them to extinction (111–115, 154, 228, 231–241). Moreover, *Through Unexplored Texas* conveys the presumed animalistic nature of the Wacos, Tawakonis, Wichitas, and Comanches through references to wild beasts. The book likens their songs and dances to animal sounds and the movements of monkeys; it calls the Comanches "wild creatures" and treats the Wacos and Tawakonis similarly: "Except [for] their greater capacity for mischief, there was no difference between [them] and…wolves" (195, 115). These stereotypes of the Amerindians also manifest themselves in the writer's terminology. Usually calling them "Indians," "tribes," or "natives," or by their nations' names, he speaks of "wild Indians" or "savages" whenever he criticizes indigenous societies. More explicitly than Marcy's reports, Parker's travelogue establishes a racial hierarchy among the indigenous nations of Texas, based on their physiognomic resemblance to Anglo-Americans. For instance, the text causally connects the Delaware guide John Conner's intelligence to both his independent, rational thinking and his fair complexion. In contrast, the volume praises a darker-skinned Shawnee scout as a "noble specimen of his race," but only with regard to his physical abilities "of wild vigor and endurance" (116–117). Similarly, another passage asks, "What clearer proof is necessary of the inefficiency of the pure blooded native to manage in a civilized community, than the fact, that in almost every instance, the leading men [of the Choctaws and Chickasaws] either are half-breeds, or have a tincture of white blood in their veins?" (62). Parker implies that not only individual Natives, but also entire nations owed their accomplishments—here, a sedentary life—to Anglo-Saxon racial influence.

Aligning with Marcy and other white travelers, Parker treated gender roles and slavery among the Native nations as a litmus test of their "civility." In line with his other judgments, he points out that Delaware women owned property and that polygyny was rare among the tribe. In contrast, a strong sexual double standard governed Comanche society, in his view, since men enjoyed sexual license while "women [were] looked upon as slaves or beasts of burden" (233). Similarly, while *Through Unexplored Texas* notes that some indigenous nations practiced slavery, the bondage of Blacks or Natives did not arouse the narrator's concern (26, 34, 57). Grossly minimizing the inhumanity of the peculiar institution, he claims that because of slaves' exposure to white civilization in the southern United States, "the humanized condition of the African race [in American bondage] differs from the brutal condition of the negro in Guinea" (63). In contrast, Parker deplores the Indian captivity of people of European descent. In one scene, he observes that an invalid Comanche "had a *slave* . . . , a Mexican, taken prisoner in some foray, dressed and painted like an Indian, and apparently quite reconciled to his degraded life" (193–194, original emphasis). Right before this passage, Parker's text pities the invalid as a "poor creature" for having to endure the hardships of nomadic life with a disability (193). But outrage at the enslavement of a young Mexican outweighs Parker's sympathy for a crippled man entirely dependent on his servant. Moreover, like Marcy and other military observers, the civilian traveler strongly disapproves of the Hispanic youth's evident integration into the Comanche Nation, as his clothes and demeanor indicated.

This episode from Comanche life exemplifies how Parker's narrative, despite its ample plagiarizing from Marcy's travelogues, goes beyond the captain's sketches of the indigenous populations of North Texas and Indian Territory. "The wealth of ethnographic detail and the rich individual portraits of Indians," George Ward writes, "make *Through Unexplored Texas* a useful resource as well as a revealing reflection of contemporary values" (xiii). For instance, the account hints at the complexity of the relations between the Delawares and white society, which goes unmentioned in Marcy's writings. While John Conner dreamed of leading an Anglo-American way of life, the Delaware Nation sought to profit politically from its members' loyalty to white explorers (Parker 214, 218–219, 225). Many other passages, however, rely on popular Anglo-American stereotypes about indigenous peoples. Written for a general audience, the volume repeatedly presents the Natives as both childlike beings requiring Anglo guardianship and as an exotic spectacle for white consumption. Most prominently, the narrator calls the North Texas Natives "dusky children of the Plains" (218). Elsewhere, he describes a group of brightly clad Choctaws as "truly picturesque," and a Kickapoo hunting camp as "a wild scene . . . [of] naked dusty savages bustling in the lurid glare of their fires, and looking like so many demons" (18, 108). Even the Choctaws and Chickasaws, whom Parker viewed as relatively "civilized," since they farmed on government-allocated lands, are framed in images of culturally deficient Otherness. Their subsistence agriculture was unprofitable, their law enforcement weak, and their practice of slavery repulsive. Moreover, the traveler attributed all these deficits to the laziness, indifference, improvidence, and inclinations to vice that he saw as innate in all Amerindian nations (25–28, 34–41, 57–62, 111–113).

Like Marcy and other military officers (S. Smith 42–50), Parker gives a more differentiated account of individual Amerindians. One particularly telling scene in *Through Unexplored Texas* portrays a Cherokee chief's daughter as an "Indian Princess," a female version of the noble savage stereotype (Parker 56). "A proud specimen of native grace," well mannered and Anglo educated but also a skilled hunter and horseback rider, she simultaneously conformed to and deviated from the prescribed Anglo gender role for women. The narrator captures her position between Native and white culture in the image of the "prairie flower" (14), which blends the Anglo ideal of feminine delicacy and innocence with the wildness associated with the Amerindians. Parker's encounter with the Cherokee woman gives rise to a motif that runs through his entire narrative: the contrast between the "ancient nobility of her race," on the one hand, and the "present degradation" and decimation of her nation, on the other (14–15). In using the trope of the "vanishing Indian," whose culture was bound to disappear soon, *Through Unexplored Texas* indulges in the American romanticist cult of primitivism, which glorified precontact indigenous cultures as idyllic and dignified and considered their "degeneration" and extinction a natural consequence of contact with the higher Anglo civilization (S. Smith 22–23, 26–27, 40). Several passages of the travelogue castigate white American society for having eliminated the buffalo and introduced the Amerindians to alcohol while withholding religious salvation from them (Parker 57, 72, 101–102, 241). But such moments of critical reflection primarily serve to confirm white America's responsibility to take care of these "children" of nature (218), and this belief entailed relocating Amerindians to allocated lands. Unlike Marcy, Parker opposed the reservation system. Considering the Natives incapable of succeeding as farmers, he wished to distribute fertile land exclusively to white settlers (63–65, 205–206).

Through Unexplored Texas also reports on army life and white immigration to North Texas. The volume gives a rare glimpse into the hardships of military service and settlement on the frontier, which were largely unknown to other Americans (S. Smith 7–8). Although the travelogue presents the enlisted men of the expedition as irascible, coarse, and given to drinking (Parker 54, 68, 72–74, 190–191), it explicitly sets out to correct widespread stereotypes about their living conditions in the West. "I would [wish] that some of our brawlers in Congress, and on the hustings, could visit these remote posts, and see a soldier's life in its true colors," the narrator exclaims. "Theirs is no carpet-knight service, but a stern reality" that required "all the energies of their natures" (217). This passage particularly targets the army's political critics. While many western settlers welcomed the military, army leaders constantly had to justify their presence in the region to easterners by emphasizing the entangled roles of the army as a guardian and a carrier of Anglo-American civilization (S. Smith 8–10, 106–107, 125–126; Tate 308). In the same vein, one passage responds to the unrealistic views of officers' lives that were circulating in the growing body of western fiction. "It is all very pretty to write on paper, and to talk of the chivalry and romance of a soldier's life, of the tented field, the glittering review, or the charging squadron," Parker writes. In reality, however, "a young lieutenant . . . [is] sent out upon a lonely prairie, to govern a company of men . . . naturally brutal and vicious . . . knowing . . . that his duty is done at the risk of health and life, and for a pittance of pay" (Parker 74).

Parker likewise addresses the difficulties of migrating to North Texas. Although his travelogue endorses European and Euro-American migration to the region, the book points out the privations awaiting settlers, the unfamiliar climate, the isolation, the long distance to towns and markets, and the perils of the wilderness (24–25, 49–50). Moreover, passing by an immigrant's grave, the narrator laments, "Poor fellow! all his hopes of home and fortune in the land of freedom, lay here on a barren hill-side in this wild Indian country—such is life, a vision, a struggle, a grave" (25). The tomb serves not only as a general memento mori but also as a specific reminder that many immigrants would find death, rather than wealth, in the West. In thus outlining the perils of frontier life, *Through Unexplored Texas* urges potential settlers to consider carefully before coming to Texas. As this passage illustrates, and as George Ward argues, Parker's "view of nature, wilderness, and frontier adventure is typical of the mid-nineteenth-century romantic mind-set; his vocabulary is dotted with its emotional language" (xii).

His journal particularly relies on the romanticist categories of the beautiful, the picturesque, and the sublime to convey his impressions of the North Texas landscape. Above all, the imposing topography and extreme weather conditions of the region provided travelers with a sublime experience. For instance, he presents the Cross Timbers as a barrier between civilization and wilderness via the image of a fortress overlooking a dark forest, which recalls European fairy tales as much as Marcy's report of the Red River expedition: "Suddenly and abruptly we found ourselves upon the brink of a steep descent. On either side large grassy bluffs stood like fortifications, terrace and bastion rising over the other, as if to guard the entrance. Below, stretching as far as the eye could reach, lay the apparently interminable forest of the Cross Timbers, like a barrier, on passing which we were to be shut out from civilization" (Parker 93).

Almost functioning as an antidote to such a scene, the narrator repeatedly depicts the expedition's campsites as veritably pastoral idylls (41, 98, 174, 187). In another passage, he praises "the glorious beauty" of scenery in the Choctaw territory: "Below . . . lay a sea of a pale green, hemmed in by timber of a darker hue; flowers of every variety . . . , trees, scattered in such perfect arrangement over the whole, as to seem as though some eminent artist had perfected the work. . . . The view, fully realized descriptions of the parks of the English nobility and gentry, wanting only the presence of animal life" (31–32). This is but one of many instances in which *Through Unexplored Texas*, following both Marcy's reports and the Mexican military exploration accounts of Texas, describes a beautiful or picturesque vista, often seen from an elevated vantage point (156–157, 162–163, 170–171). Like a later scene that calls the North Texas landscape "earth's garden" (65), the passage just cited perfectly captures Parker's engagement with the picturesque ideal of romanticist nature discourse. Whereas the Cross Timbers appeared vast and monotonous below the bluff, the landscape of the Choctaw lands was varied, fertile, and harmoniously proportioned, like an English landscape garden. Since the late eighteenth century, the often barely visible human interventions into the natural terrain that characterized English parks were viewed as improving nature (Callahan 48–54, 58, 66–67; Doughty 9, 18–19). Moreover, this aesthetic ideal had been taken up by American observers of nature. For the American cultural elite, "a beautiful view was one that reminded the observer of a European scene" (Hyde 17). In describing the Choctaw territory as a parklike English landscape, Parker's travelogue appeals to this ideal in order to present the unfamiliar western terrain as comprehensible and desirable to his target readers in the eastern United States.

Like Marcy or the Mexican military travelers, Parker further blends this sort of aesthetic description in his narrative with a utilitarian discourse. The latter engages a language of plenitude versus scarcity in order to distinguish areas suited for settlement from those that were not. The arid, treeless plains made the traveler feel "disgusted with so inhospitable a country," and like Marcy, Parker predicted that this area would remain forever "uninhabited and uninhabitable" (162, 173). Yet *Through Unexplored Texas* also praises the "fertile" soil, "rich" pastures, "luxuriant" vegetation, and "plentiful" or "abundant" water, timber, and game of other sections of the country that the explorers traveled through (43–44, 56–58, 158, 183–184). Above all, however, the narrator showed great foresight in recognizing the potential of the region for the growing cattle industry, which would soon "mark Texas as the great stock-yard of our country" (118).

Characteristic of scientific exploration accounts of the period (Hume), Parker "balances his romantic impressions with realistic and scientific descriptions" (Ward xii), at times even juxtaposing the two modes of description. Near Cottonwood Springs, for example: "Long ranges of precipitous bluffs bounded the horizon, looking like so many barriers to our future progress. These bluffs were of igneous formation, and afforded a fine field for the geologist" (Parker 121). Elsewhere, a soberer tone and scientific focus prevail. In one instance, the writer supports his observation with a scientific analysis of the soil in a footnote (155–156). Most striking, however, is his discussion of the landscape near Fort Washita in Indian Territory:

> The country . . . bears unmistakable evidence that . . . old ocean's surges rolled in all their might and majesty over these vast plains. . . . A suggestion has been made, that the days of Noah and the Flood will explain these deposits, but the depths of the strata and the size of the [fossil] specimens found, prove revolving years of submersion and procreation. . . . How ancient then must this universal system [be] . . . Its history is as unfathomable as that of the Being who formed, and now guides and directs it! (54–55)

The passage intertwines not only the romanticist aesthetic and scientific language but also religious and scientific interpretations of nature. Parker's reference to an "ocean" once covering the area offers a geological cause for the age and appearance of the region, although it falls short of the now-accepted theory that glaciers covered large stretches of North America during the last ice age and thus shaped its topography. Although the traveler dismissed the then-popular explanatory framework for reconciling geologic time with the biblical creation narrative, he nonetheless attributed this landscape to the work of a divine creator. Since humans play a privileged role in the Christian view of creation, invoking God in this scene endows humans with a greater significance than they have in the concept of geologic time. Echoing Marcy's official reports, Parker's travelogue sought to establish the United States as an internationally renowned civilization, on the one hand, and to secure the attachment of Texas to the nation through white settlement in the region, on the other.

In contrast to the Mexican military-scientific travelogues of the 1820s and 1830s, American scientific expedition accounts of Texas during the 1850s frame the territory and its exploration in a strongly romanticist imagery. In writing about their experiences, the travelers "informed others in settled places about the resources and the lay of distant lands. . . . [and] made suggestions about how to read new country and how to anticipate and cope with difficult conditions." As they "helped to diminish the 'darkness' of the wilderness," they participated in the nation's colonial policy of facilitating further white land taking in the North American West (Doughty 49–50). Marking sites for future roads, military posts, and civilian settlements, the expeditions led by Captain Randolph Marcy through North Texas in the first half of the 1850s paved the way for white encroachment on indigenous lands (Fehr 15). Since Marcy determined the site of "the first Indian reservation ever established in the West" (Hollon 166), the captain crucially contributed to the subsequent violent removal of the Texas Plains Indians, which "cleared" the region for even more whites and thus ensured the near vanishing of these Native cultures. A civilian member of Marcy's expedition to the Brazos and Wichita Rivers, Parker complemented the captain's journey account with a travelogue directed at general readers. It focuses strongly on his subjective impressions of the North Texas landscape and his ethnographic observations of indigenous nations. Like Marcy's official report, Parker's text not only participated in the ongoing discourse about Anglo-Americanizing newly obtained territories in the North American West but also explicitly pointed out the potential of the region for white settlement. In so doing, it paved the way for another type of travelogue, the journey account targeting potential settlers in order to promote Anglo-American or European colonization of Texas and other parts of the West.

PART II

Colonization and Settlement

In addition to journey accounts resulting from military-scientific expeditions, many American and European travelogues addressed the North American West from the perspective of a prospective immigrant or a traveler assessing settlement opportunities. Based on the authors' findings, these texts tend to either promote migration to the region or warn against such endeavors. As Stephan Görisch points out, "Although the propaganda against migration . . . would justify a separate study, it must be . . . subsumed among the literature about emigration, because any publication about emigration, whatever its tenor, rendered public attention sensitive to this subject" (161n1). Building on this insight, I argue that despite their opposed goals, one can understand these two bodies of travelogues as representing varieties of a single subgenre of the travel narrative: the journey account as migration propaganda, whether for or against. Even texts that claim to "objectively" present the advantages or disadvantages of migration implicitly incline toward one of these positions. By analyzing journey accounts that either advertise for or caution against American or European settlement in Texas in the second quarter of the nineteenth century, I want to foreground their formal, thematic, and argumentative common grounds. I argue that both categories of texts responded to the massive migration from Europe and the eastern United States to the West. In providing prospective migrants with information about the region, they further contributed to the international discourse about colonization and settlement.

On a formal level, journey accounts promoting and discouraging settlement in Texas often employ similar text types. Many visitors and settlers kept diaries for their private records or to send to friends and family members. Similarly, they sent letters to loved ones describing their experiences. These documents frequently circulated in the writers' hometowns, and local newspapers sometimes reprinted them. Diaries and letters, usually written in a personal tone, informed their addressees and any other readers of the promises and perils of life in the West, to either entice them to follow in the authors' footsteps or discourage them from doing so (Brenner 15, 65–68; Görisch 23–31, 170–177; Helbich 306, 310–312, 315–321).

Several visitors and immigrants penned longer narratives about their experiences in the West, often based on earlier travelers' diaries and letters. These were usually intended for publication and included both narrator-oriented travelogues and more recipient-oriented emigrant guides, a body of writings that informed prospective migrants on living conditions in a given area and how to relocate there. The travelogues often blend information culled from external sources and private, autobiographical accounts (Sundquist 144). Many of their authors refer explicitly to other journey texts, both factual and fictional, to justify their travels and their writing, either claiming the authority of the earlier works or citing the need to correct them (Görisch 201–229; Ritzenhofen 22–23). While such narrator-centric travelogues may either promote or warn against migration, emigrant guides exclusively serve as a vehicle for the former purpose. They are usually structured thematically—commonly providing information on the geography, history, agricultural and commercial potential, and population groups of their destinations—and dedicate plenty of space to practical advice (Brenner 68–75, 305; Görisch 207, 294–313; Sundquist 144–145, 170–172). Even though they emphasize opportunities and downplay the hardships of settlement, the texts warn against the migration of the ill suited and the ill prepared and caution against the exaggerated hopes raised by rival guides. This applies particularly to guides targeting European readers, for whom settlement in North America entailed making a transatlantic journey and adapting to a new language and culture (Brenner 76–80, 101–102, 311; Görisch 202, 211–213, 236–237; Helbich 298–299).

Like many exploration narratives, travel texts concerned with settlement in the North American West were deeply entangled with the colonial political projects and discourses of the writers' homelands. Accordingly, they present their subject matter and conclusions according to the backgrounds and opinions of their authors, sponsors, and target audiences (Sibley 5–8, 155–156). Moreover, many authors of such travelogues were involved in colonization endeavors, holding land titles in the West or reporting to institutions organizing emigration (Doughty 10; Sibley 154). Brigitte Georgi-Findlay points out that journey accounts employing an epistolary or diary form, in particular, mask their writers' stakes in colonization by focusing on individual experiences and points of view (25, 51).

Many authors of migration-promoting texts further belonged to a class of visitors whom Mary Louise Pratt calls the "capitalist vanguard" (143–144). Describing Europeans who journeyed to postindependence Latin America as "advance scouts for European capital," she argues that their travelogues legitimized European political or economic intervention on the continent through an aesthetic discourse that framed "unexploited nature" as hideous or perilous (146). In contrast, they found beauty either in already domesticated landscapes or in visions of future cultivation by northern Europeans, whom the texts deemed the only people capable of developing a capitalist economy (146–148). For American and European writers of settlement-promoting journey narratives about the North American West, making proper use of the soil was similarly key to advancing the region economically and socially through agriculture, trade, or mineral extrapolation. Their travel accounts prominently use not only the trope of describing the region as a plentiful and empty "virgin land" inviting Anglo-American and northern European settlers, but also the metaphor of the western landscape as a primordial wilderness. This supposed emptiness challenged the authority of white civilization but encouraged settlement with the promise that proper cultivation might transform it into a pastoral garden (Doughty 9–10, 20, 23, 62–63, 134–135; Hume 303, 305).

Rather than painting a homogenous image of the West, texts promoting migration often combine different lines of discourse in order to render the region aesthetically and economically desirable to different population groups: "[They] emphasize the plentiful game to attract trappers and traders. They promise fertile lands to attract poor farmers. They imply that the land shows signs of valuable minerals to attract fortune hunters" (Brown 59–60). More specifically, the texts present settler life as a manageable task:

The wild fauna and flora that had once symbolized the land's aboriginal hostility were seen as advantageous. Native wildlife became an important source of food and provided fun and excitement from hunting. . . . In praising the beauties of nature, [settlers] felt, to some degree, less overwhelmed by feelings of isolation and loneliness. . . . A third method of making the adjustment to strange and wild Texas was simply to make it appear like home. . . . Such similarities in environmental images suggested to newcomers that they would be able to cope with the new reality because it was, reassuringly, not so different from the old. (Doughty 37–38)

In a similar vein, the texts applied the metaphor of the western landscape as a potential garden in different ways. German uses of garden imagery predominantly appealed to migrants' wish for a modern Canaan or a *Schlaraffenland*, the land of milk and honey of European lore, paired with a desire for beauty. Nature, in this view, generously offers pleasant vistas and rich resources, thus affording settlers a comfortable life with little toil (Brenner 93–101; Ritzenhofen 63–74, 91–94). Anglo-American garden imagery, in contrast, foregrounds the need for human labor to obtain material gain. It blends biblical calls for transforming nature through cultivation (McDougall 83) with the English romanticist ideal that human intervention improves nature. American agrarianism in the tradition of Hector St. John de Crèvecoeur and Thomas Jefferson was applicable to the West: "The vast lands of the West always provide an Edenic region for the virtuous and independent yeoman farmer" (Hyde 33; Marx 107–141; H. Smith 123–142). During the second quarter of the nineteenth century, white southerners sought to counter this image with visions of the garden as an idealized plantation with "aristocratic masters . . . and devoted slaves" (H. Smith 151; see also 152). Yet, even they strategically exploited the yeoman-farming version of the garden trope to justify Anglo colonization of the North American West and its attendant subjugation of Mexican and Native populations. What would enable the region to become a garden, this line of reasoning went, was the unique ability and will of Anglo-Saxons to cultivate the land.

Therefore, they alone were entitled to make territorial claims (Doughty 63, 104, 134–135, 141; McDougall 82–84).

Implicit in this reasoning was the belief that Spanish-descendant and Amerindian civilizations were inferior to Anglo-Saxon ones. Travelogues focusing on Anglo-American or European migration to Texas align with scientific expedition accounts in their ambivalent portrayal of these populations, particularly the indigenous societies. They adopt the scientists' hierarchical division of the Texas Natives into somewhat "civilized" and utterly "savage" nations, according to the Amerindians' degree of assimilation to white culture. The texts, moreover, see indigenous racial-cultural inferiority to white civilization manifested in physiognomy and social norms, especially gender roles. They further follow the exploration narratives in treating the Natives as an integral part of nature. In so doing, they deny Native land rights and naturalize forced Amerindian removal to make room for white settlers (Allen 27–33, 56; Georgi-Findlay 56, 62, 82, 128; Ritzenhofen 154–187).

Similarly, in the tradition of the anti-Spanish and anti-Catholic Black Legend (Gibson), journey accounts focusing on Anglo-Saxon settlement in Texas frame the region's Mexican population as "immoral, indolent, and backward" (Paredes 24). Steeped in a deep rejection of miscegenation, many of these texts present all Mexicans as mestizos and thereby as more inferior than Spaniards in race and character to Anglo-Saxons (Greenberg 94, 122; Ritzenhofen 187). Once again, they draw on gender norms and physical appearance to "prove" this deficiency. They describe Mexican men as ugly, cruel, treacherous, and cowardly. Mexican women, in contrast, appear as well mannered, industrious, and charming, but also as lacking the beauty and morals of Anglo-Saxon women (Greenberg 22–23, 90–91; Paredes; Ritzenhofen 188–208). In thus presenting Mexican and indigenous cultural differences as a deficit of national character, Anglo-American and European travelogues promoting migration to the North American West justified Anglo-Saxon hegemony in the region and delegitimized Amerindian and Mexican claims to the land.

Owing to their key role in the Anglo colonization of Mexican Texas ensuing during the 1820s and early 1830s, the writings of Stephen Fuller Austin and Mary Austin Holley during these decades were of particular importance, and an analysis of their works forms the bulk of chapter 3. Austin, who became the first empresario to settle Anglos in Texas, recorded his impressions of the province in a travel journal he kept during his first trip to Texas, in 1821. He later wrote several other accounts, the most relevant of which have been published as "Descriptions of Texas by Stephen F. Austin." Based at least in part on his travels, these texts advertise Anglo-American and European migration to the province and especially to his empresario colony. The two volumes of travel writing that Austin's cousin Mary Holley penned about the region, *Texas: Observations, Historical, Geographical and Descriptive* (1833) and *Texas* (1836) were widely read and frequently cited in subsequent American journey narratives and a few German ones. The two books crucially shaped key topics and lines of reasoning justifying the Anglo-American colonization of Texas and the later creation of the state. Holley further stands out for being the only American female writer to promote Anglo settlement in Mexican Texas. Complementing and contradicting the accounts of Austin and Holley is Joshua James and Alexander MacRae's *Journal of a Tour in Texas* (1835). This travelogue is one of very few known American narratives from the period that spoke out against Anglo colonization efforts in Texas, and also a rare case of a travelogue commissioned by an emigration society to do this.

The 1830s saw the beginning of German mass migration to Texas and with it the emergence of a considerable body of travelogues catering to potential immigrants. The fourth chapter discusses German narratives encouraging German migration to Texas. Detlef Dunt's travelogue *Reise nach Texas* (1834) not only responded to the growing German interest in the region but also augmented this interest, thereby contributing to the growing German migration and the intensifying colonial discourse. Both peaked in the following decade, and one of the key actors of this German migration wave to the Lone Star State was the Society for the Protection of German Emigrants to Texas. While the association subsidized a large body of promotional texts to advertise its work, Carl of Solms-Braunfels's travelogue-*cum*-emigrant guide, *Texas, geschildert in Beziehung auf seine geographischen, socialen und übrigen Verhältnisse* (1845), stands out for its author's active role in the association. The volume exemplifies the attitude held by this aristocratic organization, not only toward Texas and Texans but also toward German emigration and its clientele. Although sponsored by the emigration society, Ferdinand Roemer's *Texas: Mit besonderer Rücksicht auf deutsche Auswanderung und die physischen Verhältnisse des Landes* (1849) pursued a dual agenda of informing both learned and general audiences about the potential of Texas for German settlement and about the geography and geology of the region. It thus provides a link with the scientific exploration of the Lone Star State and with the body of journey accounts that kept a critical distance from the unanimous promotion of German colonization.

The latter corpus of writing was published explicitly to warn prospective German migrants against relocating to Texas, arguing that the economic potential and sociopolitical conditions of the region failed to meet the expectations other texts were raising. Two narratives that specifically targeted the exploitation of migrants at the hands of colonization agents are the subject of chapter 5. Eduard Ludecus's *Reise durch die mexikanischen Provinzen Tumalipas, Cohahuila und Texas* (1837) is a highly self-reflective account that, despite its critical tenor, provides a differentiated picture of the Texas colonization experience. In contrast, Jakob Thran's *Meine Auswanderung nach Texas unter dem Schutz des Mainzer Vereins* (1848) represents the type of travelogue that is dedicated to thoroughly denouncing migration to Texas (in this case by Germans) and the work of a specific emigration organization.

THREE

A Place for Southerners
Travelogues and Anglo-American Colonization

While travel writing by Anglo-Americans promoting migration to the North American West have much in common with texts by European travelers, they more explicitly promote the region as a homeland for white settlers than European accounts do. Qualities that they identify as typically Anglo-American—perseverance, diligence, courage, self-reliance, and the appreciation of freedom—are extolled as key prerequisites for success (Brown 30–33, 36, 42, 67, 105). The establishment of empresario colonies in Texas since the 1820s attracted not only American settlers but also a series of travelers. Numerous travelogues and emigrant guides resulting from their journeys, such as Amos Andrew Parker's *Trip to the West and Texas* (1835) and A. B. Lawrence's anonymously published handbook *Texas in 1840; Or, the Emigrant's Guide to the New Republic* (1841), promoted colonization with the promise of an environment that was soon to be thoroughly Anglo-Americanized (Sibley 19, 152–170, 184–186).

Eric Sundquist observes that these and similar texts "not only offered practical advice but also carefully endorsed prevailing conceptions" of expanding the terrain and influence of the United States beyond the country's borders (44), which developed into the paradigm of Manifest Destiny (Doolen 16–19, 183; McDougall 57–98). In Texas, I argue, Anglo travel writing promoting colonization engaged in what Brian DeLay calls the "Texas Creation Myth" (227). This line of reasoning rests on three pillars: reference to geographic conditions and natural boundaries; the perception of Mexicans as ethnically and culturally inferior to Anglo-Saxons, as seen in their poor economic development of the territory; and the American discursive framing of the North American West as a region "destined to fall into American hands" (Hume 310). Against this ideological backdrop, the Texas Creation Myth claims that the political and military weakness of Hispanic rule had kept the region a largely unsettled, dangerous, wild space under Amerindian control until Anglo colonists heeded the Mexicans' call to settle the land and subjugate the Natives. Moreover, the myth argues that the Rio Grande provided the most natural boundary between Texas and Mexico and therefore should mark their uncontested border (DeLay 227–235).

Migration-promoting travel writers from the eastern United States struggled to address two controversial subjects in their journey accounts. On the one hand, they tended to express admiration for the pioneering spirit and self-sufficiency of the Texas Anglos, yet they simultaneously looked down on the materialism, coarse manners, and rough life of these people (Allen 39–42, 56; Georgi-Findlay 35–36; Sibley 88–110). On the other hand, Black slavery was a cause of disagreement within this body of texts. Writers who endorsed the peculiar institution emphasized the potential of Texas to be part of the slave-based economy, in hope of attracting settlers from the Old South. In contrast, visitors who rejected slavery were cautious about promoting colonization, which was responsible for strengthening the institution in the region (Sibley 130–151).

STEPHEN F. AUSTIN'S NARRATIVES OF TEXAS

Stephen Austin's (1793–1836) writings about his colonization endeavor in Texas were among the first texts that "expressed that colony's own nationalistic ambitions" (Sundquist 154). Born in Virginia, Austin worked in several professions in the American South before studying law in New Orleans. Though skeptical, he joined his father's enterprise to apply for a land grant and permission to settle 300 families in Texas (Cantrell 3, 8–9, 43–73, 77–88). On June 18, 1821, he embarked on what Marilyn McAdams Sibley calls "the journey [through which] the westward movement of the Anglo-Americans through Texas gained momentum" (88, 93). Shortly after the death of his father, in Missouri, Austin crossed into Texas on July 16 and arrived in Nacogdoches three days later. On July 21, his party of travelers left for San Antonio, where they stayed for ten days in mid-August, and to Goliad, which they reached on August 26. During the first three weeks of September, he explored the regions around Matagorda Bay and along the Colorado River to select a site for his colony. After returning to Louisiana, Austin reentered Texas in December 1821 with his first group of settlers. He dedicated the rest of his life to developing his colony and the region—as well as his profits from land speculation (R. B. Campbell, *Gone to Texas* 101–103, 128–138; Cantrell 89–97, 104–364).

Although Austin never published a travelogue of Texas, he penned the impressions of his first journey to the region in a private diary, "The Journal of Stephen F. Austin on His First Trip to Texas, 1821," published posthumously in 1904. Later, he published "Description of Texas" in the *Galveston News* (1828). He also wrote an unpublished manuscript, likely meant for publication in Europe (1831), and a brief statistical report (1833); all these works were published in 1924 as "Descriptions of Texas by Stephen F. Austin" (Austin, "Descriptions" 98n1). In addition, Austin produced a large corpus of Texas-related letters, memoranda, newspaper editorials, and speeches, along with a prison diary documenting his incarceration in Mexico City (1833–1835) and some of the first and most widely influential maps of Texas (Cantrell 225, 282–285, 302, 339–341). While the

"Journal of Stephen F. Austin" records his experiences and observations during his first trip to Texas, his "Descriptions of Texas" recalls the promotional journey narratives of Juan Almonte in their structure, topic, and rhetoric. Written to attract settlers from the United States and Europe to Texas, particularly to Austin's colony, these documents appear like guides for prospective colonists, for whom they paint a rose-tinted picture of the region.

"Reading Austin's journal, one is struck by the richness and variety of the land, and its utter wildness," Greg Cantrell observes (92). The empresario's search for a suitable tract of territory for his colony deeply informed his look at the land. In a relatively sober tone, the diary records the agricultural, commercial, and mining potential of the region: the quality of the soil, navigability of rivers, and the availability of game animals, timber, minerals, and water. In the same vein, Austin's "Descriptions of Texas" blends such utilitarian prose with aesthetic discourse, a combination that would become standard in depictions of Texas targeting potential immigrants. It merges anticipation of an abundant nature with enjoyment of the landscape and derives meaning from both the picturesque vistas and the agricultural wealth of the region (Doughty 20–23; Torget 59). Similarly, the "Journal of Stephen F. Austin" praises the "luxuriant growth of Grass" and "rich soil" of East Texas, and the "handsome" prairie that rendered Central Texas "the most beautiful" he "ever saw" (Austin, "Journal" 288–289, 296). Idyllic landscapes also create a vision of thriving future settlements. For example, Austin's "Descriptions of Texas" treats the Hill Country as a verdant paradise: "The round tops of the elevations . . . , the rich pale yellowish green of the small prairies . . . , the dark foliage of the cedars . . . the creeks and drains which wind their serpentine course through the small valleys and natural meadows at the feet of the undulations . . . present a landscape at once pleasing to the eye and cheering to the imagination, which in its fancy fills the scene under view with fine forms, the abode of health, plenty, cheerfulness, and happiness" (108–109).

More commonly, however, the text follows the "Journal of Stephen F. Austin" in employing a language of salubrity and abundance to advertise the economic potential of Texas. Both documents promote the region, especially to readers from the American South, by comparing the East Texas landscape to the Kentucky Pine Barrens or by pointing out that fruits typical of "a temperate Southern latitude" could grow in Texas ("Journal" 291, 293; "Descriptions" 99–100). Austin's blending of a utilitarian and an aesthetic discourse culminates in the romanticist ideal of a pastoral landscape, an unpeopled yet well-tended parklike terrain (Finney 11–12), paired with the promise of abundant crops and easy cultivation: "This undulating region is probably as desirable a country for all the wants and necessities of man as any other on earth. . . . The surface is beautifully and very fancifully diversified and checkered off into small prairies and woodland tracts, thus presenting to the farmer large fields of rich lands cleared by the hand of nature and ready for the plough" ("Descriptions" 108).

Engaging in the rhetoric of the Texas Creation Myth as a specific form of American colonial discourse, Austin's texts connect the arcadian potential of Texas with the Anglo-American economic, political, and cultural appropriation of the region, and particularly with his empresario colony. Although the "Journal of Stephen F. Austin" seems to share the Mexican Texans' joy about Mexican independence in August 1821 (296), the empresario's further comments in this text as well as in the "Descriptions of Texas" reveal how deeply his view of Mexicans was entangled with the US colonial policy of advancing Anglo settlement in the North American West. For instance, Austin's praise of a parish priest in San Antonio exemplifies how he assessed other nationals according to their attitudes to white Americans. The priest was "a very gentlemanly and liberal minded man and a great friend of the Americans" ("Journal" 298). In the same vein, he defends Anglo colonization when he writes that the Mexican government opened Texas to "the enterprising and industrious of all nations" ("Descriptions" 100). Moreover, his depiction of the Tejano settlements as poor and powerless victims of Spanish military abuse and Amerindian attacks suggests that Mexicans lacked the diligence and strength required to develop Texas ("Journal" 289, 291, 298; "Descriptions" 101).

In "Descriptions of Texas," the implied absence of civilization in Texas in 1821, manifested in the lack of significant settlements and agriculture, enables the text not only to downplay the Mexican and Amerindian presence in the region but also to imply that these two population groups had no justifiable rights to the territory. Austin articulates this view most prominently by calling Texas a "heretofore uninhabited country" and "an unknown and an entire and howling wilderness filled with uncivilized Indians" (103, 113). In his correspondence, he buttresses this image by adding the crucial argument of the Texas Creation Myth that Spaniards and Mexicans had failed to recognize the value of the land (Rajchenberg and Héau-Lambert, "Wilderness" 21–23). "My object, the sole and only desire of my ambitions since I first saw Texas," he writes, "was to redeem it from the wilderness—to settle it with an intelligent, honorable, and interprising people" (Austin to Thomas F. Leaming, July 23, 1831, in Torget and Liles). This, in turn, meant that "Texas should be effectually and fully Americanized—that is—settled by a population that will harmonize with their neighbors on the *East* in language, political principles, common origin, sympathy, and even interest" (Austin to Mary Austin Holley, August 1, 1835, original emphasis, in Torget and Liles). Against the backdrop of Spanish and Mexican failure, Austin's economically flourishing and politically stable colony shines as an almost utopian community in his "Descriptions of Texas": "Great as the obstacles were that opposed their settlements in this wilderness, their fortitude and perseverance was still greater, and success has fully rewarded their toils. . . . There probably is not at this time such an opening on the globe for industry and enterprise as in Austin's colony" (102). Even more, the success of the colonists appears in the text as a manifestation of their superior ethnic character, particularly when Austin presents them as a model of the Anglo pioneer spirit, "a most striking and highly honorable example of North American enterprise, perseverance and fortitude" (103).

The Texas Creation Myth as seen in Austin's "Descriptions of Texas" thus fulfills two interconnected purposes. On the one hand, this line of colonial discourse justifies and naturalizes the American settlers' appropriation of territory and their endeavor to gain cultural hegemony in Texas (116). On the other hand, the empresario uses this rhetoric to advertise Texas, and particularly his colony, to potential immigrants from Europe, whom his text implies to be as industrious and honest as the Anglo-Americans. The second section of his "Descriptions of Texas," written after Mexican law restricted US immigration to Texas in 1830, explicitly targets this readership and praises the prosperity and moral integrity of Austin's colonists. They paved the way for other settlers to follow, the text implies, and their ongoing labor shows readers that hard work and deprivation still await newcomers (102–103, 113–115, 118). The text explicitly responds to Mexican fears, seconded by British politicians, of Anglo separatism or US intervention (González Navarro 127–128), stressing the loyalty and economic contributions of the American settlers to the Mexican Republic ("Descriptions" 113, 116–118, 121). At the same time, Austin claims the colonists have a right of revolution against an oppressive Mexican government and thus positions himself in the American colonial discourse of his time (117). First employed in the United States to legitimize the American Revolution, the principle of the right of revolution became a key argument of US colonial and imperialist discourse and policy to legitimize the country's increasing interventions throughout the Western Hemisphere to curtail European influence and strengthen America's (Fritz 13–14, 23–24, 268–269). In his correspondence, Austin goes even further. He delegitimizes Mexican resistance to the Texas Revolution by presenting it as a barbarous war that a "mongrel Spanish-Indian and negro race [was waging] against civilization and the Anglo-American race" (Austin to Mary Austin Holley, August 1, 1835, in Torget and Liles).

The promotional function of the "Descriptions of Texas" shapes Austin's rather brief account of the indigenous population of Texas, which differs from his treatment of them in his journal. Both documents differentiate among individual Native nations but also employ the period's common generic terms "Indians" and "savages." The focus of the travel diary on the relationships between Amerindians and nonnative groups discloses the underlying concern of the empresario with assessing the safety of his colonization endeavor ("Journal" 290–291, 296–298, 300–301, 304–305). Accordingly, the text condemns Comanche, Waco, and Karankawa attacks on Tejano and Anglo settlements. The Wacos and Karankawas, Austin states, "may be called universal enemies to man—they killed off all nations that came in their power, and frequently feast on the bodies of their victims—the [approach of] an American population will be the signal of their extermination for there will be no way of subduing them but extermination" (305). This argument puts the popular colonial stereotype of Karankawa cannibalism, also reiterated in the Texas travelogues of Mary Holley, Ferdinand Roemer (both discussed in the following chapters), and the Mexican explorers, into the service of American colonial discourse. Here, it naturalizes Anglo claims to territories occupied by racially and culturally "inferior" peoples. In line with this view, the empresario's diary does not call for governmental intervention but implies the natural right and ability of the Anglo colonists to fulfill this "task." In contrast, the often-conflictive and violent relationship between the Texas Natives and the growing number of Anglo settlers increasingly shaped Austin's attitude toward the former (Cantrell 96–97, 136–145, 195; Doughty 30–31). Accordingly, to tone down prospective immigrants' anxieties about indigenous raids, the "Descriptions of Texas" only alludes to the threat of indigenous resistance to white land taking by mentioning "the intention of the [Mexican] government to keep up a considerable garrison ... to protect the northern frontier of [Austin's] colony from the Indians" (109). Thanks to the Anglo colonists, Austin asserts, it was now safe to settle there: "The Indians are subdued, and driven back and are all at peace" (102).

Similar contradictions characterize Austin's treatment of slavery in the "Descriptions of Texas." A passage that scrutinizes the practice as "that worst of reproaches against a free and enlightened people" (115) envisions a future for Texas without it: "The exclusion of slavery opens up a vast field in Texas for the enterprise and profitable employ of white laborers. Experience has clearly proved for ten years past that white men can labor in Texas as well and as safely to their health as anywhere else" (115–116). Blending ethical and economic arguments, this line of reasoning counters the popular claim of the so-called theory of climate, which was widely used either to defend Black slavery or to argue against white settlement in slaveholding areas. It claims that only people of African descent were suited to perform hard physical work in a hot climate (Paul 93, 104–105). In disputing this argument, and in emphasizing the future need for white labor in Texas, the "Descriptions of Texas" reaches out to prospective European immigrants, many of whom rejected slavery or were looking for work in the New World. This treatment of the peculiar institution was in line with Austin's repeated insistence on opposing slavery for demoralizing Anglo society and jeopardizing its existence (R. B. Campbell, *Empire for Slavery* 27–28; Torget 153–155).

In addition to expressing concern for the morals, security, and profits of white society, rather than (also) for the well-being African American slaves, the empresario's critique contradicts his investment in the colonial matrix of power represented by the transatlantic slave economy. Austin not only relied on slave labor by owning or hiring slaves (R. B. Campbell, *Empire for Slavery* 13, 18, 31–32, 50; Cantrell 9, 189, 204, 316), but also promoted the peculiar institution as an economic boon to Anglo settlers and the Mexican state. Several passages in the "Descriptions of Texas" point out the profits of the Texas cotton economy and inform readers about the possibilities for introducing slaves to the region (102, 113). Such advertisements of Texas as a cotton country, paired with Austin's lobbying the Mexican authorities to relegalize slavery in Texas, were straightforward attempts to attract prospective settlers from the southern United States, for whom cotton production was unthinkable without Black slave labor (R. B. Campbell, *Empire for Slavery* 3, 15–33, 96, 252; Torget 62–66, 72–87, 102–103, 155–156). In these ways, Austin set the stage for what became the dominant mode of promoting the opportunities of settling in Texas to Anglo-American audiences, a line of persuasion taken up most successfully by the writer's cousin Mary Austin Holley.

MARY AUSTIN HOLLEY'S *TEXAS: OBSERVATIONS* AND *TEXAS*

Only a decade after Stephen Austin penned his Texas travel journal, his cousin Mary Austin Holley (1784–1846) followed his example, becoming the only female writer from the United States to promote Anglo settlement in Mexican Texas. Born and raised in Connecticut, she lived in Boston and Kentucky until the death of her husband in 1827, when she moved to New Orleans to work as a private tutor. In 1831, correspondence with her brother Henry and their cousin Stephen Austin convinced her that Texas merited advertisement to attract American settlers and that this topic could sell books. This would not only ideologically strengthen the endeavor of Anglo colonization but also economically benefit Holley, who held land titles in her cousin's colony. She visited Texas five times, spending the first two stays, from October 22 through December 25, 1831, and from May 4 through June 13, 1835, largely at Henry Austin's plantation near Bolivar, on the Brazos. Subsequent journeys took her to Galveston, Houston, and San Luis Island between 1837 and 1844 (Holley, *Letters*; Lee 5–344).

In 1833, Holley published her travelogue *Texas: Observations, Historical, Geographical and Descriptive, in a Series of Letters Written during a Visit to Austin's Colony, with a View to a Permanent Settlement in That Country in the Autumn of 1831*. Considered "the first book on Texas ... by an Anglo-American" (Kökény 99), the volume resulted from the writer's private observations, conversations, and her correspondence with other Anglo colonists during her first journey. It takes the form of twelve letters presumably written from Henry Austin's plantation and addressed to her brother Charles in Baltimore. It made close to a thousand dollars profit, and was translated quickly into Spanish (Lee 270). In 1835, Holley published another, similarly popular account, merely titled *Texas*. (To avoid confusion between Holley's travelogues, the 1833 book is cited as *Observations* and the 1836 volume as *Texas*.) The second volume replaces the epistolary form, personal address, and blend of chronological and thematic descriptions of the earlier piece with a guidebook structure, organized by subject matter and written in a distanced tone. It also integrates practical information that Holley took from other travelogues or obtained during her second Texan journey (Holley, *Texas* v–viii, 51–52; see also Lee 252–268, 273–276). In addition, Holley wrote several Texas-themed poems; a journal of her second and third Texas journeys, published as *The Texas Diary, 1835–1838* (1965); and numerous private letters about the region, collected in 1933 as *Letters of an Early American Traveller: Mary Austin Holley, Her Life and Her Works, 1784–1846* (Holley, *Diary*; Holley, *Letters*; Lee 228, 274, 312, 331–332).

In the introductions to her two Texas books as well as in the preface to the second volume, Holley resorts to a *figura modestiae* to legitimize her traveling and writing (Holley, *Observations* 11–15; Holley, *Texas* vi–vii, 5–9). While gestures of modesty and justification frequently figure in journey accounts (Brenner 193), they were particularly relevant to female writers. The prevailing middle-class ideology of separate spheres and the cult of domesticity considered women's "natural" duty to be the care of their homes and families (Caughfield 6–8, 59–61, 142). This not only limited women's access to travel but also forced them to explain their trips and their seeking public attention through a book publication. Accordingly, female writers commonly emphasized that they had been required to travel, either as companions of family members or in order to earn a living. They foregrounded the public benefit of their writings and masked their concern with political or economic matters by focusing on social and family issues (Georgi-Findlay xiii, 16, 22–24, 51; Greenberg 202). Anticipating objections that a journey to Mexican Texas might be "too adventurous for a female," Holley stresses her kinship relations: she stayed with her brother in Texas and intended to assess settlement options for herself and her son (*Observations* 11; *Texas* 6). She also derives authority by targeting a female audience, a common strategy in women's western writing to justify female authorship and find a place in an increasingly competitive book market (Allen 52–54; Caughfield 23). Holley asserts the value of a mother's first-hand observations for female readers and provides domestic advice to prospective female settlers (*Observations* 11, 15, 123–124; *Texas* 6). Moreover, Holley's *Texas* celebrates Anglo-Texan women for combining pioneer spirit with feminine grace.

The volume points out how these women mastered masculine-coded skills required on the frontier, such as hunting and horseback riding. But the book simultaneously demonstrates that these activities would not compromise settlers' femininity. For instance, the narrator remarks that Texas women "will go fifty miles to a ball with their silk dresses, made perhaps in Philadelphia or New Orleans, in their saddle bags" (145). In this way, she tones down readers' potential anxieties about the "masculinization" of women settlers—a point that Nina Baym and Marilyn McAdams Sibley ignore in their discussions of the passage (Baym 13–14; Sibley 108–109).

Holley's *Observations* and *Texas* target not only women but also all educated American and British readers interested in the potential of Texas for colonization. The volumes repeatedly allude to American lore and landscapes, works of Anglophone literature, and classical or Oriental references likely to be known to these audiences (*Observations* 12, 43–44, 86, 119; *Texas* 7, 134, 145, 151–152). They describe the geography and history of Texas in a manner that foregrounds its enormous economic potential. They mention fertile soils, forests, navigable rivers, mineral wealth, and a healthy climate; they identify the population groups and the empresario colonies in the region. In depicting Texas as a valuable land with the potential for a bright future, the books "created a synergistic relationship between land and emigrant" and thus also between the writer and her target readers (Caughfield 25). The promotional agenda behind this depiction of Texas becomes evident, for instance, when comparing Holley's published praise of the region's climate to her privately uttered complaints about it in her journal and letters (*Diary* 12–71; *Letters* 49, 52, 72). To underline the legitimacy of Holley's writing, both volumes, moreover, document the scientific interest of the Royal Geographical Society in Texas as a destination for British emigrants (*Observations* 12, 133–140; *Texas* 7; see also Lee 225, 232).

Holley's texts engage in a colonial discourse that legitimizes both European colonization and American westward expansion as ways of furthering civilization. Modeling him after Daniel Boone, her *Observations* and *Texas* paint a eulogizing picture of Stephen Austin. He appears as a literal patriarch of his "infant colony" and as a model of bravery, sagacity, and integrity (Kolodny 101). A "hardy and bold pioneer," the empresario of Holley's texts "was enduring with the humblest laborer . . . all the exposures and privations of the camp." At the same time, he acted as a "skillful negotiator in the capital of Mexico" and the "civil governor and military commander of the people" (*Observations* 108–110; *Texas* 289–290). In line with an emphasis on familial achievements that was a typical way of legitimizing women's western writing, the narrator credits the entire Austin family with having brought "civilization" to Texas: "They have . . . been the movers . . . of the whole North American and Irish emigration to this country, and whatever good may result to the great cause of liberty, of science, and human happiness, by the introduction into this vast region of the English language, and of [the] principles of republican and constitutional government . . . , may be attributed to them" (*Observations* 113; *Texas* 295–296).

Like Austin's writings, Holley's books engage in the colonial discourse of the Texas Creation Myth to justify and naturalize the Anglo colonization of Texas. Her texts argue that Spaniards and Mexicans had neither recognized the value of the land nor succeeded in subduing its Native population. Consequently, Texas represented a veritable terra incognita before the transformative labor of the Austin family (*Observations* 5; *Texas* 1, 59):

> It is uncertain how long this extensive and valuable country would have remained unknown and unsettled, had not the bold enterprise and perseverance of the Austins . . . redeemed it from the wilderness. . . . With the settlement of [Austin's] colony, a new era has dawned upon Texas. The natural riches of this beautiful Province have begun to unfold, and its charms displayed. . . . A new island, as it were, has been discovered . . . apparently fresh from the hands of its Maker, and adapted . . . both to delight the senses and enrich the pockets of those, who are disposed to accept of its bounties. (*Observations* 9–10; *Texas* 4–5)

The notion of a newly discovered island recalls the titular land of Thomas More's *Utopia* (1516), an unknown island in the Americas with an agrarian and republican society. In alluding to this work, Holley presents Texas as a utopia for Anglo colonists. The reference to the "Maker" further connects this scene with other passages by her that liken Texas to the Garden of Eden (*Observations* 84, 127; *Texas* 78; see also Kolodny 100–101, 105). Eden, in turn, links this religious discourse with the secular argument that Anglo colonization could turn Texas into a beautiful garden, an image that rendered the Texas wilderness less threatening to readers. Holley particularly employs such garden imagery in her *Observations*. Of the Brazos River basin, for example, she writes: "Nothing was wanting, but neat white dwellings, to complete the picture. The lawns were as smooth as art could make them, and the trees . . . seemed to display the hand of taste" (31). Her text underlines its pastoral impression with lines from the popular song "Sweet Is the Vale" (c. 1807) and distinguishes it from the New England climate through a quote from Walter Scott's 1808 poem "Ettrick Forest in November" (31–32). Borrowing from Austin's "Descriptions of Texas," the Hill Country appears here as a romanticist pastoral idyll of an unpeopled park. Recalling Mary Louise Pratt's discourse of "anti-conquest," the landscape offers itself to the traveler's gaze and vision of future cultivation. It "presents a picture, not only delightful to the eye but enchanting to the imagination, which, with the pencil of fancy, would fain fill up the scene under view, with rural cottages, with the flocks of the herdsmen, and all the various indications of human activity and domestic happiness" (*Observations* 66–67; *Texas* 20; see also Austin, "Descriptions" 108).

Other passages in Holley's narratives strengthen the utilitarian discourse within the pastoral image of the Texas landscape in order to foreground the profits that diligent colonists could reap from the land. Most prominently, the *Observations* reiterates a passage from Austin's "Descriptions" (quoted earlier): "Beautifully and often fancifully diversified with prairie and woodland, [the Hill Country] present[s] to the enterprising farmer, large and fertile fields already cleared by the hands of nature and waiting, as it were, to receive the plough" (*Observations* 65; Austin, "Descriptions" 108). The volume's emphasis on the parklike diversity, rather than the vastness, of the Central Texas landscape and its reference to *domestic* happiness create a domesticated utopia. This characterization not only bowed to the societal ideal of female domesticity, manifest in the image of tamed nature, but also, and in particular, appealed to white middle-class female readers, to whom it promises a physical and social space that they could cultivate with little effort (Callahan 68–69). The vision of Texas unfolding here once again legitimized the American colonizing presence in the region as well as Anglo women's place in it. Moreover, it exemplifies the tendency in nineteenth-century women's narratives of the North American West to modify the trope of an overpowering western landscape into an image that would better accommodate female concerns. While male travelers found empowerment in the idea of conquering "virgin lands" of sublime wilderness (Kolodny 3–5; Georgi-Findlay 3–4, 7, 83–85), to female writers, "the flowered garden of the prairie beckoned" as a place of "familial security, genial climate, and physical freedom" (Kolodny 29). Accordingly, female writers frequently appropriated the garden trope, converting it into a genuinely female space where women could exert authority. Varied landscapes like those of East and Central Texas, where forests alternated with rolling hills, were particularly suited to this purpose, since they seemed more inviting for settlement than the enclosing woods or exposing deserts that many women feared (Doughty 45; Kolodny 6–10, 47–49, 54, 97, 107).

As Annette Kolodny elaborates, the "social Eden" of a garden-like Texas manifests itself in Holley's travelogues in images of social harmony and the relatively equal distribution of wealth (103, 164), a perception that recalls similar observations that European and Latin American travelers made about the United States during the 1830s (Haas, "Monroe Doctrine" 33–34, 39–40). Holley's narratives claim that the only "aristocracy" among the settlers was one of character and manners, since "there are no poor people . . . and none rich" in Texas (*Observations* 128; *Texas* 138). The Anglo colonists in Holley's *Texas* further represent an array of regional stereotypes: the entrepreneurial New Englander, the lively southern planter, and the hardy western frontiersman. Despite their differences, the texts claim, all these types display the diligence, ability, and professional skills needed to cultivate and settle the wilderness (129–130). Revising the biblical description of the promised land, Holley points out that "though the land be . . . flowing with milk and honey, the cows must be milked, and the honey must be gathered" (*Observations* 14; *Texas* 8; see also Exod. 3:8).

Although Holley's travel accounts encourage suitable colonists from all social strata to move to Texas, the texts emphasize the presence of "families of education and refinement," indicators of middle-class domesticity that may tone down anxieties about the region's rough, male-dominated frontier culture (*Observations* 38; see also Kolodny 99–100). As Holley's portrayal of one settler family's idyllic domesticity—a well-kept room with books, china, and white linen—suggests, middle-class women brought the comforts of home even to a crude shed (*Observations* 40; *Texas* 140–141). This scene shows how Holley's narratives exemplify a discourse of female domesticity entangled with the idea of a special US mission—subsumed under the rubric of Manifest Destiny since 1845—that Amy Kaplan calls "Manifest Domesticity" (48). It is based on a clear-cut distinction between the "domestic" and the "foreign" at the level of family and nation. Manifest Domesticity pitted family and nation as guardians of Anglo-Saxon civilization against the "savagery" of unsettled territories and ethnic or racial others within or beyond the household or the country (48, 50). The discourse viewed white middle-class women as carriers of Anglo-American civilization and feminine moral influence to unrefined frontier dwellers and people of color in the United States or to religious mission fields abroad. In doing that, they were supposed to help secure the safety of home and nation in areas of US territorial expansion and its "civilizing" mission (Greenberg 201–204).

As they connected discourses of domesticity and settlement in their journey narratives, many Anglo-American female travelers contributed to the discourses of colonialism and territorial expansion (Georgi-Findlay xi–xii, 18). In Holley's case, she substituted the feminizing trope of Texas as an "infant colony" in need of parental care for the "virgin land" image common in male-authored texts, thereby maintaining a key trope of colonial discourse, namely, the frontier as a space whose utter weakness and dependency required the protection and leadership that only Anglo colonization could supply (*Observations* 15). This line of reasoning legitimized the Anglo settlers' striving to transplant their culture to Texas rather than integrating themselves into established Tejano society. Both the *Observations* and *Texas* use this rhetorical strategy through reference to the colonists' labor (*Observations* 114–115; *Texas* 296–297), a key argument adopted from Stephen Austin's writings (Callahan 179), and through historical analogies that present Texas settlers as following in the footsteps of colonial Americans. One passage, for instance, calls the settlement of Gonzales "the *Lexington* of Texas" (*Texas* 115–116, original emphasis), thus establishing a parallel between major theaters of war in the Texas Revolution, on the one hand, and the American Revolution, on the other. Elsewhere, Holley refers to the ancient Greek and Roman republics, two political role models of the early United States (McDougall 18), when she states that "Texas has had her *Leonidas*, and many a *Curtius*; every man will become a *Cincinnatus*" (*Texas* vi, original emphases; *Observations* 86).

An address by Stephen Austin integrated into Holley's *Texas* claims that the American colonization sought "to keep away from the southwestern frontier . . . all enemies who might make Texas a door of invasion, or use it as a theatre from which mistaken philanthropists, and wild fanatics might attempt a system of intervention in the domestic concerns of the South" (279). In reprinting this speech, Holley sought to lure white southerners "to settle Texas as a slaveholding territory, not to annex it to the United States but to protect the South" (Baym 13). This promotion of slavery departs from her earlier critique of the peculiar institution in her *Observations* and *Texas*: thankfully, "the [Mexican] constitution and laws totally prohibit this worst of evils," since permitting slavery would turn Texas into "the receptacle of the redundant and jail-delivered slaves of other countries, all its energies would be paralyzed, and whatever oppressions may hereafter arise . . . must be endured" (*Observations* 87–88; *Texas* 133). Although Holley confirms this rejection of slavery in her correspondence, she not only owned several slaves but also edited antislavery passages out of *Texas* to appeal to southern readers (Lee 234, 240, 278). Besides depicting potential Texas slaves as "redundant," "jail-delivered," and foreign, she criminalizes the victims of slavery and disguises the domestic character of their trafficking. Other passages in the *Observations* and *Texas* explicitly encourage wealthy southerners to colonize Texas—another point absent from Marilyn McAdams Sibley's reading of Holley's works (131, 133). Holley points out the profitability of the plantation economy and reiterates the popular proslavery argument that the peculiar institution was more benign in Texas than elsewhere in the American South (*Observations* 44, 129; *Texas* 133). Despite their occasional critique, the two travelogues legitimize slavery as an integral and necessary part of Anglo colonization and the Anglo-Americanization of Texas.

In addition to justifying Black slavery, Holley "played an important role in shaping the stereotype of the Mexican population" (Myres, *Westering* 75). This disparaging characterization, in turn, formed an integral part of the Texas Creation Myth as a specific variety of the colonial discourse of American westward expansion. Early in the *Observations*, the narrator voices relief that upon arriving in Brazoria, her ship was "soon boarded, not by Spanish myrmidons, or cannibal Indians, but by friends and kinsmen . . . of the same complexion with ourselves, and speaking our native tongue" (36–37). *Texas* sets up "a hierarchy of bravery" (Paredes 9), with Tejanos at the bottom: "Five Indians will chase twenty Mexicans, but five Anglo Americans will chase twenty Indians" (*Texas* 128). In addition to denouncing indigenous peoples as weak or cowardly, this line of reasoning serves to disavow Mexico's claims to the province because of its inability to protect Anglo settlers from Amerindian raids.

Holley briefly acknowledges friendships between Anglos and Tejanos, and credits Mexican women with being financially trustworthy (*Texas* 148–150, 178). But a large number of passages endorse the religious and racial notion of national characters propagated by the Texas Creation Myth to legitimize the Anglo-American appropriation of Mexican territory. Mexican Texans are described as "very ignorant and degraded . . . timid and irresolute . . . very indolent, of loose morals, and, if not infidels . . . , involved in the grossest superstition" (128). The *Observations* and *Texas* target two of the most influential institutions in Mexico, the Catholic Church and the military, as failing to meet their own behavioral and moral standards. *Texas* mentions "an intelligent and liberal priest who had become rich enough by plundering the people in the name of . . . Christ" (178). Similarly, both accounts claim, "A more brutal and . . . more cowardly set of men does not exist than the Mexican soldiery" (*Texas* 128; *Observations* 24). They attribute the growing political conflicts between Mexican authorities and the Anglo-American settlers in Texas to Mexicans' "known jealousy of foreigners" rather than acknowledging the role of Anglo colonists in this matter (*Observations* 29; *Texas* 290). In so doing, *Texas* once again supports a primary American expansionist claim regarding the region: the inability of the Tejanos to master the Texas wilderness meant that only Anglo colonization and US annexation could "civilize" the region (13–14, 59). Holley's often purple prose goes hyperbolic on this score: "Mexico can never conquer Texas! The justice and benevolence of Providence will forbid that the delightful and now civilized region should again become a howling wilderness, trod only by savages, or that it should again be desolated by the ignorance and superstition, the tyranny and anarchy, the rapine and violence of Mexican misrule. The Anglo-Saxon American race are destined to be forever the proprietors of this land of promise and fulfillment. . . . This is inevitable" (298). By calling Mexico a "tyranny" seeking to "conquer" its insurgent province, the text, like Austin's "Descriptions," invokes the American right of revolution against a despotic government to justify the fight for independence from Mexico.

The way that the *Observations* and *Texas* repeat Anglo stereotypes and hearsay about Tejanos suggests that the writer had little direct contact with them. The same applies even more to Holley's depiction of the Natives of Texas. Like other American, Mexican, or European travelers, she considers the Amerindian nations of the region mainly in regard to their behavior toward white settlers. While her texts mostly employ either relatively neutral terms such as "Indians," "tribe," or individual nations' names to denote the Natives, in the context of hostilities, they become "savages." The narrator of *Texas* pays particular attention to the Comanches. She powerfully conveys their ethnocultural Otherness through Orientalist analogies to nomadic Cossacks, Turks, and Arabs, a common strategy in European and American travel writing to render Amerindians comprehensible to white audiences and to justify their subjugation (151–153). At the same time, both the *Observations* and *Texas* seek to tone down readers' potential anxieties about Native threats to Anglo settlers. In *Observations*, Holley argues that most of the indigenous nations either were peaceful or lacked the strength to challenge white settlement (88, 95, 97–98). Owing to favorable trade relations, the Comanches held Anglo-Americans in higher respect than Spaniards or Mexicans during the 1820s and 1830s (Hämäläinen 144–151). To Holley, this particular context translated into a generic alliance. "Though fierce in war, [the Comanches] are civil in peace, and remarkable for their sense of justice," the travelogues assert. They "call the people of the United States their friends, and give them protection, while they hate the Mexicans, and murder them without mercy" (*Observations* 90; *Texas* 153–154).

In contrast, the Karankawas appear in Holley's travelogues as truly embodying native "savagery." The texts emphasize the nation's hostility to white settlers, especially Anglo colonists. To buttress the image of their "barbarity," the two volumes reiterate the popular stereotype of Karankawa cannibalism to legitimize the Anglo settlers' war against them (*Observations* 95–96, 103; *Texas* 158–160, 284–285). Moreover, the texts characterize the tribe as an almost nonhuman part of nature: "fierce children of the woods" who "once roamed, free as the lion of the desert" (*Observations* 97; *Texas* 160). Other passages similarly denounce all Amerindians of Texas as wild creatures, describing the region as "infested" with "ferocious savages" or subject to their "predatory incursions" (*Observations* 85, 108; *Texas* 58, 289, 121). These depictions of Texas Natives sustain the common colonial trope of indigenous populations as immature and wild creatures that thus must be subjugated by Anglo-American rule (Kaplan 32). In addition, these images respond to the popular fear of white settlers that women and children might "go native," that is, lose their culture through life in the wilderness and regular contact with Amerindians (Kolodny 55–57, 68–69; Spurr 77, 82–83). In this context, the degradation of the Karankawas from "rightful proprietors of the domain" to "hewers of wood and drawers of water, to their invaders" (*Observations* 97; *Texas* 160—the allusion is to Josh. 9:21) functions simultaneously to alert Anglo colonists to the risks of settlement in Texas and to nonetheless legitimize their colonization efforts. It thus contributes to Holley's agenda of promoting and naturalizing an Anglo-American hegemony in Texas and of attracting the settlers required to realize it.

JOSHUA JAMES AND ALEXANDER MACRAE'S *JOURNAL OF A TOUR IN TEXAS*

At the time of Holley's writing, several regional emigration associations were formed in the eastern United States to assist local populations in finding suitable places of settlement in the North American West and relocating there (Sibley 154). One of these organizations was the Wilmington Emigrating Society. In the mid-1830s, Wilmington was the most populous town of North Carolina, yet economic difficulties following the Panic of 1819 made many people look for new opportunities on the Gulf Coast (Watson 101). In 1835, the town's newly founded emigration society deployed three men, Joshua James, Alexander MacRae, and Colonel Daniel Joyner, to assess the potential of Texas as a place for settling North Carolinians. The three men left Wilmington on April 23, 1835, traveling via Charleston, New Orleans, and Natchitoches to Texas. Crossing the Sabine River on June 1, they reached Nacogdoches three days later. Owing to budget restrictions and the ill health of Joyner and James, the group split up. Joyner and James explored the area between the Trinity River and the Louisiana border, especially the Neches River region. James even purchased a tract of land for himself. MacRae, in contrast, journeyed via the Trinity River and Galveston Bay to San Felipe and the Brazos and San Jacinto River regions. The parties returned to North Carolina independently of each other. James and Joyner left Texas on July 16; MacRae followed ten days later (James and MacRae 1–9, 13, 15; see also Kökény 102).

Nothing is known about the three men except what is contained in the account of their trip to Texas. *A Journal of a Tour in Texas with Observations on the Laws, Government, State of Society, Soil, etc. by the Agents of the Wilmington Emigrating Society* appeared in the same year of the journey and was advertised to local audiences in the *People's Press and Wilmington Advertiser* (Watson 101). Because of the separate itineraries of the three travelers for most of their trip, the publication consists of two parts that differ strikingly in form and opinion. James penned a chronological journal that weaves his assessment of the land into the daily entries of his and Joyner's experiences (James and MacRae 1–12); MacRae composed a thematically structured report containing his observations in Texas and the conclusions he drew from them (13–16). In line with their commission and echoing other travelogues written to promote colonization, both authors primarily looked at the agricultural opportunities, climate, transportation infrastructure, costs of living, political and justice system, and availability of land for new settlers (Kökény 102). References to crop types, methods of livestock raising, and the character of Anglo residents similar to those in North Carolina or other parts of the US South familiarize Texas for the text's target readers (James and MacRae 3, 6–7, 13–14).

The two parts of the *Journal of a Tour in Texas* diverge in their evaluation of Texas. James's diary depicts the region in a generally positive light. The text employs the familiar blend of aesthetic and utilitarian arguments to praise the splendor and abundance of East Texas: "The lands generally from the Sabine [River] to Nacogdoches . . . present one of the most beautiful prospects on the continent" and "afford facilities for all the luxuries of life" (1, 7). Characterizing the Texas Natives as dishonest drunkards who endanger Anglo settlement in the area but would soon have to leave their lands, the journal engages in a colonial discourse that seeks to justify the Anglo-American westward movement by denigrating indigenous territorial claims (6–7). In the same vein, the text portrays Tejano society as a civilization in such decline that American colonization and political intervention were justified. It characterizes Nacogdoches as "a little old Spanish village" largely "wear[ing] the aspect of decay" and criticizes the weak Mexican administration and military presence in Texas (1, 8). Writing on the eve of the Texas Revolution, James assures his readers, probably to tone down anxieties about settling in a Mexican province, that Mexico lacked the power to impose its laws and customs on the predominantly Anglo population of East Texas (8). A southerner, the narrator further endorses the practice of slavery and its extension to Texas as a legitimate part of Anglo westward expansion. He tells his target readers that slaves were not only a profitable commodity in Texas but that "this species of property [was also] looked upon . . . in the same light it is in North Carolina—equally as safe" (12).

The diarist echoes other travelers from the eastern United States, particularly women such as Mary Holley or Melinda Rankin and Teresa Vielé (whose travels are discussed in later chapters), in critically distinguishing western settlers from other Anglo populations. While James's text expresses appreciation for the hospitality, friendliness, and republican political sentiments of Anglo-Texans, it simultaneously deplores their "selfishness, meanness, and duplicity." These deficits of character find an echo in the Anglo-Texans' lack of cultural refinement. Seemingly indifferent to physical comfort, they lived in "miserable little hovel[s]" (5, 1). Like other migration-promoting texts, the journal alerts potential settlers to the hardships awaiting them: "There is nothing wanting in this delightful region, but a sufficiently numerous, industrious and enterprising population. . . . The emigrant . . . will have to encounter many difficulties on his first arrival in the country. He will find provisions scarce and dear, in consequence of the great number of persons daily arriving from the United States. . . . Neither is the country exempt from poor land" (7). In contrast to strictly colonization-promoting writings such as Austin's or Holley's travelogues, James's diary warns its East Coast readers against cunning Anglo-Texans and land speculators eager to take advantage of newcomers (2–7, 9). Nonetheless, it encourages North Carolinians to consider settling in the region.

Alexander MacRae's section of the travelogue likewise engages in a colonial discourse that not only endorses the American appropriation of Mexican Texas but also contributes to it by assessing the region's potential for North Carolinian settlement. In contrast to James, however, MacRae paints a thoroughly critical picture of the area he traversed. In pointing out both the region's agricultural potential and its lack of infrastructure, his report takes aim at the misleading advertisement of Texas to potential colonists: "the glowing descriptions given of the country, its water-courses and commercial facilities" and its "abounding in game, wild horses, buffalo, turkey, &c." The text claims that none of these elements "held out as an inducement to emigrants" were true (15–16). In contrast to James's account, Amerindians and Tejanos appear here as obstacles to the Americaniza-tion of Texas, and the latter group, moreover, as lacking a work ethic and codes of decency, seen in their penchant for gambling, even among respectable women (14–16). Since the Mexican government regulated settlements, commerce, and organized religion in Texas, MacRae denounces it as a "dictatorship" (14). In so doing, he draws on the concept of the right of revolution against a despotic gov-ernment in order to delegitimize Mexico's right to the territory and to naturalize Anglo colonization and the subsequent insurgence. Echoing Stephen Austin's and Mary Holley's journey accounts, MacRae employs the image of "throw[ing] off the Mexican yoke" as the goal of Anglo colonization in Texas (15). This seemed especially crucial regarding slavery. The nominal prohibition of the peculiar in-stitution in Mexican Texas represented a further hindrance to North Carolinian migration to the region, according to MacRae's report. More importantly, however, the text warns that the Mexican practice of debt peonage undermined the racial character of slavery because it permitted "white men [to] be held" as slaves (16). This scenario articulates the fear, common among Anglo-Americans, of losing race-based privileges and power if race no longer functioned as a basis and visual marker of social stratification (Lockard xxxi).

Although McRae's travelogue endorses Anglo-American settlement in the West, the text simultaneously asks its readers to be careful in pondering a move to a region in turmoil: "It is no doubt the policy of the government to compel the [Texans] to trade with the other Mexican States. . . . Whether this will suit the North American settlers, who do not understand the Spanish language, is a question which every one ought to settle to his own satisfaction, before he removes to the country" (James and MacRae 15). In another passage, MacRae reiterates that Anglo colonists' ignorance of Spanish signaled their refusal to integrate into Mexican society. He targets Anglo contempt for their host society. "If they did not like" the Mexican government, he writes, "they should have kept away, and not have partaken of Mexican bounty, until they have gained strength enough to kick the owners of the country out of it" (15–16). In addition to targeting the colonists as Anglo-*Americans* who consciously defy Mexican laws, MacRae's report voices concern about the formation of a veritable Anglo-*Texan* identity and its promotion among newcomers: "It is looked upon as a kind of treason for a man who visits Texas not to be pleased with it, every man he meets in the country is almost in extacies about it . . . The consequence is, that a man travelling through it is led to distrust his own judgment, if he does not happen to see it in the same light with others" (16). This critique goes hand in hand with the narrator's ambivalent attitude to what he perceived to be the Anglo-Texan character. Even though he concedes that there were both morally upright as well as degraded people in Texas, their calculation and land speculation dilute his praise of Anglo-Texan kindness, hospitality, and generosity (14–15). The Texas Anglos "are very anxious for settlers to go to the country and are therefore ready and willing to do any thing in their power to oblige a person who manifests a disposition [to] settle in their neighborhood" (14).

Whereas James regards the situation in East Texas as rather promising despite certain problems, MacRae concludes that East and Central Texas "ha[ve] all the disadvantages of an unsettled country, without laws that could give security to any man from the United States" (16). Like James, he engages in a colonial discourse that promotes American westward expansion through Anglo settlement in sparsely populated areas. But he recommends that his fellow citizens relocate within North Carolina, where they could enjoy the familiarity and security that Texas failed to provide (15). In presenting its readers with a contradictory assessment of Texas, James and MacRae's report offers a unique insight into the points of debate about Anglo-American settlement in the region, and it may have rendered its target audience a better service than a one-sided piece of praise or vilification.

Even more strongly than military-scientific exploration accounts, Texas travelogues promoting Anglo settlement in the region complement their utilitarian tenor with a romanticist aesthetic discourse of nature intended to emotionally appeal to readers and present Texas as either an attractive or a dangerous place of settlement. The writings of the empresario Stephen Austin articulate a strong sense of civilizing mission and a belief in progress that, as Robin Doughty observes, "recall the Pilgrim and Puritan call-to-arms in incipient colonization efforts in New England some two hundred years earlier" (20–21). This mission, however, had no place for either unassimilated indigenous nations or a free Black population. Despite his repeated public critiques of slavery, Austin labored to legalize the peculiar institution in Texas. In 1828 the mayor of Nacogdoches aptly observed, "Austin's colony is famous for slavery, and without it, its inhabitants ... are nothing."[1] The Texas travelogues of his cousin Mary Austin Holley played a key role in spreading the image of the region as a "land of promise" for Anglo colonization (Holley, *Observations* 21; Holley, *Texas* 298). Like the empresario, Holley legitimized Anglo settlement as a "predestined" act of creation and colonial meaning making. In contrast to her cousin, she employed the garden trope to legitimize Anglo land appropriation and lure white migrants to an earthly Eden, and elevated the task of cultivating private gardens into an act of "civilizing" the frontier and its Anglo settler population. Joshua James and Alexander MacRae disagreed in their assessments of the region and about whether to endorse or warn against Anglo settlement in Texas. MacRae's section of the travelogue in particular provides a rare American critique of both Anglo boosterism and the US colonists' refusal to integrate into Mexican society. Surveying the Mexican province on behalf of an American emigration society, the two travelers based their report on the needs of potential settlers rather than on the interest of Texas landholders like the Austins. Their text thus resembles the writings of many European visitors and immigrants to the region.

FOUR

America's Italy

Journey Narratives Promoting German Settlement

Mexico's opening of Texas to foreign settlers attracted not only Anglo-American colonists but also European immigrants. Germans came to the region in particularly large numbers during the 1840s and 1850s (R. B. Campbell, *Gone to Texas* 159, 207–208; Rese 17–19, 44–47, 51–59; Struve 43–50). Their settlement formed part of a wider German exodus to North and Latin America after the 1830s, inspired especially by growing poverty, unemployment, and political repression in Germany (Brose 119, 221, 287–288, 293; Rese 3–17; Struve 13–16). Tellingly, German discourses framed German relocation to other countries exclusively as an act of emigration from the homeland, even when discussing the destination of German migrants and their new lives there. Responding to the increasing migration and its attendant discourse, several German emigration societies began operating in Texas from 1839 (Rese 52). The most influential was the Society for the Protection of German Emigrants to Texas (Verein zum Schutz deutscher Auswanderer nach Texas), founded in 1842 by a group of aristocrats.[1] They considered German settlement in Texas a viable means to simultaneously establish a profitable overseas trading base and reduce the risk of political unrest in the founders' home regions (Kearney 1–4, 11–23, 36–62; Morgenthaler 41–47, 55–64, 71–73). The society struggled with mismanagement and diplomatic difficulties in Texas. As a result, it filed for bankruptcy in 1847 and became defunct three years later. Despite these difficulties, and notwithstanding several failed settlement endeavors under its auspices, the organization succeeded in settling many Germans in Texas (Rese 79–104; Struve 47).

Long before the foundation of the emigration society, Texas had been addressed in the *Amerikaliteratur*. The term denotes a diverse body of German writings about the United States or regions within the country. It encompasses migrants' diaries and letters, travel accounts, emigrant guides, political tracts, works of scholarship and journalism, poems, songs, plays, and narrative fiction. This text corpus capitalized on Germans' fascination with North America as well as their growing demand for information about its opportunities for immigrants. Accordingly, most works of *Amerikaliteratur* tended to promote German settlement in North America as being worth the effort, and some texts provided practical advice for prospective migrants (Brenner 45–137; Görisch 9–57, 88–182, 201–230, 264–337; Helbich; Mauch). By advocating not only German migration but also the establishment of German settlements in the New World, the *Amerikaliteratur* contributed to the growing public debate about German overseas communities as vehicles for increasing the nation's political influence abroad or providing economic relief at home (Fenske).

Though Texas lacked the key signifiers of "American modernity," that is, urbanization and industrialization (Brenner 257), during the first half of the nineteenth century, German writing had addressed the Lone Star State since the 1820s. Texts prominently discuss the region as either a suitable site for German settler colonies or a model for political change. German travelogues touching on Mexican Texas, such as J. Valentin Hecke's 1821 *Reise durch die Vereinigten Staaten von Nord-Amerika in den Jahren 1818 und 1819* (Travels through the United States of North America in the years 1818 and 1819) or Johann von Racknitz's 1836 *Kurze und getreue Belehrung für deutsche und schweizerische Auswanderer* (Short and faithful instruction for German and Swiss emigrants), praise the economic opportunities Texas offered to farmers and skilled workers (Rese 20; Ritzenhofen 28, 61–62, 94, 109–112). Between the Texas Revolution and the Civil War, the rising wave of German immigrants to Texas both produced and responded to a growing body of migration-promoting literature. A large and diverse text corpus fortified the myth of Texas as a land of liberty and a paradise of plenty. These writings included Georg Scherpf's 1841 historical study *Entstehungsgeschichte und gegenwärtiger Zustand des neuen, unabhängigen amerikanischen Staates Texas* (The beginnings and present condition of the new Republic of Texas); August Heinrich Hoffman von Fallersleben's 1846 song cycle *Texanische Lieder* (Texas songs); the successful settler Viktor Bracht's reminiscences *Texas im Jahre 1848* (*Texas in 1848*); Christine Haun's *Mit dem Paketsegler 1853 nach Texas* (With the packet ship to Texas in 1853), the only firsthand account by a female German immigrant from the period; and Armand Strubberg's 1858 adventure novel *Amerikanische Jagd- und Reiseabenteuer* (American hunting and travel adventures) (Haas, "Prairie Promises," 235–236, 249–252; Rese 1, 21–24, 26, 71; Ritzenhofen; Struve 45–46, 102–103).

To bolster their claims to accuracy and discursive authority, German writers frequently referred to documentary sources on Texas. Besides popular German travelogues such as Gottfried Duden's 1829 *Bericht über eine Reise nach den westlichen Staaten Nordamerikas* (*Report on a Journey through the Western States of North America*), these included William Kennedy's *The Rise, Progress, and Prospects of the Republic of Texas* (1841), journey accounts by Mary Holley and Josiah Gregg, and popular works of fiction such as the Austrian migrant Karl Postl's

1842 novel *Das Kajütenbuch* (*The Cabin Book*), published under the pseudonym Charles Sealsfield (Doughty 72, 110–113; Ritzenhofen 22–23, 27–28, 34–54, 63, 69, 77–79, 81, 83). In viewing the Lone Star State from the vantage point of a potential settler (Ritzenhofen 70, 271–273), German travelogues promoting their fellow citizens' migration to the region looked at Texas with a "colonial gaze" (Spurr 15–16) similar to that used by like-minded American authors. While their depictions of the region's Native and Tejano populations largely echo the American perspective, German portrayals of Anglo-Texans express ambivalent feelings of fear and admiration. These had their roots especially in diverging conceptualizations of freedom and progress in the United States and Germany. Nineteenth-century American culture emphasized the freedom of the individual and tied notions of progress to the "civilizing" of the North American continent. In contrast, German discourse stressed collective liberties, which it understood as being institutionally granted, and it linked progress to sociopolitical emancipation and cultural development (Brenner 263–271, 330–332). Accordingly, Anglo-Americans appear in German texts about North America as a foil against which writers affirmed the German national character and German approaches to solving social and political problems.

Repeating common stereotypes of Americans, specifically westerners, German texts about Texas, in line with the *Amerikaliteratur* generally (Brenner 298–344; Helbich 297–299, 311–312, 319–320), often praise Anglos' pragmatism, enterprise, and endurance but reproach them for their materialism, individualism, restlessness, and lack of intellectual and leisure culture. Literature promoting German migration to North America tends to emphasize the positive traits, whereas cautionary narratives stress the negative ones. Both categories of texts set these Anglo clichés against the equally stereotypical ascriptions of Germans' idealism, high regard for education, and attachment to home and tradition (Ritzenhofen 228–268). Moreover, attitudes to slavery, which ranged from romanticizing views of plantation life to abolitionist rejections of the institution and self-righteous claims that it was alien to Germans, divided German *Amerikaliteratur*, including texts about Texas (Brenner 357–375; Mauch 629–632; Paul 87–108, 156–160, 165). This range of views echoes public discourse both in Germany and among German settlers in Texas. While most Germans rejected slavery, the institution met with greater support among German settlers in the cotton-growing regions of the Lone Star State (R. B. Campbell, *Empire for Slavery* 215–217; Honeck 41–42, 60–61, 69; Struve 74–77). Consequently, many German travelogues of Texas either downplay the relevance of the peculiar institution or use it as yet another argument to criticize Anglo-Texans and contrast them to the presumably abolitionist Germans (Ritzenhofen 208–227; Struve 74).

DETLEF DUNT'S *JOURNEY TO TEXAS*

The earliest nonfictional travel text informing the German public about Texas was a letter sent by the German settler Friedrich Ernst from his home in Central Texas to friends in Oldenburg in 1832 (Saustrup 141–143). Although he struggled with the hardships of frontier life, Ernst paints his new homeland as a geographic and political idyll, mentioning its parklike landscape, Mediterranean climate, fertile soil, and republican government with the kind of civil liberties that German liberals desired. The letter is said to have circulated throughout northern Germany and to have enticed many readers to migrate to Texas (Saustrup 143; Ritzenhofen 35, 63–64; Struve 44). It received even greater publicity when it was included in Detlef Dunt's 1834 travelogue and emigration guide, *Reise nach Texas, nebst Nachrichten von diesem Lande für Deutsche, welche nach Amerika zu gehen beabsichtigen*, published in English in 2015 as *Journey to Texas, 1833* (Dunt, *Journey* 30–37).

Officially named Detlef Jordt, Dunt (1793–1847), a merchant's son from Holstein, settled in the Grand Duchy of Oldenburg after his marriage. Pondering migration to North America, he claims that Ernst's letter inspired him to go to Texas (Kearney and Bentzen 1–5, 8–9). He left his home on November 20, 1832, to board a ship in Bremerhaven, which left for New York on Christmas Eve. From there, he continued via New Orleans and reached the Texas coast in late April 1833. He arrived at the Ernst family farm near Mill Creek in mid-June. Dunt returned to Oldenburg in the fall of 1834 but came back to establish himself with his sons in Texas in 1836, with his wife and daughter following in 1847 (Kearney and Bentzen 9, 17–18; Struve 44–45). In penning *Journey to Texas*, Dunt sought to capitalize on the ensuing German "emigration fever" (Dunt, *Reise* 16)—a wave of German mass migration to North America that Ernst's letter had contributed to. Largely retracing the writer's itinerary to and through Texas, Dunt's volume comments on the topography, climate, agriculture, settlements, and population groups of Central Texas. It derives its discursive authority particularly from its presentation as a firsthand account of living conditions in Texas and as a guidebook providing practical advice to prospective German settlers. To strengthen his claims to authenticity, the narrator presents himself as a common man enticed to migrate by overpopulation in northern Germany, though the fact that he could afford to travel repeatedly between Texas and Oldenburg suggests that he was wealthier than most other German migrants (*Journey* 25–26, 29; see also Kearney and Bentzen 1–2, 6, 15–17).

Journey to Texas does not address the rivalry between Germany and other European nations, especially France and Britain, for influence or colonization opportunities in North America, even though the book caters primarily to prospective German migrants and their nation as a whole. Instead, the narrative follows the Mexican travelogues of Almonte and the Comisión de Límites in voicing concern about the massive Anglo-American migration to the province. But whereas the Mexican observers feared losing Texas to the United States, Dunt worried about German settlers' struggle in the competition for resources: "It could not fail that a country so rich in opportunities as Texas, with a constitution so similar to that of the North American union, would soon become well known and enticing to the Americans, who are so enterprising and venturesome" (95). At the same time, the book characterizes the United States as an ideal neighbor for Texas. In contrast to Europe, the United States was "inhabited by one of the greatest and most enlightened nations... in which thousands long ago have found a sanctuary and a government recognizing the true and just rights of humanity, dwelled in by a peace-loving people, equally alien to any wild desire to conquer and to misguiding despots, partial also to a rational rather than a fraudulent concept of liberty, with a wise and prudent government..., a nation which only draws its sword when its noblest possession, its freedom, is endangered" (99). Rather than being a firsthand observation of American reality, this view reveals the image of US society as an almost utopian model, one that implicitly outlines the political deficiencies of Europe. The memory of the Napoleonic era, with its gruesome wars but also its sociopolitical and economic reform efforts, and of the subsequent period of recession and growing repression, was surely still strong for German readers (Brose 47–65, 72–130, 155–163). In this situation, Dunt's *Journey to Texas* sought to capitalize not only on the growing movement for German emigration to the North American West but also on the public debate in German-speaking lands about the advantages and possibilities of German colonial engagements overseas.

The book's praise of the United States strikingly deviates from the way it characterizes Anglo-Americans:

> In early youth, [the American was] trained to a hardy way of life, acquainted with all the requirements of the primary cultivation of a country.... Where a European, accustomed to a softer way of life, might complain about deprivations, the American was content and cheerful, willing to be satisfied with the yields of his herds, his field, his hunting. He stands patient and brave in the face of all difficulties and dangers; nothing will mislead him, and with or without a compass he travels through wilderness untrod by human foot, merely following his sense of direction, gifted with a sort of instinct similar to that of the Indian. (103)

The passage follows both American and German colonial discourses in endorsing the settlement of seemingly uncultivated lands by Anglo-Saxon and Teutonic populations. In contrast to American justifications of westward expansion, however, *Journey to Texas* does not explain the Anglo appropriation of western territories by claiming whites' cultural superiority to other nations. Instead, the book aligns itself with many works of the *Amerikaliteratur* that treat Anglo settlers in the North American West as "savage," owing to Americans' history of interactions with Amerindian nations (Mauch 625). The passage just cited suggests that Americans' lower degree of civilization, manifest in their ability to navigate the wilderness like indigenous people, particularly qualified Anglos for colonization efforts.

Dunt's *Journey to Texas* highlights the difference between Americans and Germans in the areas of sociability and cultural refinement. The book presents the scarcity of private gardens and the lack of organized sociocultural activities like concerts or dances among Anglo Texans as signs of an Anglo disregard for the arts and the comforts of home, two core elements of the German concept of culture (60, 82–83). In the 1840s, such references to the absence of gardens would become a staple of claims to German cultural superiority over Anglo society (Ritzenhofen 228n154). They emerged from a specifically German romanticist view according to which cultivated gardens signified a person's or a society's education, cultural refinement, and diligence (Finney 49–50). While Dunt's narrator pays respect to Americans' hard work, courage, vigor, and love of freedom, he simultaneously draws on the popular stereotype of Anglos in European and Latin American cultural discourses in accusing them of crude materialism (*Journey* 95, 117, 124). "It seems, generally speaking, that Americans only cherish whatever produces money," he states. To encourage Germans to settle in Texas anyway, his book emphasizes that some "highly respectable individuals worthy of esteem," that is, members of the educated middle class, reside in the region (82, 89).

Intertwined notions of civilization and social class also shape Dunt's depiction of Mexican Texans. Strongly informed by the attitudes of the author's Anglo-Texan informers (Ritzenhofen 188–189), the book portrays the Tejanos as uncultured, unclean, and lazy (*Journey* 79, 101). Unlike Stephen Austin's or Mary Holley's writings, but soon to be followed by other German visitors' texts, Dunt's account captures the notion of Tejano Otherness in a blend of cultural differences and racial ambiguity. He describes a chance encounter with Mexicans: "[I] believed I had fallen among Indians ... [since] one of the Spaniards I encountered here had rather a brownish-yellow appearance. Such is occasionally the case in these parts since, at an earlier time, many Spaniards are said to have interbred with Indians" (79). In contrast to later travel narratives of Texas, such as Carl of Solms-Braunfels's or Frederick Law Olmsted's (discussed in subsequent chapters), Dunt's narrator becomes aware of his bias. He admits: "I was ... received in the friendliest manner.... I was shown to a very clean bed.... My concern about possibly being robbed here ... was based on the many not exactly flattering accounts Americans had given me about the local Spaniards, and according to which they are said to be strongly inclined toward thievery" (79). In revising his view of the Tejanos, the narrator attempts to tone down German readers' anxieties about yet another culturally and ethnically distinct population intent on taking advantage of ignorant immigrants. His social-class bias, however, makes him immediately qualify his correction. Echoing the observations of Juan Almonte or Manuel de Mier y Terán, Dunt's *Journey to Texas* reverts to stereotypes by pointing out that Tejanos belong "to the very lowest class of this nation" (79).

"If one is to believe ... his travelogue," Ute Ritzenhofen observes, "the reality Dunt encountered in Texas matches the expectations he must have had through his reading of previous texts" (64). The account confirms the idyllic picture of Texas that Ernst's letter had drawn. It particularly reiterates the claim of the earlier text that the region's economic potential and the benevolent Mexican attitude toward Europeans offered plentiful opportunities to industrious German settlers (*Journey* 76–78, 82–89). Like Ernst's letter as well as other German, American, and Mexican journey narratives, *Journey to Texas* blends this utilitarian discourse with an aesthetic one, thus appealing to both the reason and the emotions of prospective migrants. The text particularly draws on romanticist pastoral imagery such as unpeopled, parklike landscapes (Finney 11–12) to render the alien land familiar and attractive to German readers. For instance, the book emphasizes the "very picturesque aspect" of the prairie near San Felipe and the "little Elysium" of Ernst's farm. The latter was surrounded by "natural romantic scenery, which nevertheless cannot be referred to as wilderness," a crucial distinction that signifies the difference between desirability and danger (*Journey* 80, 85, 84). By emphasizing the beauty of Texas and by comparing it favorably to European nature—the Italian sky, the landscape of Holstein, and the Rhine Falls—the narrator familiarizes an alien and remote terrain for his German target readers (72, 84, 100).

Responding to the widespread German fear of political instability, an oppressive state, and material loss, based on experiences at home and prejudices about Mexico, Dunt's *Journey to Texas* minimizes the conflicts between Anglos and Tejanos and exaggerates the legal security and the political and religious freedoms that settlers enjoyed in Texas (90–103). The volume denounces, as products of irresponsible minds, travelogues by returned German emigrants that warned against settlement in North America (107–108). But, possibly informed by the controversy that Duden's unanimous praise of North America, in his *Report on a Journey through the Western States*, had aroused in Germany (Brenner 77–78, 113–120; Ritzenhofen 46), Dunt's book does not blindly promote German migration to the region. Instead, it cautions readers against exaggerated expectations of "nothing but an Eldorado in the New World" and points out the hardships and uncertainties awaiting settlers in Texas (*Journey* 25, 105–107). The narrator further thwarts naïve expectations of German immigrant solidarity there, pointing out that some established German settlers capitalized on the needs of newly arriving fellow citizens (107–108). Accordingly, he advises readers to ponder with care their ability and willingness to adapt to life in Texas: "Many people here, in a free America, would gladly pay more taxes if they had the fine roads, good police protection, etc., enjoyed in Germany under many truly good and honorable ruling princes. . . . Many who could live quiet, satisfied lives in their familiar settings regret too late that they have given up a secure subsistence for an uncertain one. Secondly, every emigrant would do well to test his physical capabilities, to make sure he can endure what hardships, deprivations, and physical labor might be required" (27–28). Nonetheless, the tenor of Dunt's *Journey to Texas* remains one of boosterism for German migration to Texas. The book strikingly concludes with the utopian vision of a "little Germania," a German settler community, to develop soon in the region (122; see also Ritzenhofen 112, 250). This claim serves to reassure readers fearful of an isolated life in a distant land and an unfamiliar culture. It further ties in with the conviction that Germans should settle abroad in large groups rather than as isolated individuals, a common view in the German colonial discourse of the time. Forming larger settlements, in turn, would allow Germans abroad to maintain their native culture. While proponents of German migration stressed the role of thus strengthening the German element in the world (Fenske 94–95), individual settlers, as Dunt's text argues, likewise stood to profit from the opportunities the New World offered them. Despite its shortcomings, the travelogue thus paved the way for a growing wave of German migration to Texas that ultimately made them the third-largest ethnic settler population in the region.

CARL OF SOLMS-BRAUNFELS'S *TEXAS*

While Dunt's travelogue was a pioneer work, reflecting the emerging German migration to Texas, the 1840s saw a massive increase in German texts about the region (Ritzenhofen 30, 60, 269). Among that body of works, Walter Struve points out, "numerous books and articles subsidized by the Adelsverein presented an enticing image of Texas" (48). One of these was written by one of society's stockholders, the travelogue-*cum*-emigrant guide *Texas, geschildert in Beziehung auf seine geographischen, socialen und übrigen Verhältnisse mit besonderer Rücksicht auf die Deutsche Colonisation: Ein Handbuch für Auswanderer nach Texas* (1846)—translated into English as *Texas, 1844–45* (1936).[2] Its author, Carl of Solms-Braunfels (1812–1876), was a Hessian prince and captain of the cavalry in the Austrian Imperial Army. He became interested in the Lone Star State around 1840, was among the founding members of the Society for the Protection of German Emigrants to Texas, and was appointed its commissioner general to Texas in April 1844. One month later, he set off for North America and reached Galveston on July 1. From there he traveled via Houston and Washington-on-the-Brazos to arrive at Nassau Farm, the society's Central Texas plantation, on July 8. Several trips took him to San Antonio and the Medina River, to Washington, Houston, Galveston, and Gonzales. The prince's duties in Texas included managing the plantation and the finances of the society, negotiating with governmental officials and public representatives, securing land tracts, and organizing the reception of settlers. In December, the first group of German migrants supported by the society arrived, with whom Solms founded the town of New Braunfels the following March. Replaced as scheduled, he left Texas in June 1845 to resume his military career in Germany (Kearney 77–90; Morgenthaler 41–43, 73–77).

During his journey, Prince Carl recorded his observations and experiences in a private journal, published only in English translation as *Voyage to North America, 1844–45: Prince Carl of Solms's Texas Diary of People, Places, and Events* (2000), and in twelve reports to the emigration society (Solms, *Voyage*; Geue and Geue 21–72). After his return, he compiled his notes into a travelogue. When the book appeared, in 1846, it met with broad acclaim in the German press but also with criticism for its portrayal of Anglo-Texans (Ritzenhofen 40–41). As the German title indicates and the preface confirms, the book responded to the country's growing popular interest in emigration to Texas and thus contributed to the wider public discourse on German colonization endeavors in the New World (Solms, *Texas* 7–9). Characteristic of emigration-promoting texts, Solms's *Texas* advocates the Lone Star State as a suitable location for German settlement. It underlines its relevance by claiming to be more accurate than earlier publications on the topic, and it bolsters that claim by recommending writings that confirmed the prince's observations, particularly William Kennedy's historical study of the Texas Republic (*Texas* 7–9, 16–17, 139). The first part of the volume describes and evaluates the geography and society of the region, and the second part provides practical information for potential migrants and promotes the work of the emigration society. Like other German travelogues of North America, the text regularly employs English geographic terms, followed by translations or explanations in German. In so doing, it reveals the role of language as an instrument of power, which was already visible in the Mexican travelers' complaints about the growing dominance of English in East Texas. Accepting the hegemony of English as a lingua franca in the region, Solms's book acted as an intercultural contact zone for its German readers, whom it familiarized with the alien geography and terminology in order to facilitate their settlement (Ritzenhofen 75–76).

Prince Carl's travelogue stands out among the emigration society's texts for its somewhat differentiated portrayal of the Amerindian population (Ritzenhofen 168). Usually calling them "Indians," the narrative follows Mexican, American, and other German travelogues in dividing the Texas Natives into "hostile" and "friendly" nations, depending on their way of life and degree of submission to Anglo rule (*Texas* 17, 40–47). Despite making this distinction, the text tends to homogenize the Amerindians as perpetual nomads, repeatedly referring to "wander[ing]" or "roving tribes" who "roam[ed]" throughout Texas as skilled hunters and horseback riders (41, 40, 44). Based on their lack of fixed abodes and failure to systematically cultivate the land, the prince's travelogue denies Natives the status of civilized nations. It thereby legitimizes whites' appropriation of indigenous territory, which the colonization endeavor of the emigration society, among other actors, represented. To promote this project further, the book presents the resident Amerindian population as a manageable threat that was not impeding German settlement in Texas. Even though it warns against indigenous cunning, fraudulence, drunkenness, and thievery, Solms's *Texas* assures its readers that "when one [shows the Natives trust and frankness and] treats them justly and honestly, they can be trusted and one can rely on their promises" (43; see also Hoerig 424–425).[3]

Solms's view did not emerge from actual contacts with indigenous people (Hoerig 425–426). Rather, *Texas* uses the Amerindians to distinguish the Germans from the Anglo-Americans in Texas and to criticize the latter: "When a drunken American mistreats or kills an Indian, not even a rooster would bother to crow." He cites the Anglo murder of Comanche negotiators in the San Antonio Council House Massacre of 1840 to exemplify this claim (40, 42; see Hämäläinen 217). Solms implies that the Natives accordingly differentiated between Anglo-Americans and Europeans, following the line of German public discourse that postulated a special relationship between Germans and Amerindians, one based on greater mutual respect (42; see also Ritzenhofen 169–170). This myth was often employed to justify German involvement in the rivalry between the United States and European nations for influence in North America. In a "Memoir on American Affairs," addressed to Queen Victoria in December 1845 and published with his journal, Solms presents the Comanches as likely allies in a British military intervention against the recent US annexation of Texas (*Voyage* 223; see also Morgenthaler 174–177). In contrast, when the Texas Natives were in the way of his colonization project, Solms did not hesitate to use force against them. For example, he advised the emigration society in one of his official reports to remove a Comanche band in order to settle one of their land tracts, which was located within the tribe's hunting grounds (Solms, "Third Report from Texas to the German Emigration Society," August 26, 1844, in Geue and Geue 36). In his migration-promoting travelogue, of course, the prince did not address this matter so as to not arouse concern among prospective German settlers for their safety in Texas.

Solms's *Texas* is deeply entrenched in the tradition of unequal exchange that marked European-Amerindian relations in the Americas. Since the colonial period, the European colonizers and their North and Latin American descendants had exchanged goods with Native nations in trade and as goodwill gestures. This practice resulted from the Europeans' desire to receive valuables in exchange for trinkets and from their belief in Amerindians' ignorance of material value (Greenblatt 13, 110). Solms advises German settlers to pay for precious Native merchandise with cheap bric-a-brac from Germany, perpetuating this tradition and its underlying colonial ideology. In so doing, he undermines his claim to have treated the Amerindians with respect (*Texas* 131–132; see also Ritzenhofen 169).

The character traits that *Texas* attributes to the Tejanos similarly reiterate those from the American and European colonial discourses that established a hierarchy of civilizations based on race or ethnicity, culture, and social class. The narrative particularly draws on Black Legend–inspired stereotypes in appraising the pleasant physique and "polite and pleasing manners" of the Mexican Texans while denouncing them as "deceitful, cunning" cowards and "a slave to all vices" (47). Their flawed character manifested itself to Prince Carl in their failure to preserve the Spanish colonial heritage in Texas. Speaking about the Spanish missions near San Antonio, he argues, "Since the Mexicans freed themselves from Spain, they have been constantly disputing and fighting, and so it has happened that these beautiful institutions have been destroyed" (46–47).[4] This conclusion, in turn, reveals a contradictory attitude toward Spain: it was an oppressive colonial power, which legitimized Mexican independence as liberation, yet it was also a European civilization worth preserving. Solms's *Texas* further delegitimizes the Mexican presence and land claims in Texans by indigenizing the Tejanos. The text emphasizes not only their history of miscegenation and physical resemblance to Amerindians but also their almost Native equestrian and hunting skills (46, 27). Finally, the writer advertises the Mexican Texans in his "Memoir on American Affairs" as useful allies of a British military operation in Texas (*Voyage* 220–221). Yet he downplays their military strength in his travelogue to assure his readers that German settlements in Texas were not at risk of being regained by Mexico.

Although Solms's travelogue acknowledges the settlement opportunities an American Texas provided for Germans (*Texas* 135–139), it echoes the reservations about US annexation of the region that Prince Carl voiced in his "Memoir" and in his reports and correspondence during his Texas journey (Solms, "Fifth Report from Texas to the German Emigration Society," October 25, 1844, in Geue and Geue 44).[5] In contrast to both Mexican and American discourses, Solms's *Texas* does not equate "American" with Anglo identity but describes the nation as a multiethnic blend of people from the lower social strata. Slightly revising a passage from his "Memoir" (*Voyage* 206–207), the narrator states:

> If we look back to the formation of the so-called American [nation],
> we find the conglomeration of all nationalities, from Norway and
> Sweden to Sicily, and from Russia to Portugal and Spain. . . . Those
> various immigrants left their homes to enter the new promised land
> either for the sake of gain or for other pressing causes, in which
> case they may not have belonged to the better parts of their nation.
> Hence . . . we also find among them the vices of all nations, but with-
> out their good qualities being transplanted. (*Texas* 47)

In the context of the author's monarchical political views and ethnic and class prejudices, this passage delegitimizes the non-Anglo-Saxon migration to North America as well as the nation resulting from it. Strikingly, however, other passages of the travelogue connect the materialism it criticizes with the Anglo population exclusively. Like Dunt's *Journey to Texas*, Prince Carl's *Texas* expresses admiration for Anglos' adventurousness but denounces their rugged individualism, disobedience, and lack of European manners: "The American is brave, possesses an enterprising spirit and is persistent in following out his plans and speculations." And although "warlike by nature," the Anglo male is an "undisciplined soldier" (50, 48, 86–87). According to Solms's *Texas*, ruthless materialism was the all-determining impetus of American life, which was visible in the individual's weak ties to places and people: "The home of parents, tokens from friends . . . , and many other things which are dear to [Germans], are merely mercenary to the American, who enjoys them only as long as he can make pecuniary gains thereby" (47–48). This line of reasoning reiterates the German societal discourse of the period. Its anti-Americanism articulates the widespread uneasiness among German conservatives about the sociocultural and geographic mobility that was challenging the established social order of their societies (Brenner 36–41). Hence, the prince's travelogue sets the relocation of German migrants, inspired by the purpose of finding a new, permanent home, against and above the supposedly greed-driven, perpetual wandering of the Anglo-Americans (*Texas* 47–49, 94–98).

In addition to Anglo materialism and mobility, Prince Carl depicts the institution of slavery as a key symptom and marker of Anglo cultural deficiency (Ritzenhofen 213–214). His travelogue explicitly targets the racial double standard of Anglo society, which denied its African American population the opportunities for freedom and social mobility that it cherished for itself (*Texas* 50, 52–53). Solms further scrutinizes the peculiar institution by showing the dehumanization of slaves, as seen in their treatment. The Black slaves were to Anglo-Americans "like horses, dogs, or any other animal which we can buy or make our own." They were accordingly "raise[d] ... with the whip, like cattle," and when slaves ran away, they were "chased like the wild beasts of the forests!" (50, 52–53). But like most Anglo-American and European witness texts about slavery in North America (Lockard; Mauch 626–635; Paul 7, 87–108, 163–165), Solms's depiction of the slaves was deeply steeped in racist prejudices and colonial thought. According to Joe Lockard, it was not the injustice to Blacks but the fear of losing white racial privilege that shaped most antislavery discourses: the insight that "but for facts of racial birth [the white observer] could be standing on the auction platform, working in a field, or living in a crude shack" (xxxi). Prince Carl's *Texas* counters the popular proslavery argument that African Americans lacked the intelligence and capacity for feeling and therefore did not qualify as humans. As the narrator points out, "among the darkies who were not so oppressed in their early age as to be irrational, I have found [a greater] honesty, faithfulness, attachment, ... gratitude and ... a far nobler disposition than [among] many Americans or Americanized Europeans" (53). Yet, in contrast to Ute Ritzenhofen's reading (213), this does not mean that Solms preferred Blacks to Anglos. On the contrary, the statement falls in line with the German *Amerikaliteratur* of the period. While viewing African Americans as humans, this body of writing tends to depict them as "natural" servants and ethnocultural inferiors to whites. In so doing, it criticizes slavery but also strengthens the position of German immigrants within American society, since many of them struggled with poverty and Anglo hostility (Paul).

In this vein, Prince Carl's portrayal of Black Texans enabled him to cater to the concerns of the German professional class, which he sought to win as settlers. Just as his journey account distinguishes the voluntary loyalty of African Americans from their enforced servitude, it denounces the latter as evil while simultaneously naturalizing the former. By emphasizing Blacks' loyalty and subservience, the text tones down the anxieties of German migrants about unfair labor competition with slaves. Elsewhere in *Texas*, the narrator somewhat contradicts this line of reasoning, as when he affirms the theory of climate, according to which only people of African descent were suited to manual labor in hot climates (25, 53). Moreover, although Solms argues that "the principle of slavery does not appeal to the German mind" (25), he criticizes the emigration society's practice of slavery at Nassau Farm only in his private letters and official reports from Texas (Solms, first, fourth, and sixth reports from Texas to the German Emigration Society, July 15, September 20, and December 23, 1844, in Geue and Geue 21–25, 39–41, 45–53).[6] He does not mention the society's slaves in his travelogue, nor does he address his personal involvement in the peculiar institution as manager of Nassau Farm in any of his writings (Kearney 5–6, 77–80, 84, 89).

Besides indicating a likely lack of self-reflection, the prince's public silence about slavery at Nassau Farm relates to his strategy, common in German *Amerika-literatur*, to present the Anglo-Americans as the opposite of the idealized Germans. The latter appear in his journey account as the model nation conforming to a feudalist ideal, since they possessed everything the republican, more egalitarian Americans supposedly lacked (Ritzenhofen 214, 252). Diligent and disciplined but also loyal and generous, the Germans drew their physical robustness and mental strength from a strong attachment to place, family, and culture. Hence, they appear as morally and culturally superior to other nations but simultaneously as vulnerable to exploitation by cunning, materialist minds (*Texas* 25, 40, 47–48, 56). This line of reasoning not only voices a misunderstanding resulting from a European aristocrat's encounters with an Anglo culture he cared little to understand, it also reiterates national images of Germans and Anglos prevalent in German social discourses on emigration and colonization. Like Dunt before him, Prince Carl captures this difference by juxtaposing American and German ways of interacting with nature and with other people. While "the American is usually too lazy to prepare a garden" in Texas, "the German settlements . . . are distinguished by their beautiful gardens, vegetables, and flowers," Solms argues. In so doing, he frames the colonists' well-tended private yards as markers of German diligence and appreciation of beauty (25). At the same time, the prince's travelogue concedes that the more "savage" Anglo-Americans were particularly suited to mastering the Texas landscape, since they knew how to survive in a hostile environment, handling inimical Natives and wild animals alike, whereas the more sociable Germans struggled with frontier life (33, 38–39, 75, 94–97). These oppositions apply the distinctions made in American travelogues between "indolent" southerners and westerners—who showed little will to carry out farm labor—and "diligent" New Englanders (Sibley 98, 165).

Nature and agriculture played a crucial role in advertising not only German migration to Texas in general but the colonization endeavor of the emigration society in particular. Characteristic of accounts promoting migration to North America, Solms's narrative blends utilitarian rhetoric with aestheticized landscape descriptions into enticing images of beauty and abundance. For instance, in one scene, tellingly plagiarized from Postl's *Kajütenbuch* (Ritzenhofen 78), the prince writes, "The prairies . . . spread themselves out before [the traveler] like a costly carpet, richly green, with an embroidery of exquisite flowers of diverse colors. One cannot help but be apprehensive that the hoof of his horse does not trample these marvels of nature and disarray their harmony" (*Texas* 35). Other scenes in *Texas* emphasize the economic benefits the region offered the industrious German colonist: a healthy climate, fertile soil, and mineral wealth; plenty of game animals, water, and timber; and a nascent infrastructure of settlements, roads, and navigable rivers. By comparing the region's potential for viticulture to the wine-growing areas of Germany and France, the volume seeks to further advertise Texas as resembling Europe (114; see also Ritzenhofen 77). Like the Mexican and Anglo-American journey narratives or like Dunt's German travelogue, Solms's volume perpetuates the myth of almost labor-free agriculture in order to argue for the superiority of Texas to other areas of North America: "The Texas farmer devotes neither time nor work to this purpose, because his cattle finds good grazing on the prairies in the winter as well as during the rest of the year. . . . Since the virgin soil has no need of any fertilizer and needs a rest only every three years at the most . . . , there is no reason for keeping the cattle in a pen" (34). In contrast to this image of a Texan *Schlaraffenland*, other passages in the prince's book remind readers that even such a bountiful region will not yield harvests without the settlers' labor. "All the garden vegetables grow abundantly if one takes the pains to plant them," the narrator remarks. The same is true for animals: "Horses roam wild in . . . Texas. But they are hard to catch and much more so to tame for riding" (*Texas* 24–25, 27). Like Dunt, Solms seeks to entice only those Germans to come to Texas who had the vocational skills, physical abilities, and financial means to make a living under frontier conditions—and hence reap profits for the emigration society and help establish a flourishing German colony in the region. *Texas* accordingly points out that settlers would face dangers, drudgery, and deprivation before their efforts would pay off: "Texas is the land where, after the first few years of strenuous and tedious toiling, the well-being of life blooms, and [one] can even consider with certainty prospects for a future" (118–119).

Logically for a text composed by a representative of an emigration agency, Prince Carl's travelogue promotes German settlement in Texas via his sponsoring organization. The text praises the emigration society for offering German colonists a set of services that facilitated settlement and provided security from abusive empresarios and raiding Natives. But the narrator never mentions the profits the organization sought to reap from its colonization project, nor does he specify the almost feudal character it envisioned for its colonies in Texas. Moreover, in exchange for support and protection, the emigration society demanded settlers' loyalty: "Whoever freely enters the Verein should have unwavering faith in [its] officers . . . by following their orders punctually, and by showing them respect" (*Texas* 139). The prince further bolsters his promise of protection to prospective German migrants by citing the example of a group of Alsatians whom their French empresario had abandoned without provisions: "I have seen much misery among gypsies in Hungary and among the lower classes of Jews in Poland, but all this was nothing compared to the wretchedness of these unfortunate people" (38). In German societal discourses, the figures of the eastern European Jew and the Gypsy represented familiar images of cultural difference and marginalization from which the average German in Texas could usually feel safely removed by geography, ethnicity, and social class. By implying that a group of Gentile European settlers could find themselves in the position of these dreaded others, Solms's *Texas* expresses the vulnerability of European colonists in a distant land. At the same time, the book distinguishes the German colonization effort, embodied by the emigration society, from similar endeavors of French empresarios.

In his journey account, Prince Carl refutes accusations made against him during his journey that his goal was to establish a German state in Texas. Yet he urges German settlers to maintain their identity abroad (Ritzenhofen 126–127, 252–253): "Leave your country with the firm resolution that you will always remain worthy of its name and that you will ... be faithful to [its] ideals" (*Texas* 141). He supports this appeal by portraying Americanized Germans in Texas as treacherous and despised (49, 100, 136). In addition to concerns that the emigration society would soon lose influence over an Americanized German community in Texas, these words voice the unease of a European aristocrat about the growing appeal of a young nation with a decidedly republican and meritocratic capitalist society for a populace once loyal to their nobles (Ritzenhofen 238). In the main, though, his text aligns with the wider German colonial discourse of its time that promoted not only German migration to Texas as an economic opportunity for hardy individuals but also advocated larger immigrant communities in the region to preserve their original culture within a hegemonically Anglo-American environment.

FERDINAND ROEMER'S *ROEMER'S TEXAS*

Such concerns with maintaining a German identity abroad also characterized many later German travelogues of Texas. Soon after Solms's return to his native land, another German began a lengthy tour of the Lone Star State, including a visit to the settlement the prince had founded. Karl Ferdinand von Roemer (1818–1891) was the first German scientist to study the geology of North America. Born and raised in Hildesheim, he obtained his doctorate in paleontology from the University of Berlin in 1842. In April 1845, he sailed to the United States with funds provided by the Berlin Academy of Sciences and the Society for the Protection of German Emigrants to Texas. From New York, he journeyed for several months through New England, Quebec, and the Midwest before reaching New Orleans. Curiosity about the Lone Star State led Roemer to Texas, where he arrived in Galveston on December 22, 1845, and in Houston the following January. He continued to New Braunfels, which he made his base for the following months. Scientific excursions took him to the state's recently founded capital city, Austin, and to the Brazos River valley, San Antonio, Fredericksburg, and the San Saba River valley. Departing from Galveston on May 8, 1847, Roemer traveled through the United States for another four months before returning to Germany. He subsequently held positions as a university lecturer and professor in Germany (Göbel and Stein 337–374).

During his lengthy academic career, Roemer published widely on the geology of central Europe and North America, and he has been acknowledged as the "father of the geology of Texas" (Göbel and Stein 368; Ritzenhofen 51). Probably inspired by a member of the Berlin Academy of Sciences, to whom he reported about his journey, Roemer penned a series of newspaper articles that appeared between March 1846 and August 1847 in the *Allgemeine Zeitung*, a leading German daily of the time (Göbel and Stein 343, 354–358, 363–364). He subsequently enlarged them into a travelogue-*cum*-scientific study for general audiences. Entitled *Texas: Mit besonderer Rücksicht auf deutsche Auswanderung und die physischen Verhältnisse des Landes nach eigener Betrachtung geschildert* (1849), the volume appeared in English as *Roemer's Texas: With Particular Reference to German Immigration and the Physical Appearance of the Country* (1983). Following the tradition of the scientific journey account, the book includes three sections: a general introduction to the geography and history of Texas, a chronological report of the writer's journey, and an appendix systematically presenting the results of the author's scientific studies. Roemer's use of scientific terminology to describe the geology, flora, and fauna of Texas, and his numerous references to other travelogues or scientific studies to support his observations, underline the scholarly character of his text. In a discussion of these sources, he follows Dunt and Solms in distinguishing his own work from similar-themed publications (Roemer, *Roemer's Texas* 32–34), a by-then common strategy to support the claims of a travelogue to objectivity, novelty, and practical value for readers.

As the subtitle of the volume indicates and the author's foreword confirms, Roemer's mission was twofold: to conduct a geological survey of the country and to assess the settlement potential of Texas and the situation of German colonists there (xii; see also Göbel and Stein 340, 368).[7] In so doing, the volume contributed not only to scientific knowledge but also to Germany's public discourse on establishing German settlements abroad. The latter aspect manifests itself especially in the geologist's taking part in the expedition to the San Saba River valley, mounted by the emigration society in 1847 to negotiate a peace treaty with the Comanches that enabled the organization to settle a land tract on the tribe's hunting grounds (Roemer, "Roemer's Account"; Hämäläinen 306). Moreover, Roemer's travelogue became one of the few German writings about Texas the association officially recommended to its colonists (Ritzenhofen 50–51). The way that *Roemer's Texas* looks at the Lone Star State indicates the writer's intertwined concerns with science and settlement. The text presents Texas as "a beautiful, promising land" whose "wide, green prairies" the narrator hopes will "become the home of a large and happy population" (xii, 301). Moreover, Roemer follows both Mexican and American explorers in assessing the topography of the region with an eye to its agricultural value. Echoing Berlandier in particular, he renders this alien land meaningful to his German target readers by comparing the Texas landscape to that of Europe (Doughty 52). For example, the area around Nassau Farm recalled "a certain region of the Rhine," and some of the stones used to build the Spanish Mission San José near San Antonio could also be found in Germany. In poetic exaggeration, Roemer even claims that Texas buffalo resemble the—already extinct—German aurochs (*Roemer's Texas* 165, 128, 199).

As in the writings of other travelers, the Lone Star State appears in *Roemer's Texas* as a land of unique natural abundance, one whose vegetation was "luxuriant" and thus required little effort to make a settlement flourish (115, 175, 299). "Texas is a natural grazing land, unsurpassed by any in the world," the book claims. "The cattle thrive and multiply . . . without the care and help of human beings" (9). In describing the San Saba River valley, the text blends the notion of the land of milk and honey with the myth of the gold-clad Seven Cities of Cibola, which inspired the Spanish conquest of the Mexican North (Gonzales 29–30). To the narrator, the area represented "the unknown, almost mythical wonderland with which every Texas settler associated the idea of unsurpassed fertility and loveliness and at the same time a wealth of precious metal, promised to satisfy both" (*Roemer's Texas* 218). As the reference to "loveliness" indicates, Roemer's depiction of nature is indebted to the aesthetic concepts of the beautiful and the picturesque. This connection becomes evident particularly in passages that show a benign nature fit for desirable leisure activities, another strategy of rendering Texas attractive to German readers. For example: "To drive along the beach in the evening in a light cabriolet drawn by a spirited horse and fanned by a cooling breeze affords the inhabitants of Galveston much pleasure. This pleasure is enhanced by the beautiful view of the Gulf, where the waves, rolling in ceaselessly, tumble over each other in the broad, white foaming surf" (42).

Like Randolph Marcy, Roemer views nature's bounty ambivalently, both as a demi-paradise and as a peril to itself. The fur trade and white settlements were heavily decreasing buffalo and other game animals, depredations that endangered Amerindian survival (151, 192–193, 231, 265). In addition, like other exploration narratives, *Roemer's Texas* identifies not only those areas that showed potential for agriculture and trade but also those parts excluded from such consideration by having barren soil, an unhealthy climate, or no transportation routes. The latter type of landscape appears in the text as the downside of the metaphor of the "virgin land": an utterly hostile, untamable nature. For instance, the book calls the Nueces Strip (the region between the Nueces River and the Rio Grande) a "wilderness, where no settlement will ever be made." Similarly, even parts of the Hill Country "present a picture of original primitiveness undisturbed by human activity" (4, 146).

Roemer's aesthetic ideal becomes manifest in the way his travelogue frames the Texas landscape. An area near San Antonio is described thus: "The prairie appeared...more as a charming natural garden or park on a large scale. Countless blossoms...formed natural flower gardens miles in extent" (156). Images of parks and gardens—restricted spaces of "cultivated naturalness" (Trott 74)—symbolically tame the wilderness of the Texas prairie in order to appeal to prospective German migrants and present the region as a desirable destination of settlement. American colonial discourses likewise presented Texas as a garden in order to legitimize Anglo land claims against Mexicans and Natives. Both lines of reasoning put forth the argument that turning the Texas wilderness into a cultivated and cultured space required not only labor and knowledge but also a higher civilization, which only white populations possessed. In this sense, Roemer muses about San Antonio's possibilities: "What an earthly paradise could be created here through the hands of an industrious and cultured population.... The soil is of great fertility and this could be still more increased by restoring and expanding the irrigation system used under Spanish rule" (*Roemer's Texas* 133).

As the reference to the irrigation system indicates, the German geologist appreciated some of the achievements of colonial Spain. Elsewhere, *Roemer's Texas* praises the Spanish policy of converting the Natives to Christianity and teaching them a sedentary way of life (127). Moreover, although the Spanish towns, missions, and garrison buildings in Texas appeared "foreign" to the traveler (120, 125), he views the region's colonial architecture as a symbol of the Spaniards' objective to spread European civilization to the New World. For example, at the Presidio San Luis on the San Saba River, the narrator admits his "astonishment to see in this wilderness... the indisputable evidence of a former permanent abode of the white man" (256). The narrator contrasts Tejano settlements with Spanish colonial architecture in Texas to signify the cultural decline brought forth by de-colonization. "The entire place gave the impression of decay," Roemer writes about San Antonio, "and apparently... had seen better and more brilliant days" (120).

That the German visitor treats the shift of power in Texas from the Spaniards to the Mexicans as a social and cultural falling-off becomes even more evident in his portrayal of the latter. Although Roemer expresses a genuine interest in Tejano culture, the volume comports with the predominant Anglo-American and European perceptions of Mexicans. On the one hand, *Roemer's Texas* frames their cultural difference in unthreatening images of consumable exoticism, for instance, by describing the "primitive workmanship" of Mexican oxcarts, the "natural charm and grace" of Tejanas, and the "dignified" and "picturesque" appearance of Mexican men (135, 120–122). On the other hand, the volume reiterates the negative stereotype of Tejanos as gamblers, thieves, cowards, and brutes (11, 122–123, 158; see also Ritzenhofen 204–205). The book further renders the cultural Otherness of Mexican Texans visible by indigenizing them, a rhetorical strategy particularly employed in American discourses. "It is a general opinion in West Texas that the Mexicans have the same inclination and skill for stealing horses as the Indians," the narrator states. He similarly connects the presumed idleness of San Antonio's Tejano residents to their mestizo and working-class identity (158, 11, 120). These means of Othering this population contributed to the European and Anglo-American colonial discourses that declared Mexican civilization inferior in order to justify the US claim to terrain and power in Texas.

Given Roemer's entanglement with Eurocentric colonial ideas, it is no surprise that *Roemer's Texas* depicts the Texas Natives much as it does the Tejanos (Ritzenhofen 171–173). Usually calling them "Indians," the book differentiates individual indigenous nations but also adopts the Mexican and American distinction between "wild" and "tame" tribes, based on their degree of assimilation to white society. The Comanches stand out in the German travelogue for their bravery, mastery of the horse, hospitality, and ingenuity (*Roemer's Texas* 245, 266, 275, 279–280). The text similarly does justice to the Karankawas. It remarks that their much-purported cannibalism, mentioned in both Mexican and Anglo-American texts, was hearsay (14). Nonetheless, like Mexican Texans, most Native nations appear in Roemer's travelogue as lazy, thievish, and warlike. The book links these negative traits causally with the "primitive" cultural and racial identity of the Amerindians (13, 158, 275–276). In line with the period's racial discourse, the text argues that whites might obtain advantageous indigenous traits by living close to nature, whereas Natives could acquire but the bad habits of Europeans or Anglo-Americans, being unable to rise above their "primitive" state (237, 241, 278).

In Roemer's text, the Natives' presumed lack of civilization at times manifests itself in images of a populace living in a perfect natural state. The volume asserts, for instance, that a band of Caddo Indians "live in harmony and that bickering and strife are unknown," and it describes a Comanche chief in traditional regalia as providing "the genuine, unadulterated picture of a North American Indian" (202, 269). Yet this harmony and cultural purity were in peril. Like Marcy's writings, *Roemer's Texas* acknowledges the genocide that interaction with Europeans had brought upon the region's Native population, pointing out that European diseases had carried off entire tribes and that alcohol had hastened the survivors' downfall (278). The book particularly deplores the US government policy of Amerindian removals. "It is apparent that the Indians of Texas, as well as the Red Race in North America, will be driven from their homes and eventually be exterminated," the narrator argues. "The most beautiful lands have already been taken from them, and restlessly moving forward, the white, greedy conqueror is stretching forth his hand to take their new hunting grounds also" (14). Yet rather than blaming white settlers for this genocide, Roemer's travelogue fully endorses the European and American discourses and practices of colonization. The volume depicts the Texas Natives as animalistic creatures who had to be subjugated, along with the wilderness they inhabited, in order to "civilize" the region. It describes the "untamed ferocity" of a Shawnee guide and speaks of indigenous nations as "marauding" in the wilderness. Similarly, the text argues that "roving" bands of Natives hindered the land's "cultivation by civilized man" (238, 4, 150, 1).

Most striking among the imagery of Amerindian cultural difference from European and Anglo-American norms is the way *Roemer's Texas*, once again prefiguring Marcy's accounts, characterizes Native nations according to Orientalist stereotypes of Middle Eastern peoples, depictions that would have been familiar to American and European readers. Watching a band of Natives arrive at a trading post, the narrator muses, "To see the long train, resembling a caravan, appear . . . presented a picturesque and fascinating sight for a European" (195). Similarly, in a Lipan Apache camp, he notes "a young Indian of effeminate, Bacchus-like appearance, stretched out on soft buffalo hides, holding a pipe," amid two women and a child: "This whole scene of an Indian family life with the man seemingly taking a domineering position, reminded me of a picture from the orient" (103). By calling up the Orientalist clichés of male effeminacy, decadence, and despotism, the scene highlights Amerindian cultural Otherness in order to justify white settlement and indigenous subjugation. In a similar vein, echoing the perceptions of Mexican and American travelers, Roemer's description of Comanche society blends notions of absolute patriarchal rule and inverted gender roles into a veritable counterimage of European cultures. "Unlike civilized people, the men and not the women among the Indians lay special stress upon outward finery," *Roemer's Texas* states. "The poor squaws are the slaves to the men, and . . . they are concerned only to adorn their lord and master and to gain his approbation" (244).

The "primitiveness" of the Natives and Tejanos contrasts with the respect the German travelogue voices for Anglo-Americans' achievements. The text praises their work ethic and practical skills as well as their determination, courage, and perseverance in confronting the dangers and hardships of settling the West (36–37, 57, 65–66, 82). The traveler reads a scene in which a German aristocrat turned Texas tavern owner served working-class clients with courtesy as an indicator that the United States was, indeed, "the land of perfect equality and brotherhood" (97). Alluding to a famous battle lost by ancient Sparta, the narrator exclaims in yet another passage that "in the ruins of the Alamo, Texas had its Thermop[y]lae" (126). While such enthusiasm for the Texas Revolution was common among German liberals of the 1830s and 1840s, Roemer deviates from the hopes articulated in parts of German public discourse of establishing better trade relations with an independent Texas Republic. Instead, *Roemer's Texas* adopts an Anglocentric point of view when justifying the region's annexation to the United States: "Texas needed the protection of the United States, as Mexico still had designs of reconquering the lost province. It was profitable for the United States as annexation removed the possibility of having [Texas] come under the sway of European diplomacy" (52).

At the same time, the seeming Anglo-Texan disregard for a comfortable home life disturbed the German geologist. Roemer shared the German romanticist view of gardens as signifiers of diligence and cultural refinement, and so he notices with consternation that in contrast to the gardenlike landscape, actual kitchen gardens were an "unusual sign in Texas" (*Roemer's Texas* 188). Moreover, the state of towns convinced the German visitor that he had reached the borders of civilization. In many Anglo settlements, houses showed signs of decay or neglect (64, 86, 171). In Houston, "the streets were unpaved and the mud bottomless"; San Felipe presented itself as a "dismal, deserted place" (63–64, 77). Against this backdrop, *Roemer's Texas* hails any sign of education or class distinction among the Anglo-Texans, such as "a small but carefully selected library" in a rough log cabin or separate parlor rooms for middle- and working-class patrons in a guesthouse (60, 64–65).

The German journey account ambivalently portrays the capitalist materialism of American culture. The volume praises the freedom of trade in the United States (95), but laments that people's desire for profit was greater than their attachment to private possessions: "A Texan is ready at any moment . . . to trade or sell anything he wears . . . , if he can make an advantageous trade" (89). In remarking on their fondness for drinking, gambling, and horse racing, their sloppy manners and jealousy of foreigners, *Roemer's Texas* places the Anglo-Texans only a step above their Tejano neighbors (67–68, 122–123, 132, 190). Although the book explicitly approves of US annexation of Texas, and is indebted to a Eurocentric hierarchy of civilizations, it deviates from the specifically American colonial discourse that claimed Anglo political, economic, and cultural superiority over other populations of European descent.

Unlike many other foreign visitors, the German geologist does not criticize Anglo-American society for its slaveholding. But *Roemer's Texas* does target slavery whenever the enslaved were persons of European descent. Firmly grounded in a Eurocentric hierarchy of peoples and echoing Mexican and American observers, the narrator voices his incomprehension at why an Anglo boy would choose to remain with his Comanche captors rather than return to "civilization." Similarly, he pities the same Native's Mexican slave, although he points out that unlike southern slaveholders, indigenous nations allowed acculturated captives to become free members of their tribes (242–243, 271). Other than this small critique of Amerindian slave ownership, *Roemer's Texas* joins the American proslavery discourse, presenting a series of common arguments to justify the bondage of Blacks. By pointing out certain parallels between the slavery systems of the United States and ancient Rome, the book suggests that slavery was perfectly compatible with a complex civilization (Ritzenhofen 218). The text further asserts that African Americans' purportedly limited intelligence placed them close to domestic animals, which made it legitimate to treat them as such.[8] The volume frames the master-slave relationship in Texas as that of a family patriarch and his wards. Roemer not only states that slaves were often called their owner's "black family" but also depicts them as children (*Roemer's Texas* 61–62, 71–72). The narrator remarks, "It requires a combination of great determination and a certain amount of indulgence in order to strike a happy medium" in managing slaves. "And one must have an intimate knowledge of [their] disposition" to succeed therein (164).

The only aspect of the peculiar institution that *Roemer's Texas* criticizes is its socioeconomic impact on Texas. Roemer was one of the few observers to question the profitability of slavery, because it required high capital investments and because free states showed higher rates of wealth, population growth, and property value (31, 36, 58–59). But what particularly concerned him was the way that slavery shaped social differences among whites in Texas. African American slaves, *Roemer's Texas* argues, not only "form the basis for gauging the wealth of a person in this country," but also determine their owner's social prestige: "The social standing of a slave-owning planter is always quite different from that of the farmer who has to till his own soil by the sweat of his brow" (187, 89). Consequently, most German settlers in Texas would suffer economic and social disadvantages compared to their slaveholding Anglo neighbors, because the newcomers would lack the money and knowledge to buy and manage a slave labor force (31, 164; see also Sibley 149). To underline his point, Roemer cites the case of a slave from Nassau Farm who successfully negotiated favorable treatment from his novice German slaveholders. Rather than advising Germans to avoid settling in a slave state, the geologist's journey account endorses their joining the ranks of slave owners, as its sympathetic depiction of the plantation implies (162–165).

Roemer's worries about the fate of the Germans in Texas related directly to his mission of assessing the situation of the budding German settlements in the region and the potential for further immigrants. His travelogue therefore charts the brief history of German colonization in Texas, delineates the program of the emigration society, and describes its major settlements (15–24, 92–99, 227–230). Even though the organization supported his stay in the Lone Star State, *Roemer's Texas* did not blindly promote its colonization endeavor. Instead, the volume points out the flaws of the society, above all the mismanagement that caused many German settlers to struggle with diseases, desperation, and death (21, 24–32, 284–290; see also Göbel and Stein 367–368, 382–383). In a particularly compelling passage, the travelogue resorts to Orientalist imagery—otherwise only applied to the Texas Natives—to describe the living conditions of a group of the emigration society's protégés in Galveston: "Various families were crowded into the rooms among their ... baggage and boxes piled up high ... Continuous cooking and baking was maintained on impoverished hearths in the yard. The whole scene reminded me of an Oriental caravan. ... These people had no foreboding of the privations and sufferings awaiting them" (46). The last sentence endows the scene with a cautionary character, warning that not everyone considering emigration from Germany was suited to succeed in Texas. Roemer's journey account especially blames German migrants' misery on their often-unrealistic dreams and lack of diligence, perseverance, and relevant skills (154, 289, 215). Consequently, the text admonishes readers: "May the young men of the educated class inform themselves in the future as to what they may expect. May all who have not the firm intention and the necessary qualifications to establish themselves as farmers remain away, where instead of the dreams of good fortune, nothing but disappointment and a tragic end await them" (102).

Despite these warnings, the geologist's travelogue argues in favor of German migration to Texas, emphasizing the region's agricultural potential and expressing patriotic pride in the advancement of German settlements there. However, like Solms, Roemer was concerned with Germans maintaining social-class distinctions and standards of cultural refinement in the New World. In both his book and his private correspondence, he repeatedly complained about German immigrants such as the aristocrat turned innkeeper or German peasants and workers who had welcomed the more egalitarian culture of the United States (Roemer, *Roemer's Texas* 84–86, 97, 233; Roemer to Rudolf Ihering, January 10, 1846, qtd. in Göbel and Stein 354). Roemer notes with ambivalence how these and other German colonists in Texas negotiated a new cultural and social identity. *Roemer's Texas* shows sympathy for the financial constraints that made the owner of a New Braunfels eating house take to the Anglo custom of serving beef, the cheapest food available, for breakfast (98–99). Yet immediately afterward, the narrator comments with a mixture of curiosity and bewilderment on the unconventional dress of some German settlers: "The component parts [of their garb] were borrowed from the Indian, the Mexican, the American, and the German costumes, but the greater part was a production to suit the capricious taste of the individual" (99). The reasons he gives for this exotic apparel again reveal the traveler's uneasiness with Germans who shed the social restraints of their native culture. His book blames their "recklessness in dress" not only on "the almost total absence of cultured women" among the Texas Germans but also on the colonists' wish "to compensate" for the stricter dress code they had to submit to in the old country" (100).

The attention that Roemer pays to matters of mores and manners in his journey account results from his sharing the then-widespread belief among Germans in the superiority of their native culture. For example, the text comments on a planned German colony on the Pedernales River: "The first settlement of civilized human beings was to be found in the northwest hill country of Texas.... Whereas the Anglo American was always the first to advance into the western wilderness, here the German was to be assigned this role" (154). Similarly, the narrator remarks about the Christmas tree at New Braunfels: "On the same place where today the symbols of a happy German family life [are] planted in the midst of a cultured population, scarcely two years ago the camp fires of the wild Comanches were burning" (215). As these and other scenes demonstrate, *Roemer's Texas* engages in the period's discourse about establishing German colonies in overseas territories. Aligning itself with earlier writings such as Dunt's and Solms's travelogues, the text asserts that Texas provided unique opportunities for establishing entirely German communities, where residents could enjoy the economic benefits of living in the United States while resisting cultural Americanization (17, 23, 26–28, 165).

Like their American counterparts, German authors of journey narratives of Texas tended to either recommend future German settlement in Texas or warn against it. Both Detlef Dunt and Prince Carl of Solms-Braunfels capitalized on and further stimulated the first major German migration wave to Texas. Their travelogues crucially modify the Anglocentric Texas Creation Myth to accommodate the concerns of their German target audience, emphasizing the opportunities for farmers and workers and downplaying the conflicts with Native nations. In particular, they employ the motif of the garden as a marker of German national character that would strengthen German cultural identity and immigrant-community cohesion amid an Anglo-dominated society. Ferdinand Roemer's travelogue about the region holds a special position in this body of writing, since it combines an interest in natural-science observation with a German-migration-promoting review of social conditions in Texas. His geological findings in Texas would lay the foundation not only for Roemer's academic career in Germany but also for the subsequent scientific study of the Lone Star State. His assessment of German migration to Texas indicates the influence of German colonization discourses and endeavors on his mission. In a letter from 1850 to one of the officers of the Society for the Protection of German Emigrants to Texas, Roemer revised his earlier, more critical observations on the budding German settlements in the region. Nonetheless, he urged the organization to ensure the success of its Texas settlement projects (Roemer to Freiherr von Bibra, April 3, 1850, in Roemer, "Roemer's Account" 71–74). His writings, while endorsing the German colonization of Texas, thus acknowledge the problems the settlers were likely to face in the Lone Star State, problems that another body of texts, the travelogues of disappointed migrants, would focus on and profit from.

FIVE

Newcomers' Plight

Travel Accounts Warning against German Migration

In addition to a large body of writing that encouraged settlement in the North American West, a smaller number of texts circulating in both Europe and North America sought to discourage migration to the region. Like the migration-endorsing literature, this corpus comprises several formats: migrants' private and public letters, journalism, tracts, pamphlets, travelogues, and antiemigration guides (Görisch 28–29, 168–169; Rese 93, 99–100). Some German texts are known (or assumed) to have been published on behalf of public authorities eager to retain taxpayers and laborers. But there was neither a concerted governmental effort nor a political agenda behind these works (Görisch 161–169). Instead, in both Germany and the United States, disappointed settlers or emigration agents seem to have penned most of the texts that warn against migration to the North American West. While Texas was rarely the subject of American antimigration propaganda, the writers of several German travelogues voiced their disillusion with the region. Prominent examples include Friedrich Höhne's 1844 account, *Wahn und Überzeugung: Reise des Kupferschmiede-Meisters Friedrich Höhne nach Nordamerika und Texas* (Delusion and conviction: Travels of the master coppersmith Friedrich Höhne to North America and Texas"); Alwin Sörgel's 1847 compilation of letters, *Für Auswanderungslustige! Briefe eines unter dem Schutz des Mainzer Vereins nach Texas Ausgewanderten* (*A Sojourn in Texas, 1846–47*); and Louis Constant's 1848 report, *Texas: Das Verderben deutscher Auswanderer in Texas unter dem Schutze des Mainzer Vereins* (Texas: The ruin of the German immigrants in Texas under the protection of the Mainz Society") (Ritzenhofen 39, 47, 84–87, 167).

The texts warning against migration provide cautionary tales of failed settlements. They emphasize the difficulties awaiting the migrant: the hardships of farming on poor soil, the lack of other labor opportunities, the privations of living in isolated, undeveloped areas, the prevalence of dreaded diseases like cholera, and the threat posed by hostile Natives. German works commonly also voice concerns about having to adapt to a capitalist American society that lacked the social safety and cultural refinement Germans enjoyed in their native states (Görisch 162–169; Ritzenhofen 186, 239–240, 255). Many works of antimigration literature particularly accuse emigration agents and emigration societies of luring migrants to the West with hyperbolic promises, efforts that provided profits only for these mediators and for local businesses, whereas migrants suffered from poor conditions (Görisch 125, 166–169; Sibley 156–159, 163–164, 166–167). Authors frequently bolster their authority and accuracy by pointing out their social status and migration experiences as well as by providing factual documents or references to other travelogues. Nonetheless, this body of writing generated much less public interest than migration-promoting narratives catering to readers' desire for economic advancement through emigration (Görisch 163–164, 167–168).

EDUARD LUDECUS'S TRAVEL LETTERS FROM TEXAS

While most empresario colonies in Mexican Texas were located in the central part of the region, one famous exception was the settlement endeavor of the British entrepreneur John Charles Beales. Starting in 1828, he secured four empresario grants to settle foreign immigrants in the Texas-Coahuila-Tamaulipas border region. In the fall of 1833, he managed to gather fifty-nine colonists interested in settling on his most recently acquired tract, known as the Grant and Beales Grant (Dr. James Grant was his partner in the scheme) or the Beales River Grant, in the area between the Nueces River and the Rio Grande (Brister, introduction xvi–xvii). One of these settlers was the German Eduard Ludecus (1807–1879). A native of Weimar, he had worked for a trading company in Braunschweig for several years before health problems and wanderlust made him consider migrating to the United States to become a farmer in the Missouri Valley. Already well read about North America, he further prepared for his emigration by learning to speak English, to swim, to ride a horse, and to shoot a rifle (Birk 11–12; Brister, introduction xi–xiii; Brister, "Ludecus's Journey" 369–371). Sailing from Bremerhaven on August 29, 1833, he reached New York City in October, where he met Beales and decided to join the empresario's colonization endeavor. On November 11, 1833, Beales's group of settlers embarked by ship from New York to Texas; they anchored at Copano Bay in December. Their overland journey led them via San Antonio to the Rio Grande, and they reached their destination on Las Moras Creek, a tributary of the larger river, on March 12. There they established the settlement of La Villa de Dolores. Owing to the unsuitable territory, constant risk of Amerindian raids, and Beales's poor organization, the colonists struggled fiercely. In July 1834, they abandoned Dolores (Brister, introduction xiii, xvii; Brister, "Ludecus's Journey" 371–382). Ludecus then traveled to Matamoros, from where he continued in October by boat for New Orleans and up the Mississippi River. He spent the rest of his life working in different professions in the southern and eastern United States (Birk 13; Brister, introduction xiv–xv).

From his departure from Bremen through his stay in New Orleans, Ludecus wrote nineteen letters to friends and family in Germany, which he sent home in a single package (Ludecus, *Reise* iv; see also Birk 13 and Brister, introduction ix, xi). They were published in 1837 under the editorship of his father, Wilhelm Ludecus, as *Reise durch die mexikanischen Provinzen Tumalipas, Cohahuila und Texas im Jahre 1834: In Briefen an seine Freunde—John Charles Beales's Rio Grande Colony* (2008) in English translation. (While the book will be referred to by its more proper, German title in the text, page references are usually to the English edition, cited as *Beales*.) In contrast to the travelogues penned to promote migration to Texas, Ludecus did not compose his text retrospectively or with a preformulated agenda. Instead, he articulates his views based on his experiences during the journey. While the first letters have a witty tone that both entertains and educates their readers, the correspondence increasingly shifts to informing prospective German colonists about conditions in northern Mexico. Accordingly, the correspondence moves from a rather humorous account of the traveler's individual experiences to more general observations, in a soberer tone, on the colony of Dolores and the different cultures Ludecus encountered (Birk 14; Brister, introduction ix–xi; Brister, "Ludecus's Journey" 384). The narrator justifies his writing by pointing out his intention "to show what unpleasant situations one can encounter and the difficulties and dangers emigrants must risk" in northern Mexico. He views his text as "a warning to my compatriots not [to] entrust their fate so unconditionally to people and especially to a country they do not know" (Ludecus, *Beales* 77, 94). In addition, the German edition of his book contains a preface by the editor that explains Ludecus's motives in going to North America and provides readers with additional information on the history, geography, and population of the Mexican North (*Reise* iii–xvi; see also Ritzenhofen 189–190).

In contrast to texts promoting migration to the New World, Ludecus's *Reise* provides only little practical advice for German settlers (*Beales* 17, 41–42, 45–46). Like Carl of Solms-Braunfels, the writer commonly uses English or Spanish terminology with German explanations to familiarize his readers with unknown plants, animals, everyday objects, and cultural practices (Ritzenhofen 193–194). He frequently alludes to figures and incidents from European history, mythology, literature, and the arts that would be known to educated Germans in order to convey his and his fellow colonists' experiences, thoughts, and feelings (Brister, introduction x). For instance, he describes the food in Dolores as being "strongly reminiscent of the soup of the Spartans." Upon leaving the failed settlement, he imagines the destructive force of the Roman Empire: "I was standing there like Scipio on the ruins of Carthage and . . . looked out without pity at the forsaken heroic city" (*Beales* 145, 183). And by claiming that a group of Mexican soldiers "had the faces of the most genuine scoundrels that only a [painter like] Salvator Rosa could select" (65), the text adds to a colonial discourse that turned representatives of the Mexican Republic into an exotic spectacle in order to signify European cultural superiority. In so doing, the volume justifies and naturalizes the American colonization endeavor that Ludecus had joined.

The German writer's Eurocentrism shows strongly in his perception of the natural world. In European romanticist discourse, nature in the Americas appears as an original and untamed force. Although it threatened European travelers, it simultaneously provided them with unfamiliar physical and spiritual experiences, and it was available for conquest (Birk 21–22). Ludecus's *Reise* frames the wild nature of Texas and Tamaulipas as a source of danger, adventure, and survival, and the text recounts numerous hunting expeditions and struggles with ferocious animals (*Beales* 111–113, 123–124, 162–166; see also Brister, "Ludecus's Journey" 369). Other passages voice the writer's typical romanticist fascination with dark forests, rugged mountains, mist, and moonlight (Trott 75–76, 80–81). In an "extraordinarily Romantic scene," Ludecus's narrator admires "a dense forest of trees, some of them tall and majestic" (*Beales* 113). Elsewhere in the book, he voices a powerful European colonial fantasy of contact with nature and other cultures: "Around the fire you see sitting, standing, or lying in a semicircle some men and women, boys, girls, and children, the masters and their servants, Englishmen and Scotsmen, Irishmen, Germans, Frenchmen, and North Americans in a colorful blend. Also, there are the Mexicans . . . Their sunburned faces and bodies form a natural transition from the whites to the Indians sitting next to them and completing the circle. The bright light of the fire is hardly able to make the dark brown figures distinguishable and visible before the dark background" (137). Here the text familiarizes the potentially hostile nature of the North American West through the image of a multicultural human society whose harmonious interactions naturalize the underlying social stratification. The mix of genders, ages, nationalities, and social statuses somewhat blurs the differences among the Europeans. In contrast, the arrangement of the entire group in the scene establishes an ethnoracial hierarchy with the Europeans at the center, the Mexicans next to them, and the Amerindians on the margins (Ritzenhofen 159, 193). The Natives' blending into the surrounding landscape stresses their presumed proximity to nature, whereas the Europeans' command of the fire, as a source of light, heat, and nourishment, articulates their claim to higher civilization and control of the land.

Ludecus paid special attention to the economic and political potential of his destination for settlement. *Reise* identifies those areas of Texas and Tamaulipas that feature the topographical and climatic prerequisites of successful white colonization. Echoing travelogues promoting settlement, the book describes these regions in a language of abundance and fertility. For example, near the Nueces River, "the land . . . resembled a garden," the narrator states. "The luxuriant vegetation gave testimony to the great fertility. . . . A large pond . . . was enclosed by beautiful oak trees. Behind the pond … a delightful spot of meadow … resembled a large yellow carpet of flowers" (*Beales* 116). By thus blending the aesthetic discourse of tamed nature with the utilitarian rhetoric of land cultivation, the garden imagery tones down readers' anxieties about an alien land and legitimizes white colonization. Ludecus's narrative aligns itself with other German travelogues by viewing gardens as signs of a population's cultural refinement: "The Mexican is too lazy to plant more than he needs for himself and he understands nothing at all about horti-culture. … Only a small number of Americans have gardens" (230). By blaming the absence of kitchen gardens in Texas on the presumed idleness and ignorance of Anglos and Mexicans, the volume undermines their claims to control the land.

Reversing the discourse of abundance and fecundity prevalent in literature promoting migration to the North American West, Ludecus stresses repeatedly that many parts of Texas were not suitable for colonization. For example: "No luxuriant vegetation [was] to be seen" near the Rio Grande, and "the sight of [the river], its murky, sandy water and its bare banks … made a very depressing impression" (118). Elsewhere the text compares the area to a "desert" or a "wilderness" and calls it "an impoverished savage country"—a term that evokes the dual threats of a hostile topography and a dangerous Amerindian presence (117, 164, 185). In a similar vein, Ludecus praises Mexico for having opened Texas to foreign coloniza-tion, but more strongly foregrounds the downsides of settling there (Birk 26–27). Ludecus's *Reise* particularly voices concern that "this province is now the object of interest among North American land speculators, and many inhabitants of the [US] western states are leaving their homes in order to seek new ones in Texas" (*Beales* 44). Consequently, "the great multitudes of wild horses and buffalo, which used to roam over the land in such large herds …, have almost disappeared" (243). The increasing presence of white people, the text argues, had thus already taken a toll on the land, and further settlement would aggravate that harm.

With great irony, Ludecus's journey account unmasks the illusory claims that the empresario Beales had made to attract colonists, as well as the settlers' naïve belief in his promises. For example, the narrator compares a dirt road in Dolores to Berlin's Friedrichstraße, the most elegant shopping street of the Prussian capital (132). Later, in a poem on the failed development of Dolores, he muses: "Probably never will a mansion be glimpsed in you, / If an Indian … / Does not erect his wigwam of dry branches there" (184). Elsewhere his journey account draws on the biblical Exodus to convey the settlers' disappointment with their condition: "Everyone was talking about leaving the flesh pots of Egypt behind and seeking the blessed promised land, wherever it may be" (168). The ironic analogy of the fondly remembered fleshpots of Egypt to the barren, torturous Rio Grande colony savagely lampoons the unfulfilled promise of the colonization project and the deprivations it caused.

The subjects of freedom and material welfare run as leitmotifs through Ludecus's *Reise*. One of the letters contains a telling anecdote about one of Beales's often authoritarian-acting representatives in Dolores: "Swarming wasps, perhaps French liberals transformed in the process of reincarnation, were resisting the raising of the white flag and had inflicted several red and blue spots on Mr. Egerton's deathly pale face. If he had shown himself [in that condition] in Germany, he would have certainly been brought to Mainz as an arch-demagogue" (*Beales* 169). The passage alludes to the Mainz-based Central Investigative Commission, installed by the Carlsbad Decrees of 1819 to identify and persecute revolutionary activities in Germany (Brose 91). Treating the wasps as French revolutionaries who turn Mr. Egerton's face into the tricolored French flag, which would have led to his political persecution in Germany, the narrator criticizes the lack of political freedom in his native country and voices his support for the liberal goals of France's July Revolution of 1830. Elsewhere in his travelogue, Ludecus explains how his desire for liberty and adventure more than made up for the hardships of frontier life. "In Germany ... I had plenty of everything ... and yet I was dissatisfied," he confesses. "Now I am in the interior of Mexico ... without a cent of money ... traveling through an arid desert over inaccessible roads and exposed to wild Indians and predatory Mexican robbers—and yet I am content" (*Beales* 175). What the passage does not mention is the crucial impact that the writer's situation as a healthy single white man with considerable language skills had on his success in the New World. Other scenes in *Reise* address either the importance of knowing English and Spanish for anyone hoping to settle in the United States–Mexico border region or the role of translators to enable communication and cross-cultural understanding among Anglo-Americans, Mexicans, Germans, and Amerindians. Ludecus repeatedly fulfilled this function (*Beales* 71, 128, 159). Thus privileged, the traveler endorses his "participat[ion] in this cross-country crusade," and he advises his German readers accordingly: "It is very impractical to make plans in Europe and expect to carry them out in America without having a thorough knowledge of the country. ... Here in America the moment matters" (231).

Although the abilities that Ludecus identifies as prerequisites for "seizing that moment"—pragmatism, flexibility, and perseverance (231)—are the same ones that North American and European public discourses associated with Anglo-Americans, the German did not unequivocally endorse Anglo culture. Instead, his *Reise* squarely falls in line with the tendency of the *Amerikaliteratur* to look at white America with special regard to how its political institutions, economy, values, and customs might affect German immigrants to the United States. Ludecus's travelogue praises the republicanism and hospitality of Anglo-Americans but complains about their lack of manners, bias against foreigners, and economic materialism. For instance, the book characterizes an Anglo resident of San Fernando as "one of those people who have come to Mexico to get rich at a galloping pace." Elsewhere, the narrator calls religion "a good business in America and very lucrative" (*Beales* 194, 144). In Matamoros, the traveler warns against the negative Anglo influence on European immigrants: "The [Germans], as well as the French, seem to have become somewhat coarse, particularly through the example of the North Americans [in town] who really can be held up as models of crudeness" (229).

Ludecus echoes European and Latin American travelers to the United States in noting the comparatively little amount of poverty among the white population of New York, but provides a more complex picture of Anglo society and manners elsewhere in the United States and among colonists in Texas and Tamaulipas (37–42, 49–51, 115, 130). Like Solms's emigrant guide, Ludecus's *Reise* does not question the ethnic stratification of labor that naturalized the inferior or enslaved status of Blacks in the United States (*Beales* 38). Quite tellingly, the single African American among Beales's colonists, a servant or slave named Henry, is the only member of the expedition always called by his first name (146). Ludecus's travelogue aligns itself with that of Joshua James and Alexander MacRae or that of Jane Cazneau (discussed in a later chapter) in criticizing the Mexican system of debt peonage for jeopardizing the freedom of the white lower class. But in contrast to these proslavery Anglo-American texts, which differentiate poverty-induced servitude in Mexico from race-based slavery in the United States, the German travelogue likens peonage to other forms of institutionalized bondage. Moreover, Ludecus's indignation that peonage was "a *modern* form of slavery" indicates that his frame of reference was not the peculiar institution of the US South but bygone systems of slavery such as those of classical Greece and Rome, which an educated German like him was surely familiar with (97, my emphasis).

The German traveler follows Anglo-Saxon discourse in depicting Mexicans as closely related to the Amerindian nations of the North American West. *Reise* foregrounds not only physiognomic similarities between Natives and Mexicans but also cultural values common to the two groups, such as their liking for guns and horses (*Beales* 77, 87, 119). The text sketches a pastoral idyll, depicting the Mexicans as happy people with modest needs, yet also criticizes their seeming lack of ambition (86–87, 190–191, 196, 230). At the same time, the journey account praises the loyalty, helpfulness, and courage of those Mexicans who served the American and German colonists as guides, guards, or hosts (123, 127–128, 145–146). Both images serve as a foil for Ludecus's cultural critique. On the one hand, Mexican servility contrasts positively with the contemptuous behavior of the Anglo leaders of the Rio Grande colony toward their German colonists (188, 194, 208). On the other hand, Ludecus portrays all other Mexicans as the opposite of those who served him—as gamblers, thieves, idlers, and cowards whose sexual libertinage was shared by even the Catholic clergy (88–89, 91, 167, 234–235;

see also Birk 34–35, 37). He thereby advances the belief that Mexicans were at a lower stage of civilizational development than Anglo-Saxons and hence were "naturally" suited for a life of want or servitude (Ritzenhofen 192, 194).

Ludecus's depiction of Tejano and Tamaulipecan society reveals the way that intertwined preconceptions of ethnicity and social class shaped his assessment of Mexicans (*Beales* 190). Several scenes of his travelogue depict Mexican dances as exotic spectacles lacking grace and harmony. In one of these passages, the narrator compares the dance to a "cockfight" and describes one of the musicians as "a fat fellow ... screaming the lyrics to the *fandango* in a terrible falsetto voice" (91). By likening the dance to a sport associated with a lower-class milieu and by describing the male singer as a parody of manliness and musicality, the scene articulates the presumed lack of Mexican cultural refinement and respectability. In a similar vein, Ludecus's narrative reverses the widespread Anglo-Saxon view that Mexican men were ugly and the women attractive. At another Mexican ball, the German narrator calls his Mexican dance partner "the ugliest skeleton that may have come to the Brocken mountain on a Walpurgis Night" (189). In alluding to the annual witches' Sabbath of German lore, the narrator employs an image of transgressive femininity—the ugly, uncontrolled, and harmful witch—to articulate the Mexicans' presumed social, cultural, and ethnic inferiority. In another passage, his ethnic bias blends with social-class prejudice when he describes Mexican children as animalistic creatures: "Small children ..., even those of the upper classes, crawl and run around up to a certain age completely naked.... The children of the lower classes look more like little pigs than people and are rarely or never washed" (89).

In his *Reise*, Ludecus ascribes a similar lack of civilization to the Mexican nation-state. Asserting his original commitment to settle in Mexico and "live under [its] flag" (*Beales* 110), the narrator blames the political instability and weakness of the Mexican government for its failure to develop the country (105, 161, 230). Unlike Anglo-American travel texts such as Mary Holley's or Stephen Austin's writings, the German travelogue does not use this critique to justify the Anglo-American appropriation of Texas. Instead, in line with German colonial discourse, the text limits itself to cautioning against European migration to Mexico: "No matter how enlightened and political the government may be, given the Mexicans' jealousy of foreigners and their aversion to them settling in the country, I am convinced that foreigners will encounter all kinds of difficulties and intolerance in the execution of a colonization plan, and ... gain no security for their property" (230). In Ludecus's travelogue, the poor state of the Mexican body politic reveals itself most powerfully in the appearance of its settlements. The text acclaims the rapid development of the Tamaulipas port town of Matamoros from a "rancho" into a settlement where "one sees buildings ... which might adorn the most attractive plazas of Europe's capitals" (229). In contrast, San Antonio, the "metropolis of Texas," disappoints the German visitor because it does not meet his "expect[ation] to find [it] resembling more a European city" (92, 100). Instead, it and other Spanish towns of South Texas appear as exotic spaces in decay. In Goliad (then La Bahía), for example, the narrator calls the Mexicans an "alien race of people" and notes the presence of "Indian huts" on the central plaza (85). Like many Mexican, Anglo, and fellow German observers, including Jean Louis Berlandier, Jane Cazneau, and Ferdinand Roemer, Ludecus further views the transformation of the Spanish mission buildings of South Texas and Tamaulipas from proud symbols and instruments of European colonial grandeur to dilapidated structures indicating Mexican social degradation (78, 101, 120). In its depiction of Mexican Texas and Tamaulipas, the book thus falls in line with European and American colonial discourses that presented the Mexican Republic as politically deficient and its population so culturally inferior as to require Old World or US guidance and colonization (Ritzenhofen 194–195).

The same line of reasoning characterizes Ludecus's portrayal of indigenous populations. They appear in his *Reise* as even greater impediments to European colonists than Anglos or Mexicans. The narrator denotes them as "Indians," "Natives," or "tribes," or gives their nations' names, but also uses derogatory terms such as "savages" and "redskins." To convey their cultural Otherness, he even turns to Orientalist rhetoric. Visiting a Karankawa settlement, he describes how he "stepped into the first [hut] and right away I thought I had been transported into a tale of 'A Thousand and One Nights'" (*Beales* 86). In this resort to Orientalism, he echoes German and Anglo writers such as Roemer, Mary Holley, and Randolph Marcy. Even more than through their clothes and dwellings, the Natives' alterity manifests itself in bodily differences between Amerindians and other population groups of northern Mexico (79, 126, 180–181). The journey account largely frames the physical appearance of the Amerindians of Texas and Tamaulipas according to the popular stereotypes of the noble savage and the savage threat (Birk 29–30; Ritzenhofen 157, 160). For instance, the narrator aestheticizes a young Karankawa couple: "Never have I seen a more beautiful anatomy, neither in art nor in nature. When I saw [Antonio] Canova's statue of Hebe in the Berlin Museum, I thought that nature could never produce anything like her. Now I am persuaded that it can. A more or less faithful copy of the [couple] would make an artist immortal" (*Beales* 86). Although the handsome couple surpass art, they are brought within the purview of European culture, appearing only as potential models for European artists, not as creators or carriers of civilization themselves.

Moreover, although this passage and another one describe native physiognomy as appealing (138), such approval does not extend to Amerindian culture (138). On the contrary, *Reise* predominantly frames the Amerindians of Texas and Tamaulipas as a threat to colonization. The text repeatedly mentions Native violence against white settlers in the region (Ritzenhofen 157–158). Elsewhere, the narrator characterizes the Karankawas as being "still completely wild," a remark that serves to justify the military campaigns by Mexicans and Americans against the tribe during the 1820s and 1830s (*Beales* 78). In the same vein, Ludecus's travelogue explains Comanche hostility toward Mexicans by reference to "the cruelty with which the Spaniards conducted a war of extermination against" the Comanches. But the text fails to connect Comanche violence against white settlers in Texas and Tamaulipas with the colonists' encroaching on tribal territory or with the economic role of raids in Comanche life (Hämäläinen 245–247). Instead, Ludecus quotes at length from Holley's *Texas* to support his negative portrayal of the Comanches and to legitimize American and European settlement (*Beales* 80–82, 128, 160; see also Holley, *Texas* 91–94; Ritzenhofen 155).

The German traveler, in line with Enlightenment and romanticist aesthetic discourses, depicts Amerindians as an integral part of "wild" nature, to be subdued, like the landscape itself, by North American and European colonization. In one scene, he invokes the specter of cannibalism to convey the indigenous threat to white settlers: "When I thought about how I would perhaps quench my thirst soon in camp . . . , I immediately remembered also that it was much more likely that a savage would quench his bloodthirst with my life" (*Beales* 108–109). Another passage blends Natives and wild animals into a tableau of perilous dangers: "The innocent pleasures [in Dolores] are very often spoiled by the thought that a Comanche is sneaking up out of the nearby brush to fire a fatal arrow into the circle of unsuspecting settlers. . . . Meanwhile, maybe there is an ambling bear or a cunning panther prowling around the woods and threatening to attack the person who goes out there alone" (139). As in other German travel texts about Texas, the two tropes applied to the Amerindian population function within the colonial discourse and policy that Ludecus's *Reise* engages in. The noble savage serves as a justification to deplore Mexican and Anglo land taking and indigenous subjugation. The savage threat confirms the European's sense of possessing a superior civilization and thereby justifies German immigrants' participation in such land-seizing endeavors as Beales's Rio Grande colony—or the even larger colonization endeavor of the Society for the Protection of German Emigrants to Texas, which followed a decade later.

JAKOB THRAN'S *MEINE AUSWANDERUNG NACH TEXAS*

Thirteen years after Ludecus's failed settlement in Texas and only one year after Carl of Solms-Braunfels advertised the efforts of his emigration society, Jakob Thran migrated to the region under the auspices of Solms's organization. Thran had worked as a schoolteacher in his native Duchy of Schleswig as well as in

Lithuania and East Prussia, where he turned to trade and first heard about German migration to North America. A publication explicitly promoting the endeavor of the emigration society inspired him to settle in Texas. Together with his family, he boarded an emigrant ship departing from Bremerhaven on August 23, 1846, which reached Galveston in October. While his wife and children remained there, Thran set out with a group of fellow immigrants to assess the conditions of the emigration society's settlement of New Braunfels. In early November, they went via Houston, San Felipe, and Gonzales to their destination. Thoroughly disappointed, Thran returned to Galveston within the month. In December, he left with his family for New Orleans, from where they departed for Germany in March 1847. They reached Bremerhaven on April 23 and subsequently settled again in East Prussia (Pawel 12; Ritzenhofen 48–49).

In 1848, Thran published an account of his experiences, *Meine Auswanderung nach Texas unter dem Schutz des Mainzer Vereins: Ein Warnungsbeispiel für Auswanderungslustige* (My emigration to Texas under the protection of the Mainz Society: A warning to those desiring to emigrate). This is one of several travelogues that harshly criticize the activities of the emigration society. Among these texts, Louis Constant's *Texas* is probably the most prominent example. But it is not based on the author's firsthand experiences. Thus, although Thran's account is less well known than Constant's, it represents, as Ute Ritzenhofen points out, "the only printed book of a returned emigrant who attempted his migration under the wing of the Verein" (48). It draws on the author's personal migration experience to contest the claims that Carl of Solms-Braunfels made about the emigration society in his travelogue. Thus, Thran's narrative "marks a turning point in the development of the German images of Texas." He had been "enticed to emigrate by a text that conveyed an extremely positive image," but "the confrontation with reality turned Thran's exaggerated expectations into a one-sided rejection of the land that had disappointed his hopes." Thran's book on Texas added nuance to the German conception of the state: "He sketched a new picture, many aspects of which oppose the positive image dominant until the 1840s" (Ritzenhofen 83–84).

As the subtitle of the travelogue indicates, the book presents the writer's journey as a cautionary tale warning German readers against moving to Texas as protégés of the emigration society. To bolster his claim of providing his target audience with a "faithful, true account" of conditions in Texas, based on firsthand observations and verified sources (Thran viii), Thran integrates testimonies of other German migrants and excerpts from newspaper reports into his journey narrative. Many of these were culled from other returned-emigrant narratives such as Karl von Sommer's 1847 *Bericht über meine Reise nach Texas im Jahre 1846* (The story of my trip to Texas in 1846) and Alwin Sörgel's 1847 *Für Auswanderungslustige!*

without acknowledging these sources (Ritzenhofen 86–87). A preface written by the German law scholar August Theodor Woeniger asserting the relevance and accuracy of Thran's *Auswanderung* further buttressed the authority of the text in the German societal discourse on German migration to North America (Thran i–iv). Thran frequently reprints and cites from documents of the emigration society or from writers supporting its endeavor to explain how he could have fallen prey to the organization's promise of a thriving German colony in Texas. Unlike the emigrant texts he plagiarizes, he explicitly identifies the texts that deceived him, obviously to strengthen his accusations—a point Ute Ritzenhofen overlooks in her discussion of Thran's sources (86–87). The narrator's contrasting ways of dealing with the precursors to his account reveal not only his highly selective reading of these works but also his equally one-sided perception of Texas.

Thran's *Auswanderung* does not reject the idea of German overseas emigration or organized settler colonies out of hand, but critically interrogates the suitability of Texas for such a purpose. Like travelogues promoting settlement in the region, the narrative blends a utilitarian discourse on the agricultural and trading potential of the Lone Star State with picturesque descriptions of nature. Moreover, references to German landscapes and animals or incidents from European history seek to familiarize German readers with the alien land (Thran 31, 35, 54). But unlike travelogues advocating German migration to Texas or Eduard Ludecus's more balanced account of an individual colonization project, Thran's volume claims that Germans cannot successfully settle in the region. Its line of reasoning establishes a set of topoi that were to become typical of German returned-emigrant narratives. Whereas migration-promoting texts depict the Texas prairie either as an open plain promising freedom or as a fertile garden offering a harvest, Thran's book presents it as endless, unsettled, bald, and moor-like. "It is boring and disconsolate," the narrator comments, "to work oneself through such a flooded plain, of which there is no end in sight" (54).

In contrast to this view, the few instances in the *Auswanderung* that foreground the aesthetic qualities of the Texas landscape convey a counterimage of density and overabundance. In one scene, the traveler observes an overcrowded forest: "Tall, mighty trees . . . pressed tightly against each other. . . . Their growth was yet suppressed by all too rapidly sponging, creeping climbing plants that formed picturesque garlands. . . . Slim and tall reed covers the ground here and there and edges out the underwood" (52).[1] Elsewhere in his travelogue, the narrator highlights the presence of predatory animals and warlike Amerindians near the migrants' travel route to challenge the image of the Texas wilderness as a pleasurable hunting ground (27–28, 50–51; see also Ritzenhofen 86). In the same vein, Thran's *Auswanderung* argues that the Texas climate endangered the health of any European immigrant: "Diseases, especially pernicious fevers, shorten his life span. . . . This climate . . . undermines his body, his mind" (66). The volume supports this point by painting a particularly bleak picture of Galveston as a town in almost fatal dilapidation: "The harbor . . . announces horror and ruin to the newly arriving. . . . Between the piers and up to the dry land one beholds . . . the debris of stranded ships, skeleton-like, a truly deterrent sight." The houses in town are "tacked together out of planks, like huts, which is why many of them, although only a few years old, are already in decay" (30–32). References to heat, floods, and swarms of vermin complete the picture of the city as a veritable "entrance gate to the great grave of German emigrants and Texas as the grave itself" (34).

Thran's *Auswanderung* targets the discursive framing of Texas as a paradise, put forth in American and German writings such as Mary Holley's and Detlef Dunt's journey accounts, which were intended to attract settlers to the region. Thran's narrator responds to the biblical promise of an easy life in plenitude when he points out the deprivations that many settlers had to endure and thereby argues that "Texas is not the land where milk and honey flow" (75, 73; see Exod. 3:8). As Peter Brenner argues, in nineteenth-century travel texts, a discourse of paradise or similar metaphors powerfully captures all those hopes that fact-based information on migration to (or within) North America could not honestly supply (94–97). Thran's polemical assertion "If Texas is a paradise, there is truly no Eden" uses biblical imagery to deflate the exaggerated expectations that migration-promoting literature often aroused in German readers (Thran vi). In contrast to that body of texts, Thran's volume emphasizes the hardships of cultivation in Texas not to justify colonization but to warn against German settlement in the Lone Star State. The region "must be left to nature," the narrator argues, since there was no "hope of turning Texas into a flourishing province through cultivation" (75–76). The German terms *kultiviert* and *Kultur* originally referred to agriculture but have come to primarily denote "cultural refinement" and "culture." The writer's use of these expressions tellingly points to the close entanglement of notions of cultivating the land and the mind, which resonated strongly in German romanticist discourses of horticulture (Finney 11–12).

The inhabitants of Texas fared little better than its landscape in Thran's *Auswanderung*. The book completely ignores the Tejano presence in the region (Ritzenhofen 203). It further frames the Amerindian nations of Texas, whose members it refers to as "Indians" or "savages," primarily as an integral part of the wilderness that jeopardized the spread of civilization in the Lone Star State. To underline this point, the volume repeatedly mentions instances of Native horse theft or attacks on white people (Thran 58, 78–79). Following the racialist discourse of the time, which causally connects notions of national character and physical features, the narrator asserts that "the perfidy of [the Natives'] way of thinking and acting articulated itself in their physiognomy" (57). His text singles out the

Comanches as a particular threat to the German colonization of Texas, pointing out correctly that some of the lands of the emigration society were located on indigenous hunting grounds, which Solms did not address in his travelogue. In contrast to the Hessian prince, moreover, Thran states that the true peril was not the Comanches harmed white colonists but that the latter stole indigenous land (27, 37, 80).

Common in texts by returned emigrants warning against migration to the United States, yet also in many other works of the *Amerikaliteratur*, such as Dunt's and Solms's settlement-promoting travelogues, Thran's volume finds fault with Anglo culture. In distinguishing the "civilized condition" of a society "from a rampant, arbitrary, American one," the narrative denies the claim of the United States to be considered culturally on a par with Europe (87). In what was becoming a stock image, Anglo-Americans appear here as selfish individuals driven solely by a desire for profit. "The American is never more willing to accommodate a German than when the latter is ill and provided with good clothes and a certain wealth," the book states. "He rarely errs in his intrigues to gain possession of these things" (115). In contrast to Solms's *Texas*, however, Thran's *Auswanderung* does not criticize Anglo-Texans for practicing slavery. Rather, like Ferdinand Roemer's journey account, the text exclusively targets the peculiar institution as a pernicious economic factor (Ritzenhofen 216). Adhering to the theory of climate, Thran's book presents slavery as an essential prerequisite for successfully operating a sugar or cotton plantation in Texas. Since slave ownership and management were beyond the means and knowledge of most German settlers, the text argues, the peculiar institution excluded them from a significant sector of the Texan economy (Thran 68). Thran's application of the theory of climate to Black slave labor contradicts his earlier comment that the Texas climate was insalubrious to Europeans, Americans, and Africans alike (66). Other passages indicate that the narrator, despite his limited criticism of slavery, shared the prevalent view among Europeans and white Americans of his time that a subordinate social status was natural for Blacks. Even more, his text confirms Joe Lockard's observation that white travelers' concern did not emerge out of compassion for African American lives. On the contrary, what frightened these observers of slavery was the awareness that they, too, could be enslaved if they were Blacks (Lockard xxxi). In this vein, Thran's *Auswanderung* grotesquely exploits the Middle Passage, comparing the situation of German steerage passengers on emigrant ships with that of human captives on a slaver, in a misguided attempt to arouse compassion among German readers for the fate of their migrant compatriots (Thran 22–23, 113).

The key target of Thran's journey narrative, however, was the German emigration society. The volume is correct in criticizing its exaggerated promises, organizational incompetence, and ignorance of conditions in Texas, all of which brought misery to many of the society's charges. But Thran's highly fraught language relentlessly denounces the organization primarily for profiting from poverty in Germany and for betraying the idea of relieving it through overseas colonization. "The Society's agents became wealthy people," the text claims (37). What was worse, "Nobody has seen, not to mention received, a single crumb, yet several thousand people have been deceived and thus lost one or several years of their lives, their work, their fortunes. Thousands have died as victims of the ignorance and carelessness of the Emigration Society; many parents have lost their children, many children their parents—in a distant, alien, raw, and desolate land" (64). This passage takes up images of German migrants' misery, loss, and disorientation that recur throughout Thran's travelogue. Widows and orphans wander about or wait in vain for provisions, others lose their possessions to scheming Anglos or thievish Natives, and yet others succumb to infectious diseases. Taken together, the images paint a picture of Germans triply victimized: by the Texas landscape, by its resident population, and by the German organization that failed to protect its clients from these depredations (26–28, 60–68, 82–87).

Meine Auswanderung nach Texas powerfully captures the situation of the German migrants by observing their settlements. Galveston marked the entry to "the grave of those who believed they would find paradise" (60), and the major German settlement of New Braunfels ("deterrent and unbearable the sojourn") fully embodies the doom of the colonists. Thran does not find "the bursting strength of flourishing American towns, which carry the guarantees of growth," but instead "an impoverished little place" full of "sickly, weak, and destitute" inhabitants. He decries the overall wretchedness without qualification: "This is the locus of desire and attraction for so many of my . . . brothers in the German fatherland! Truly rather a place of mourning, death, and tears" (59). In its paired oppositions, this highly emotional passage articulates the stark discrepancy between the popularized image of New Braunfels in Germany and the depravity that Thran saw there. It further highlights the settlement's sharp contrast to the vigor and promising future—a characterization contradicting Thran's earlier judgments—of many Anglo towns (31–34, 45–46, 53).

In a similar vein, failed German settlers are described as "human skeletons, black like the mulattos, weak, careworn" (29), and references to immigrants' succumbing to fevers create an image of the Germans in Texas as a community facing a dreaded epidemic. Thran's *Auswanderung* thereby uses the widespread fear of large-scale infectious diseases to carry its cautionary message. Another scene even likens the large midcentury emigration wave from Germany to North America to an "epidemic disease" (89). The book thus joins a line of nineteenth-century societal discourses, whether motivated by political nativism or social reform, that framed the massive migration of the lower classes and ethnic or religious minorities within Europe and to North America as an imminent socioeconomic peril to the receiving countries. By medicalizing migrant populations and their mobility through the rhetoric of epidemics, these discourses legitimized radical public policy measures that policed these groups in the name of the "health of the nation" (Kraut).

In line with the anti-American strain of the *Amerikaliteratur*, including emigration-promoting texts like Solms's *Texas*, Thran's *Auswanderung* argues that conditions in North America jeopardized the well-being of German newcomers and that emigration did the same to the German nation. According to Thran, most Germans experienced only loss in the New World. Rather than gaining freedom of speech and economic opportunities, their lack of English, skills, money, and entrepreneurial knowledge placed them at the bottom of America's unbridled capitalist economy (Thran 39–41, 92–94, 106–108, 116–118). Germany gave "rich offerings to both body and spirit," but in the United States, "maintaining the body fully absorb[ed] one's . . . thoughts and strength, whereas the sublime and noble in man are wrecked" (103). Elsewhere, the narrator urges his readers, "Don't follow the allurements; you will not find your dear good fatherland in the New World again" (112). In line with this position, Thran frames the cultural assimilation of German immigrants in North America as an act of moral failure. Although the Americanized Germans mentioned in his book tend to have "made it" in the United States, they subsequently either estranged themselves from or took advantage of their less fortunate compatriots (41–42, 108–111). As Ute Ritzenhofen observes about returned-emigrant accounts, viewing German settlement in Texas as leading to either economic or moral failure "serves to justify the authors' activities, since it allows writers to retrospectively transform their return to their home country from an escape or defeat into a success" (253). Rather than undermining his credibility, Thran presents his struggles as a migrant as a source of his authority to speak on the subject. Yet, ironically, despite his critique of German emigration and the emigration society's Texas settlement project, Thran contributed to German colonial discourse by publishing his book, and profited from public debate and the German "emigration fever," which he blames for his misery in Texas.

Though this body of writing is considerably smaller than the corpus of migration-promoting texts, a few travelogues penned by returned colonists or emigration agents cautioned against settling in the Lone Star State, pointing out that the region was not the paradise it was widely advertised as being. Somewhat as Joshua James and Alexander MacRae did within Anglo-American discourse and travel writing, two disappointed German colonists, Eduard Ludecus and Jakob Thran, drew on established conventions of migration-promoting travel accounts of Texas to argue against further German settlement in the region. While Ludecus's differentiated narrative targets an unsuitable landscape, greedy emigration agents, badly prepared colonists, and a deficient Mexican culture equally, Thran's account is largely a diatribe against the Society for the Protection of German Emigrants to Texas, which the text singles out for causing the misery experienced by German colonists in Texas. Both travelogues agree, however, on the risks of settlement for migrants lacking the financial means, language knowledge, and practical skills that were necessary to establish oneself in this multiply contested border region and Amerindian contact zone.

PART III

Professional Journeys

In addition to explorers, settlers, and visitors involved in settlement endeavors, other groups of travelers journeyed through Mexican, independent, and antebellum-America Texas and recorded their experiences and observations in written narratives. Their accounts include diaries; letters to friends, family members, and business partners; travelogues; and memoirs. All of them depict the journeys of a type of travelers I call itinerant professionals. The term encompasses people whose professions required them to relocate to distant places or regularly travel long distances; thus, the impetus for their journeys and their itineraries were provided by their work. Although this definition also applies to scientific explorers, their "pioneer" role of reconnoitering territories little known or unknown to the travelers' cultures makes them a unique subgroup of itinerant professionals (see part 1).

Several trading routes connecting the eastern United States with the southern Rocky Mountains and Mexico ran through Texas, and several travelogues by traders address the Lone Star State as part of their authors' itineraries (Goetzmann, *Exploration* 65–67; Padget 79–82; Sundquist 153–154). The most prominent examples include the memoir of the Santa Fe Trail trader Josiah Gregg, *Commerce of the Prairies* (1844), and *Down the Santa Fe Trail into Mexico*, the private diary that Susan Shelby Magoffin penned about a trip along the trail with her trader husband two years later (Bryan 52, 64–66, 129; Georgi-Findlay 92–103; Padget 81–82). Because these and similar travelogues from the second quarter of the nineteenth century cover journeys that reached far beyond the borders of Texas, they are not discussed here. The same holds true for most journey accounts written by officers and soldiers about their participation in military campaigns during the period. Some of these texts echo the traders' accounts in reporting on territories other than Texas, such as New Mexico and Mexico in George Kendall's *Narrative of an*

Expedition (1841) about the Texas military campaign to take control of the Santa Fe trade in 1841–1842. Other texts, such as Herrmann Ehrenberg's 1843 reminiscences *Texas und seine Revolution* (*Adventures of a German Boy in Texas' Revolution*), or the Mexican General Adrián Woll's 1842 report on a failed attempt by his unit to reconquer Texas, *Expedición hecha en Tejas, por una parte de la 2a División del Cuerpo del Egército del Norte* (Expedition to Texas by a part of the 2nd Division of the Northern Army), focus largely on military matters (Myres, "Army" 178; Sibley 182–184, 190–191, 196–198). Therefore, this body of writings is excluded from the present study, too.

Three other groups of itinerant professionals who journeyed through parts of Texas between 1821 and 1861 and wrote about their impressions of places and people in the Lone Star State include Christian missionaries, the wives of US Army officers, and American journalists. Catholic clergy had been active in Texas since the Spanish era. From the time of the Texas Revolution, US Protestant denominations also sent teachers and missionaries to the region to care for budding congregations, evangelize the unchurched, and convert Catholics. While only a French priest is known to have written a Catholic missionary journey account of Texas, several American Protestant missionaries penned narratives about their sojourns in the area. Chapter 6 analyzes the writings of two of them. The preacher Orceneth Fisher recorded his observations in Texas with the specific intention to inspire religious migration from the northern and eastern United States. His *Sketches of Texas in 1840* (1840) is the only Methodist missionary journey account written during the Texas Republic, testifying to the denomination's religious labor in the region before the US-Mexican War. The Presbyterian educator Melinda Rankin was active in East Texas, the Rio Grande Valley, and northern Mexico. Her travelogue-*cum*-emigrant guide, *Texas in 1850* (1850), sought to entice Protestant religious migration to the Lone Star State. Although written after the period under consideration, her memoir *Twenty Years among the Mexicans* (1875) significantly complements the earlier volume, since it accounts for the writer's itinerant labor in the Texas-Mexico border region.

The armies of Mexico and the United States were another institutional presence in Texas from 1821 through 1861. Some US Army officers were accompanied to their Texas posts by their wives, and several of these women recorded their experiences in diaries and travelogues. Unlike their husbands, they were little concerned with military affairs, and instead foregrounded daily life on the roads and in army camps. The seventh chapter examines two such accounts. Teresa Griffin Vielé's *Following the Drum* (1858) largely depicts the writer's life at Fort Brown in the Rio Grande Valley as a series of adventures otherwise unavailable to a white middle-class woman at the time. Eliza Griffin Johnston's posthumously published "Diary of Eliza (Mrs. Albert Sidney) Johnston: The Second Cavalry Comes to Texas" (1957) foregrounds not only the daily toils of regimental travel but also women's specific struggles with army life on the road.

A third major institution that informed both life in antebellum Texas and popular knowledge about the region was the press. The Lone Star State gained prominence in national and international media coverage during the US-Mexican War and its aftermath. Most journalists who reported on Texas were from the United States, and most were residents rather than temporary visitors. Exceptions such as the German journalist Friedrich Kapp based their writings about the Lone Star State on sources other than firsthand observation. Chapter 8 looks at the accounts of Texas written by two renowned journalists of the period. The reporter and land speculator Jane McManus Cazneau intended to lure Anglo settlers from the American South to Texas with her travelogue and historical sketch *Texas and Her Presidents: With a Glance at Her Climate and Agricultural Capabilities* (1845). Her West Texas narrative *Eagle Pass: Or, Life on the Border* (1852) blends a journey account, a settler memoir, and a pamphlet against Mexican debt peonage into a work that lobbies against abolitionism and advocates US territorial expansion into Mexico. Frederick Law Olmsted took a contrary stand in his travelogue *A Journey through Texas, Or: A Saddle-Trip on the South-Western Frontier* (1857). The volume employs the format of an anecdotal travel chronicle to scrutinize the state's slavery-based economy and culture as well as to promote a communitarian society and free-market capitalism in Texas.

SIX

Missionary Messages

Narratives of Itinerant Religious Labor

Among the itinerant professionals who journeyed through Texas in the period 1821–1861, Christian missionaries left the earliest records. This achievement reflected the important role that religion and religious missionary activity played in the colonial and postcolonial history of the region and of the Americas as a whole. Works of missionary travel writing testify to the role of evangelization in processes of colonization and the postcolonial formation of nations. Attempts to win souls for the faith formed part of the political striving to submerge cultural Otherness, since converts were urged to submit to the sociocultural norms and ways of life of the missionizing denomination in order to achieve salvation (Gründer 7–9, 11–14; Kunow). But as Hilde Nielssen and her coauthors point out, "The missionary enterprise had an ambiguous relationship to colonialism" (6). Believing that all human beings could attain salvation and civilization by adopting their brand of faith, Christian missionaries were repeatedly at odds with secular discourses that justified policies of indigenous removal and extermination by pointing to the Natives' presumed unchangeable "savagery" (9–10). Besides indigenous nations, Christian evangelization in the nineteenth-century North American West targeted unchurched whites and members of rival Christian denominations. Anglo-Protestant churches directed their missionary zeal particularly at Catholic populations in order to contain the growing influence of Catholicism in the region (Banker 12–13, 29, 31–32; Barton 29, 34–38).

Especially through its engagement in education, health care, and social reform, Christian missionary work was one of the few professional fields open to women in the nineteenth century. Rising numbers of Protestant American women served in domestic and foreign missions, particularly as teachers (Banker 72–74, 84–86; Georgi-Findlay 238–285). The entangled ideologies of Anglo-Saxon racial supremacy and female domesticity charged white women with instilling the values of American civilization in children and the mission subjects under their tutelage; therefore, religious labor was promoted as their contribution to the US policy of extending the nation's territory and sphere of influence (Caughfield 14–16, 60, 62; Kaplan 29, 31–32). The mission field further gave women freedom from the restraints of domesticity. Although subject to patriarchal structures within the churches, women enjoyed a position of power over their missionary target groups (Nielssen et al. 15–17; Renda 368, 371–372, 376–377).

Another aspect of women's greater liberty in the mission field was mobility. Evangelization is inextricably tied to movement, since it "mobilize[s] both the faith and the faithful" (Kunow). Missionaries displace themselves by journeying, and they employ their creeds and cultures to inspire conversions (Kunow; Gründer 12–14). Through narrative accounts of their activities, many nineteenth-century missionaries sought to testify to their experiences, mobilize religious believers, and inform the sponsors of their activities about their work. Often reaching large audiences, missionary travelogues, letters, memoirs, novels, and journalism formed part of a "transnational missionary aesthetic" that "link[ed] disparate parts of the missionizing world together as an imagined community with a shared missionary imaginary" (Nielssen et al. 8). In line with the principles and goals of evangelization, these texts commonly frame members of other cultures simultaneously as radically different from the missionaries' fellow believers and as members of the same human family. This dualistic representation allowed missionaries to accommodate pluralism and still affirm their cultural identity. By showing how religious and cultural conversion "improves" the cultural Other, missionary literature justifies the proselytizing labor to the missions' financial and spiritual supporters and to the public (Banker 23–24; Nielssen et al. 10).

While Texas belonged to Spain and then Mexico, Catholicism was the only officially permitted religion in the province, even though many of the Protestant Anglo-American colonists of the 1820s and 1830s managed to avoid the required conversion, since neither the Catholic Church nor the Mexican authorities were strong enough to enforce it (Moyano Pahissa 80–82; Weber 69–82). After the Texas Revolution, American Protestant denominations began to send missionaries and establish congregations in the region (R. B. Campbell, *Gone to Texas* 110, 227). Although the Catholic Church attempted to counter these activities by deploying more priests, the Methodists, Baptists, and Presbyterians were particularly successful in their efforts. As elsewhere in the North American West, their religious doctrine, modes of worship, educational efforts, and community structures appealed to many Anglo-Americans, Europeans, and Mexicans in the region (Barton 27–112; Finke and Stark 55–116). Missionaries' efforts manifested themselves in their written narratives about their labor. The only known travelogue by an antebellum Catholic priest is Emmanuel Domenech's 1857 *Journal d'un missionnaire au Texas et au Mexique, 1846–1852* (*Missionary Adventures in Texas and Mexico: A Personal Narrative of Six Years' Sojourn in Those Regions*). Protestant missionaries produced a considerably larger body of journey accounts. Prominent examples of this body of writings include the memoir of the Presbyterian minister Daniel Baker, *The Life and Labours of the Rev. Daniel Baker, D.D., Pastor and Evangelist* (1859), and the travelogue of the Methodist bishop George Foster Pierce, *Incidents of Western Travel: In a Series of Letters* (1859) (Sibley 185–186, 191–192, 195–196). Pioneering work, however, was carried out by the first missionaries deployed to Texas on behalf of their denominations.

ORCENETH FISHER'S *SKETCHES OF TEXAS IN 1840*

Enticed by widely publicized appeals from Methodist settlers in Texas, the Methodist Episcopal Church of America began its organized religious labor in the new republic in 1836 (Ledbetter 83–86; Schloeman 7–8). One of the first Methodist missionaries deployed to the region was the circuit rider Orceneth Fisher (1803–1880), an itinerant preacher who served circuits of small congregations in sparsely settled areas (Finke and Stark 73, 82). Born in Vermont, he took up the ministry in Indiana and Illinois. He came to Texas in December 1839, inspired by the new missionary opportunity. A year later, his family joined him. For the next fourteen years, Fisher preached on several Methodist circuits in the region, served as chaplain to the Texas Congress, and edited the church's weekly *Texas Christian Advocate*. In March 1855, he moved farther west to California and Oregon to continue his labor (Schloeman 5–30).

Throughout his life, Fisher published several theological works and pieces of journalism in the *Texas Christian Advocate* and the *Texas Wesleyan Banner*, another Methodist weekly (Ledbetter 107–108, 112–113, 116). While preparing for his family's move to Texas, Fisher composed his observations on the region in a small book entitled *Sketches of Texas in 1840: Designed to Answer, in a Brief Way, the Numerous Enquiries Respecting the New Republic, as to Situation, Extent, Climate, Soil, Productions, Water, Government, Society, Religion, etc.* (1841). As revealed in the subtitle of the text and confirmed in its introduction, the volume follows in the tradition of the migration-promoting travelogue, particularly the emigrant guide, in structure and purpose (Fisher vii–viii). According to Robert Edgar Ledbetter, "The chief value of the book at this point is the fact that it portrays the country during the period when Fisher visited the region" (70). Structured thematically, *Sketches of Texas* provides readers with basic knowledge of the geography and society of Texas, with a clear focus on the republic's economic potential as well as its social, political, and cultural conditions. In addition to practical advice for American settlers in Texas, Fisher pays special attention to their spiritual concerns. He reiterates his hope to write a virtuous and prosperous text in a hymn at the end of the text, and he appeals to the American Methodist Church to engage more in the region. Finally, a brief recommendation by two eminent Methodist ministers to read this "very useful and instructive manual" (Fisher n.p.) strengthens the legitimacy of *Sketches of Texas*. Fisher supports this validation by stressing his reliance on firsthand observations and trustworthy secondary sources (vii–viii).

In line with both his mission and the conventions of the emigrant guide, Fisher "gives a glowing account of the physical properties of the Republic," combining a utilitarian with a romanticist aesthetic discourse (Ledbetter 70). On the one hand, *Sketches of Texas* emphasizes the region's natural riches in a language that repeatedly stresses plenitude. Texas offers "some of the richest valleys," which yield bountiful crop harvests, and "prairies [that] afford a never failing and rich pasturage" for cattle (Fisher 13, 32). Similarly, references to the "abundance of fine timber" and "streams . . . afford[ing] a vast amount of hydraulic power" (23) hint at the manufacturing potential of the republic. By comparing the Texas soil favorably to that of Illinois, the volume further seeks to render the alien land familiar and desirable to audiences from Fisher's home region. The book contains several descriptions of the Texas landscape that foreground its aesthetic appeal without losing sight of its usability (12–13, 27–28, 32). For instance, an area near the Trinity River seems to have it all:

> The surface is occasionally gathered up into a vast magnificent
> mound . . . crowned with valuable timber. Then, again, a noble,
> gentle ridge stretches away in the distance for miles, watered on each
> side with a gurgling little stream . . . and richly studded with valuable
> cedars and other timber. Upon one of these prairie eminences an
> observer may take his seat, and cast his eye upon the rich vale of
> woodland below him. Raising his eye a little, he beholds beyond
> this another noble ridge of black rich prairie, inviting as it were the
> plough of the farmer. (12)

Speaking from an elevated vantage point, the narrator reiterates the "monarch of all I survey" scene of travel writing, known from narratives of scientific exploration and from literature promoting migration (Pratt 197–210). As in these text types, Fisher's gesture of surveying the land entails a sense of entitlement not only to view the territory but also to possess it. The narrator's remark that the fertile land was "inviting . . . the plough" borrows a phrase from Stephen Austin's and Mary Holley's writings (Austin, "Descriptions" 108; Holley, *Observations* 65). To justify Anglo-American settlement, *Sketches of Texas* draws on the American aesthetic-political ideal of nature being improved by human cultivation. The narrative adds a spiritual dimension to this reasoning by framing the Texas Revolution as a divinely supported Protestant uprising against the "evil" forces of Catholicism and Mexican rule. The text thereby covers up the Anglo-Texans' colonial program of codifying white land claims, establishing a slave-based plantation economy, and exercising political and cultural hegemony in the region. Fisher's travelogue describes Spanish and Mexican Texas as both "an unbroken wilderness" and "a great moral desert." It had fallen "prey [to] either . . . savage heathenism, or . . . Romish superstition and bigotry," under whose "blighting influence . . . the country could not prosper" (Fisher 34, 44, 43, v). The freedom-loving and "moral[ly] and intellectual[ly]" enlightened Anglo-Protestant population was forced to revolt, since its people "could never consent to be the dupes and slaves of ignorance and superstition." And it was worth reminding readers that the insurgents would not have succeeded if not for the divine support of Protestantism's "great tidings of salvation" (v, 44).

In line with this discourse, Fisher's journey narrative employs stereotypes of ethnic difference in a manner that seeks to tone down readers' anxieties about a hostile Mexican and indigenous presence in Texas. Blending Protestant religious bias with Anglo-American ethnic prejudices, the narrator indicts Catholicism's fostering of "ignorance, superstition, and bigotry" and deplores the Mexican nation's "low . . . worthless character" (v–vi). He never mentions Tejanos, and his references to other Mexicans are limited to unthreatening images of soon-to-be-defeated bandits and friendly residents of a hostile but powerless neighboring republic (46). Similarly, *Sketches of Texas* looks at the indigenous nations of the region through the lens of the religiously imbued Texas Creation Myth. Claiming that large parts of Mexican Texas had been "under the dominion of the roving and ruthless savage and the wild beast" (34), the text describes the Natives as a ferocious force of nature that the Mexican authorities had failed to subdue. By contrast, Anglo settlements inspired fear and retreat even among the most powerful Native nations. At the time of his writing, the narrator claims, incorrectly, that the Comanches "recede as fast as encroachments are made upon their territory" (47). In thus arguing, the book joins Anglo migration-promoting travelogues that proclaim Native cowardice in the face of Anglo-American arms and power (DeLay 241).

Fisher's *Sketches of Texas* responds to the then-popular image in the United States of a community consisting mainly of "desperados and outlaws" by asking readers to be patient with the young Texas Republic (Fisher 41). Although the volume calls Galveston "the New York of Texas," it points out that none of the towns in the Lone Star State are comparable to any major American city (35). The book seeks to counter the stereotype of immoral Anglo-Texans by arguing that the new republic had attracted an "intelligent and enterprising" population of "moral worth" (41). The major obstacle to the progress of Anglo-Texan society, the text claims, is its practice of Black slavery (38, 51, 55): "The long experience of the Christian world has proved [slavery] to be a great *political* if not *moral* evil; and it is devoutly to be hoped that the day is not far distant when this foul stain shall be washed from the escutcheons not only of the proud American States but also from every nation under heaven" (38–39, original emphases). The narrator then immediately qualifies his critique: the "slavery of Texas is only an attenuation of American slavery," and is practiced in a rather mild form (39). In downplaying the impact of slavery in his text, Fisher sought to minimize the deterrent effect that a slaveholding Texas might have on attracting US religious immigrants and missionaries. While most northern branches of Methodists, Baptists, and other Protestant denominations opposed slavery, southern branches tended to be vociferous in their support for the peculiar institution (Finke and Stark 105–106). Moreover, the book's depiction of slavery falls in line with the author's personal dealings with it. Although Fisher privately rejected the practice and never owned a slave (Schloeman 36), the preacher defended his church's policy of tolerating the peculiar institution in Texas. Moreover, despite his critique, he ministered to the state's slave population without intervening politically on their behalf (Fisher to the Reverend J. C. Simmons, c. 1878, Ledbetter 249; see also Ledbetter 104–105).

As Robert Edgar Ledbetter points out, "upon his entrance into the Republic in the winter of 1839 . . . Fisher found a struggling, partially organized church," adding, "Methodism was not new to this region, but it was hardly organized" (71). To encourage Methodist immigration to the Lone Star State, Fisher dwells at length on faith. In addition to framing the Texas Revolution in spiritual terms, *Sketches of Texas* acclaims the new republic as a fruitful mission field where religious settlers and clergymen would find budding Protestant congregations, schools, and media outlets (Fisher 41–44, 60–61). At the end of the book, the narrator calls for the Methodist Church to send more preachers and missionaries to Texas as well as for regular church members to settle there (52–57). It was not only the church's charitable obligation to help this spiritually needy region, but also an opportunity for religious labor to toil in the "whitened field" of a nation "destined to take a high stand among the nations of the earth" (53). Here "whitened field" refers to acreage ready to harvest.

Yet, the color white evokes cotton farming. This connects Fisher's religious mission with slavery, which the book presents as a special opportunity for evangelization. His volume describes Black slaves in Texas as eager recipients of the gospel and claims that both slaves and masters are worthy and in need of salvation (54–56). In line with its earlier acquiescence in slavery, *Sketches of Texas* never calls for either individual or organized intervention to abolish the peculiar institution. The book asks readers in free states to remember that they, too, profit from slavery, since they conduct business with the American South and consume goods produced with slave labor. Pointing this out serves to remind readers that moving to Texas would not further corrupt them. The narrator understands slavery as an infringement not of human rights but of moral principles. "As much as you may be horrified . . . at the evils of physical bondage," he asks his audience, "is not the bondage of sin indefinitely worse? . . . Break first the hard bondage of sin; then [the slave's] condition will be tolerable" (56). Religious salvation was a prerequisite for political deliverance, he argues, since converting slaveholders to believers was the way to move them to better treat or even liberate their slaves (55–56). Theologically, this argument, though criticizing slavery, fails to acknowledge that it was a *manifestation* of sin rather than a consequence of it. Politically, by reducing slavery to a moral evil and by not calling for religious ministries to work toward its abolition, Fisher is an accomplice of the peculiar institution.

Seeking to entice practicing Protestant Americans to settle in Texas, the preacher's narrative aligns itself with other migration-promoting travelogues by both praising opportunities for newcomers in the young republic and cautioning immigrants against having false expectations (vii, 49–50). *Sketches of Texas* explicitly warns potential settlers against striving for quick material gains from mining or land speculation. To appeal to potential white settlers concerned about hardships, Fisher stresses that farming and livestock raising in Texas were easy and profitable (27–33, 48–50). The book simultaneously admonishes readers that diligence was needed to advance the young country economically as well as morally. "As good as Texas is," the argument runs, "people cannot . . . live there without labor, and retain a good character" (51). The text calls its target audience of Anglo-Protestant believers to duty by appealing to both their sense of obligation and their desire to do good in the eyes of God and society (50). It thus contributes a religious agenda to the widespread Anglo-American discourse of settling the North American West. Fisher's focus on spreading Protestantism in the region strengthens and justifies the ongoing Americanization of Texas and the subjugation of Mexican and indigenous populations entailed by it.

MELINDA RANKIN'S NARRATIVES OF RELIGIOUS LABOR

After pointing out the potential of Texas for Protestant religious missionary activity, Orceneth Fisher concludes his volume of travel writing by asking, "Have we not reason to believe that God will soon call us into Mexico? and should we not be in readiness?" (Fisher 57). This proposition ties in with the interest that American Protestant churches expressed in evangelizing Mexico during the nineteenth century. Owing to widespread Anglo prejudices against Mexicans, only a few Protestant missionaries in Texas considered proselytizing the Tejano population before the Civil War. And those few considered their work there a mere step toward future endeavors in Mexico (Chavez 13–14). One of the earliest, and probably the first female among them, was Melinda Rankin (1811–1888). Born and raised in New Hampshire, she worked as a teacher in Kentucky and Mississippi starting in 1840 and continued this line of work in the East Texas town of Huntsville from 1847 to 1852. Encouraged by a report about the prospects for Protestantism in the region, Rankin moved to Brownsville, in the Lower Rio Grande Valley, where she founded a girls' school and a Protestant seminary. From 1855, she also traveled the region as a Bible reader and colporteur. When a new Mexican constitution permitted Protestant missions to operate in the country, she extended her religious activities beyond the border. Her work was interrupted only by a forced retreat from the region during the Civil War, and she retired in 1873 (Chavez 14; González-Quiroga and Bowman ix, xii–xxiv).

As William Huntzicker points out, evangelical religious periodicals "rapidly spread west in the 1840s–50s," and many of them endorsed the ideology of Manifest Destiny and the US policy of westward expansion (60). These newspapers and magazines empowered women as both writers and readers (Renda 375). During her years in Huntsville, Rankin wrote a series of articles about Texas for the weekly *Texas Presbyterian*, which she compiled into the travelogue-*cum*-emigrant guide *Texas in 1850*, published in the titular year. The title likely alludes not only to Fisher's narrative but also to the missionary A. B. Lawrence's popular guide *Texas in 1840*. In Brownsville, Rankin continued her journalistic activities, contributing numerous articles about her work in the Texas-Mexico border region to the monthly *Christian World*. After her retirement, she integrated some of these works into her memoir, *Twenty Years among the Mexicans: A Narrative of Missionary Labor* (1875). The volume offers insight into the lives and customs of Mexicans in the Texas-Tamaulipas border region as well as into a female missionary's struggle to achieve her goals in a male-dominated world (González-Quiroga and Bowman ix, xii, xxix).

Whereas *Twenty Years among the Mexicans* chronologically follows Rankin's religious career and journeys from her beginnings until her retirement, *Texas in 1850* is structured thematically. In line with its stated agenda of promoting the Lone Star State as a worthy mission field for Protestant proselytizers, especially from New England (Rankin, *Texas* 3–5), the text outlines the physical and social conditions of life in Texas, along with the region's potential for agriculture, manufacturing, trade, and Protestant mission. In addition to its religious focus, the volume stands out among Texas writing of the period for being "the first book to make towns rather than farms the end of settling" (Baym 15). This emphasis affects the narrator's use of comparisons to familiarize readers from other parts of the United States with the unknown territory. For example, besides the staple comparisons of the Texas climate to that of Italy, and the beauty of its landscape to the picturesque scenery of New England or Switzerland (*Texas* 15, 189), the book quotes an article from the *Texas Wesleyan Banner* that suggests that San Antonio could become "the Manchester or Lowell of Texas, if not the South" (184). Rankin's emphasis on the economic prospects of Texas towns also stems from their apparent lack of aesthetic appeal, particularly for her target readership of Anglo-Protestant settlers from the South and Northeast. "Though [the city of] Austin has no claims upon artificial beauty," she writes, "its natural scenery compensates very materially" (154).

This comment falls in line with the attention the text pays to the nature of Texas. Echoing both exploration accounts and journey narratives promoting migration, Rankin's *Texas in 1850* intertwines utilitarian and aesthetic discourses. The book emphasizes the beauty of the landscape and the fecundity of the soil in an appeal to readers' emotions and reason (24–25, 122–123, 153–154, 197). For example, a passage depicts the Texas plains as a veritable seascape, an image going back to William Cullen Bryant's 1832 poem "The Prairies" (Ritzenhofen 82): "The luxuriance of their vegetation presents the appearance of seas of verdure. The grass . . . is waved by the winds like the rolling billows of the ocean. Without a tree in sight, except the thick forest which bounds them, as the beach limits the sea, they stretch far away beyond the power of vision. Those immense prairie regions are susceptible to a high state of cultivation, and their utility is equal to their beauty" (*Texas* 86). Based on the belief that human intervention improves nature, Rankin follows other writers promoting Anglo-American migration to Texas, from Stephen Austin to Orceneth Fisher, in claiming that the land must be properly worked to fully develop its potential (21, 24, 93, 125–127). Her travelogue resorts to the familiar trope of the garden, inspired by the biblical image of Eden as well as Jeffersonian agrarianism, to paint a picture of an arcadian space and to urge settlers to undertake the effort required to cultivate it: "In beauty and fertility [Texas] is the most perfect garden of nature, and if those advantages which the State possesses were brought into use and exercise, what a brilliant prospect would open through the darkness of the future!" (88). In an earlier passage, she substantiates this prospect with a vision that connects advancements in agriculture, trade, demography, and transportation. She foresees "fertile lands in a high state of cultivation, . . . rivers improved to ensure safe and successful navigation, railroads constructed to facilitate inland commerce, and the country towns and cities teeming with population" (65–66). Furthermore, like Holley's texts or German emigrant guides, Rankin's *Texas in 1850* praises actual gardens as the highest form of improved nature. By indicating settlers' diligence and cultural refinement, gardens signify the degree of civilization a given region has attained, especially in a fertile region "where so little trouble is required to render every garden like another Eden" (26).

Like other writers promoting American migration to Texas, Rankin presents Anglo-Texan society as a (nearly) perfect match for the splendid landscape it inhabits. Taking her readers along on her physical and mental journey, she describes her first entrance into Texas in *Twenty Years among the Mexicans*: "The miserable and desolate looking country which I had . . . imagin[ed] Texas to be, became transformed into one of the most beautiful regions I had ever before beheld. The splendid trees, the verdant plains, and great variety of wild flowers, conspired to make the scene an enchanting one. Instead of a wild and uncultivated population, I found many highly refined and intelligent people, who had but a short time previous emigrated from the Southern States to Texas" (Rankin, *Twenty Years* 22). In *Texas in 1850*, Rankin explicitly engages in the Texas Creation Myth, writing, "Where but a few years since, the stillness of the forest was only broken by the war-whoop of the Indian, is heard the constant hum of civilization, having become the abode of an industrious and intelligent population" (24). The book never addresses the violent removal of indigenous nations from their farming and hunting grounds, violence that enabled this transformation. The only other context in which the book mentions Amerindians is a passage that calls for US military engagement in the Rio Grande Valley to stop ongoing Comanche raids of the area's white settlements (171–173). Since the Natives seem to almost naturally vanish in Rankin's version of the Texas Creation Myth, and Spanish colonizers and Mexicans remain completely absent, the Anglo settlement of the region appears less "heroic" but simultaneously less violent in *Texas in 1850* than in Austin's or Holley's writings. In a similar vein, the volume calls the Mexican period of Texas "the anti-Texan era." By limiting the causes of the Texas Revolution to the Anglo-Texans' "love of freedom and honor," and by suggesting that God supported their insurgency, the text further obliterates the economic causes of the independence movement as well as the conflicts surrounding the US annexation of the Lone Star Republic (145, 196, 145–146).

Another crucial omission in Rankin's depiction of Texan history concerns the subject of slavery. *Twenty Years among the Mexicans* criticizes the denial of education to African Americans in the US South and views the Union sympathies of many Mexicans during the Civil War with favor (75, 84). In contrast, although *Texas in 1850* refers to the Texas plantation economy, the text never mentions its reliance on slave labor or the presence of a slave population in the region (163, 186, 197). The volume focuses its critique of the Texas Anglos on common "vices" such as uncouth manners, intemperance, materialism, or Sabbath breaking. In so doing, the text, like Orceneth Fisher's travelogue, seeks to tone down the anxieties of readers in the eastern United States about a society widely believed to be rough and immoral. Rankin's narrative emphasizes the beneficial impact of the Anglo-Texans' perseverance, enterprise, and rising level of education on the economy and social mores in the region (14–15, 26–28, 66, 126). In line with this approach, the book warns potential colonists against harboring exaggerated hopes of making quick and easy money in the Lone Star State. It points out employment opportunities for the diligent and morally upright and urges such people to come to the region (15, 22–23, 42–44, 197).

Rankin was convinced that "the people must not only be enlightened but also religious" (50). In keeping with this view, *Texas in 1850*, echoing Fisher's narrative, reads like a promotional religious tract. The volume argues that the Lone Star State offered a promising mission field, since the growing Protestant communities desired to improve themselves but lacked the financial means and qualified personnel to establish and maintain churches and schools (31–46, 94–98, 129–133, 159–166). The book argues that the spread of Protestantism and education in Texas would yield both spiritual and political benefits: "The efforts in establishing the institutions of a pure and spiritual Christianity, are heaven's appointed means, not only in saving souls . . . but also of national and social salvation. Upon the religion of the Bible [rest], as upon a corner stone, the hopes of the country" (50). Convinced that the Northeast was culturally more advanced than other parts of the United States, Rankin appeals especially to New Englanders' sense of obligation to spread their brand of faith and civilization to Texas by sending money, missionaries, teachers, and settlers there (*Texas* 43, 68–73, 165–169; *Twenty Years* 43). To inform and inspire them, *Texas in 1850* explicitly addresses the dangers and hardships awaiting Anglo-American Protestant prose-lytizers in Texas, but it simultaneously stresses the higher purpose these privations serve. "One soul brought in [to the fold of Christ]," the text claims, "adds to the Saviour's crown a gem of more real value than all the glittering mines of Mexico or California" (19). In line with the American colonial discourse of the period, particularly the ideology of Manifest Destiny, the missionary's travelogue frames such efforts as part of a larger political endeavor of westward territorial expansion and cultural Anglo-Americanization. "Every church . . . is bound, when her number and ability will warrant, *to colonize*," the text contends. "In this way, and in this way only, can the land be possessed" (167, original emphasis).

Rankin's writings present the Lone Star State as a particularly fruitful location for converting Catholic Mexicans and unchurched Anglos and as an entrance to the even vaster field of activity waiting in nearby Mexico (*Texas* 17, 54–56, 176–177, 183). In line with nineteenth-century American Protestant religious discourse, a Black Legend–inspired blend of American anti-Catholicism and ethnocultural bias against Mexicans shaped Rankin's view of Mexico. *Texas in 1850* and *Twenty Years among the Mexicans* strongly engage in the period's Protestant religious rhetoric, which likened Catholicism to paganism and ex-cluded it from the rubric of Christianity. The two volumes depict the Catholic Church as an evil empire whose degrading reign by a despotic priesthood kept a benighted population in spiritual and cultural bondage (*Texas* 56, 177, 182,

194–195; *Twenty Years* 17, 23, 29, 81). For instance, once again quoting from the *Texas Wesleyan Banner*, Rankin describes the decadence of San Antonio: "The moral depravity . . . , instead of being checked and subdued by Romanism, had been encouraged and promoted . . . by the example of the Roman priests, who had been more devoted to the pleasures of the card-table and the billiard room, than to the appropriate duties and functions of their high office" (*Texas* 182). In this line of reasoning, the presence of Catholicism in Mexico and among Tejanos justifies both Protestant religious action and American political intervention. Rankin's *Texas in 1850* maintains that the Mexicans not only "appear . . . ripe for the gospel" and want "to get rid of the domination and oppressive exactions of their priests," but were ready for political change as well: "Moreover, they are better pleased with our laws and government" (177; see also *Twenty Years* 93). In *Twenty Years among the Mexicans*, the narrator recalls, "I felt that the honor of *American* Christianity most imperatively demanded that some effort should immediately be made" to evangelize the Mexicans (17, original emphasis; see also *Texas* 56).

This conflation of Protestant religious and Anglo-American ethnonational identity was a response to a resurgence of Catholicism in the antebellum United States, which many Protestants in the country perceived as a threat to the Protestant character of the nation. Consequently, Anglo-American Protestants "frequently framed their struggle with the Catholic Church in terms of a holy war" or a "crusade" (Barton 37–38), and Rankin was no exception. Using a military language of "spiritual conquest" (González-Quiroga and Bowman xx), *Texas in 1850* calls for combatants who will take up the cause of Protestantism: "A contest is [being] waged . . . against the power of darkness, the spiritual enemy. Soldiers are called upon for rallying around the standard of freedom, equipped with spiritual weapons, drawn from heaven's armory" (198). Similarly, in *Twenty Years among the Mexicans*, she calls the Bibles that her supporters smuggled into Mexico "missiles . . . of a character to do powerful execution." They would cause "essential damage . . . [to] this kingdom of darkness, where Satan had so long reigned with undisputed sway" (30).

Despite her conviction that Americans should spread Protestant civilization into Mexico, Rankin, unlike many other Anglo writers of the period, neither advocates further American territorial expansion after 1848 nor the removal of Mexicans from the territories then gained. Instead, she explicitly criticizes Anglo-Americans' ethnic bias against Mexicans as a key obstacle to performing religious labor among them (*Twenty Years* 38, 41). In line with the principles of Christian mission, she regarded Mexicans as potential proselytes capable of improvement and salvation by the adoption of Protestantism and American civilization (45). Even more, she confesses her deep loyalty to the Mexicans. Recalling her arrival in Brownsville in her memoir, she confesses, "A new sensation seized me when I saw, for the first time, a *Mexican.* . . . I did not feel . . . that the *sight* of a Mexican was enough to disgust one with the whole nation. A heartfelt sympathy was revived, not by the prepossessing exterior, surely, but because a priceless soul was incased in it for whom the Savior had died" (25, original emphases).

During her narrative, Rankin repeatedly stresses the Mexicans' positive responses to her presence, particularly in education. The Presbyterian Church placed great emphasis on schooling as an instrument of spreading both Protestantism and American civilization (Banker 49–65). Rankin admits that her Brownsville school attracted Mexicans mainly because "the parents were greatly desirous their children should learn the English language and become Americanized" (*Twenty Years* 41). Rather than downplaying their secular motivation, *Twenty Years among the Mexicans* foregrounds it as an example of Mexican intelligence and desire for learning. Elsewhere the text attests to the people's "calculating minds with quick and ingenious penetration" and concludes that "if born and reared under other circumstances, [the Mexicans] might have become lights in the world" (27, 127). The missionary's narrative thus counteracts the prevalent Anglo stereotypes of Mexican ignorance and indolence, which were often deployed as an argument in favor of US territorial expansion and economic-cultural hegemony in North America.

Although Rankin primarily worked as an educator, Miguel Ángel González-Quiroga and Timothy Paul Bowman observe that she "placed more emphasis on her work as a [Bible] colporteur . . . than she did on her teaching" in her memoir (xiv). This surely relates to the importance of scripture in the Protestant tradition, but also serves to justify the support the missionary received from American Protestant organizations to distribute religious literature among the Mexicans. Her narrative recounts numerous instances demonstrating Mexicans' receptiveness to the Bible and their conversion to Presbyterianism (*Twenty Years* 41, 45–47, 55–56, 59–60; see also Barton 29, 38–39). *Twenty Years among the Mexicans* further validates the work of converted local Mexican preachers and teachers, claiming that their familiarity with Mexican culture represented an advantage for their religious labor that easily compensated for their lack of theological training (87, 93–94, 104, 117). In so doing, the book crucially deviates from many works of American or European missionary writing. Even though local evangelists and believers carried out the bulk of everyday work, textual representations of missions tend to render their labor (almost) invisible. Commonly motivated by ethnic bias as well as by the need to justify missionary deployments to distant regions, missionary writings usually depict nonlocal proselytizers as the sole agents of religious labor (Nielssen et al. 13–14).

Its validation of the Mexicans notwithstanding, *Twenty Years among the Mexicans* establishes their positive national character at the expense of the indigenous nations of Texas and northern Mexico. In contrast to examples of Mexican peacefulness, kindness, and loyalty to Americans, the Amerindian population of the Texas-Mexico border region appears in the memoir as notoriously insurgent and inclined to robbery (27, 53, 111, 125–129). Moreover, both of Rankin's volumes regard all other ethnic groups as inferior to Anglo-Americans and express unease with interethnic mingling. For instance, *Texas in 1850* deplores that in Mexico and West Texas "the wild Indian, Mexican, European, and American blend their contrasting influence" (175–176). Unlike this ethnic mix, the "enterprise and public spirit" of Anglo-Americans brought prosperity to Texas, whereas resident Tejanos represented "an evil to contend with" (191, 185). In a similar vein, *Twenty Years among the Mexicans* undermines its validation of Mexicans by presenting them as indolent and undisciplined "children of nature." Moreover, even after their "liberation" from Catholicism, Mexican converts to Protestants remained "babes in Christ" in need of further Anglo tutelage (128, 127, 103). By characterizing the Mexicans as immature and dependent children requiring American "parental" guidance, Rankin's book resorts to a popular trope of colonial discourse and policy. In so doing, the volume once again justifies not only the Protestant American religious and civilizing mission to Mexico but also the ideology of Manifest Destiny and US religious-cultural hegemony beyond the country's borders.

Despite all of Rankin's hard work as an educator and missionary, she assures her readers that she never transgressed the social boundaries of female domesticity and respectability. She strategically opens *Twenty Years among the Mexicans* by engaging in a discourse on feminine modesty that was characteristic of women's writing in the nineteenth century, and is seen in Mary Holley's, Jane Cazneau's, and Teresa Vielé's Texas travelogues, among others. A key element of this discourse was the female writer who downplayed her achievements and professional ambitions. Rankin states in her memoir: "To a very great extent the prevailing sentiment among Christ's people has been, that women's work should be necessarily circumscribed, lest she transcend the delicacy of her sex. To unwomanly aspirations I am as much opposed as anyone. But had public sentiment been my guide some forty years ago, I should have probably settled down in my New England home" (13). Here and elsewhere in *Twenty Years among the Mexicans*, the missionary presents herself as an instrument of Providence, selected for her usefulness and faith. She thus legitimizes not only her own work and writing but also female missionary labor in general (5–6, 23, 42–43; see also, González-Quiroga and Bowman xxviii, xxx). More specifically, she defends her venturing as a single woman into Texas and Mexico by pointing to the acknowledged role of Anglo women in extending Protestantism and American civilization to other territories and cultures. "Although I could not preach the Gospel to [the Mexicans]," she writes, bowing to the exclusive maleness of the Presbyterian ministry, "I felt that [I] could, in some way adapted to my appropriate sphere, do something for bringing its blessing among them" (17).

In *Texas in 1850*, Rankin exploits the ideology of women's "civilizing" influence when she calls for state and church efforts to improve girls' education in Texas: "The well-being of this new and interesting State requires that the important element of power, female influence, should receive the necessary preparations for the extensive sway it is destined to exert over society" (119). *Twenty Years among the Mexicans*, on the other hand, singles out the respectful treatment of women in Mexican and Tejano society to counter Anglo-American prejudices against these populations and to support Rankin's claim for public recognition. Since "a Mexican never harmed a lady," she argues, "I would not presume to say that it was the wisdom of God to put a woman in the front ranks of Protestantism in Mexico, but I do say that a woman has stood firmly on ground on which a *man* would have been dispossessed" (129–130). By connecting faith, nation, and gender, Rankin's narratives participate in the entangled social discourses of American religious and "civilizing" missions—Manifest Destiny and female domesticity. While the texts largely affirm the hegemonic lines of reasoning and their ultimate political goals of expanding American political and economic influence as well as the Protestant faith across the hemisphere, their validation of Mexican culture undermines the racial Anglo-Saxonism entailed therein (Barton 157).

"Whoever comes to Texas to do good, might consider himself upon missionary ground," Rankin wrote in 1852 (*Texas* 98). Like many other Protestant missionaries from the eastern United States, she regarded it as New Englanders' obligation to spread their education and civilization to the socially rough and religiously "destitute" North American West. One of the few missionary journey narratives set during the Texas Republic, the travelogue of the Methodist circuit rider Orceneth Fisher complements the format of the emigrant guide with a discussion of religious matters in order to inspire Protestant Anglos to migrate to the region as well as win financial support for the Methodists' Texas mission. Similarly, Rankin wrote her Texas travelogue and her memoir to solicit funds, attract followers, and justify her work. Rankin surely antagonized many people and overstated the spread of Protestantism among the Mexicans in both Texas and Mexico. Yet her activities and narratives make an important and successful claim not only for women's agency but also for intercultural understanding within, and at times beyond, the paradigms of Manifest Destiny and Protestant mission in mid-nineteenth-century North America. This plea for understanding links her narratives with the Texas travelogues written by American officers' wives during the period, with their strong commitment to their husbands' "civilizing" military missions in the region.

SEVEN

Reporting from the Regiment

Journey Accounts of US Army Officers' Wives

The need to reconcile feminine gender roles with the rigors of life and travel in the North American West crucially informs the Texas journey narratives of another group of female travelers from the 1820s through the 1850s, namely, the wives of US Army officers accompanying their husbands to frontier assignments. Hailing predominantly from the educated Anglo middle class of the eastern United States (Myres, "Women" 107; S. Smith 4), many officers' wives penned journals, letters, travelogues, and memoirs of their time in the West. A number of these texts appeared in newspapers and magazines or as books (Georgi-Findlay 106, 169; Myres, "Army" 176–177). Although they present themselves in their writings as women bravely facing the hardships of army life as well as enjoying some freedom from social constraints, many army wives nonetheless stress their adherence to prevailing gender norms. Their texts often emphasize their domestic activities and justify their journeys (Georgi-Findlay 114–116, 120–125, 129–131; Myres, "Women" 107–110). In so doing, they contribute to the phenomenon of Manifest Domesticity, the interaction of the ideologies of female domesticity and Manifest Destiny that endowed white middle-class women with an active role in American discourses of territorial expansion and cultural imperialism. Besides women engaged in education, social reform, and religious labor, settlers' and army wives' homemaking in the indigenous and Mexican contact zones was considered a valuable contribution to spreading Anglo-American "civilization" to these areas (Kaplan 23–50).

Like female civilian travelers, army wives often felt overwhelmed by the vast, monotonous landscapes and extreme weather they encountered in the West. Their depictions of nature commonly find beauty in areas that resemble their home regions, whereas prairie and desert landscapes often appeared desolate to them (Georgi-Findlay 129; Myres, "Women" 102–103). While women's migration-promoting travelogues tended to project "domesticating" visions of flowering gardens and cultivated fields onto an alien landscape, officers' wives—echoing female settlers—foregrounded the need for white control over the terrain and its native residents in order to safely enjoy the land (Georgi-Findlay xiv, 77, 128–133). Army wives' narratives also express curiosity about Amerindians, yet frequently voice prevailing Anglo-American stereotypes about them (Myres, *Westering* 51,

63, 80; S. Smith 18, 78). Despite adhering to the widespread distinction between "civilized" sedentary and "savage" nomadic Native nations, officers' wives depicted the diverse indigenous population as a rather homogenous group. Their journey accounts often provide moralizing interpretations of sordid living conditions and unfamiliar gender roles as signs of Amerindian cultural "inferiority," which rationalized the "need" to spread Anglo-American civilization in the West (R. D. Campbell 12–14; S. Smith 62–64, 75, 135). Yet, although they tend to exaggerate the risks of Amerindian attacks and abductions (Georgi-Findlay xii–xiv, 85–87, 122; S. Smith 17–19, 45, 75, 135, 147), many army wives' narratives criticize the government's cruel treatment of Amerindians (Myres, "Women" 104–105; S. Smith 21–22, 145–147). Moreover, their texts often feminize or aestheticize indigenous men, a common practice in colonial discourses to exert power over "alien" populations (Said, *Orientalism* 206–207; Spurr 170–173). It allowed officers' wives not only to tone down readers' anxieties about white women's contacts with indigenous men but also to empower the women, since it symbolically reduced gender differences by maintaining the racial hierarchy that placed white women above Native men (Georgi-Findlay xiv–xv, 151, 155–157).

In contrast to their portrayals of indigenous people, white army wives distinguished different classes of Mexicans in the North American West. Their travelogues frequently reveal a deep fascination with both the Spanish colonial heritage and current Mexican customs. But they often present Mexican Catholicism as a sign of cultural backwardness, and Mexican peasants and laborers as lazy and ignorant (Myres, *Westering* 79–81; Myres, "Women" 105–106). Similarly, many officers' wives looked down on the enlisted men in their husbands' regiments as well as on the civilian Anglo frontier dwellers. Their narratives characterize both groups as ignorant, immoral, ill mannered, and violent. Accordingly, the texts frequently endorse rigid army discipline, even though they occasionally deplore the brutal treatment of common soldiers or criticize officers' misconduct going unpunished (Myres, "Women" 106–107; Tate 277). Nonetheless, their travelogues usually express the loyalty of officers' wives to the US Army. Largely eschewing any explicit discussion of political questions, the narrators voice pride in their contributions, as officers' spouses, to "making history" (Georgi-Findlay 107, 116, 123, 128; Myres, "Army" 179, 194–195). Although many private letters and diaries of army wives articulate conflicted views of the military presence in the Indian and Mexican contact zones, other narratives, particularly those written for publication, tend to obscure or justify the army's mission in the North American West (Georgi-Findlay 126; Myres, "Women" 112). In this way, even seemingly private accounts "become an important medium for a colonial discourse" and its attendant practices of subjugating Natives and Mexicans in the name of spreading Anglo-American civilization to the region (Georgi-Findlay 115).

TERESA GRIFFIN VIELÉ'S *FOLLOWING THE DRUM*

Among the travelogues of officers' wives from the antebellum North American West, only a few are known that depict journeys to or sojourns in Texas. Among them, Martha Hopkins Barbour's journal of her stay in Galveston in 1846, published in *Journals of the Late Brevet Major Philip Norbourne Barbour . . . and His Wife Martha Isabella Hopkins Barbour* (1939), does not address army life, as her husband fought in the US-Mexican War. And Lydia Spencer Lane penned her reminiscences of living in the region in the 1850s only much later, in her 1893 memoir *I Married a Soldier; Or, Old Days in the Army* (Vielé 259, 266–267). This makes Teresa Griffin Vielé (1831–1906) the only officer's wife to publish a travelogue before the Civil War about army life in Texas. A few months after marrying Egbert Vielé, a lieutenant of infantry, in 1850, she accompanied her husband on his assignment to Ringgold Barracks near Rio Grande City on the Texas-Mexican border. When he resigned from this post three years later to work as a civil engineer, his wife followed him back to New York before embarking on an independent life after her divorce (R. D. Campbell 142). In 1858, Vielé published her travelogue *Following the Drum*. The chronologically arranged text charts the experiences of roughly the first two years of her marriage, including her one-year stay in Texas.

The writer's romanticist frame of mind manifests itself in her numerous references to American and European literature in order to provide key scenes with poetic qualities or to characterize incidences and people. For example, her text frames life on a Tejano ranch as a pastoral idyll by quoting from Friedrich Schiller's 1802 poem "The Four Ages of the World." Another passage conveys the loyalty of Vielé's Black manservant by comparing him to the faithful family retainer Caleb Balderstone in Walter Scott's novel *The Bride of Lammermoor* (1819). And a chapter on the history and prospects of Texas opens with two stanzas from Alfred Lord Tennyson's 1842 poetic appeal to patriotic sentiment, "Love Thou Thy Land" (Vielé 126, 131, 235). This strategy reveals how *Following the Drum*, like Mary Holley's Texas travelogues, targets an educated middle-class Anglo readership likely to be familiar with these references, since the text usually does not indicate the sources of quotations. In the same vein, Vielé's volume refers to Oriental settings or Muslim culture—neither of which she knew firsthand—to show the exotic qualities of certain places or the narrator's fascination with them. For example, the US Military Academy, at West Point, attracted the young officer's wife "like a pilgrim [to] the shrine of Mecca," and she likens the Rio Grande to the Nile, "only want[ing] a few swarthy, turbaned men, and a sphinx or two, to complete the illusion" (16, 99). Elsewhere the narrative resorts to stereotypical regional American character traits to familiarize its target readers in the eastern

United States with the alien "nature" of Anglo-Texans: "In the Texan are combined the raciness of the Kentuckian, the Creole impetuosity of Louisiana, with the reckless heart-in-hand spirit of the Southwest" (149–150).

According to Nina Baym, Vielé "presented herself simply as an observer of the Texas scene" (16). I want to argue that the lieutenant's wife did precisely the opposite. Instead of limiting herself to the passive position of the officer's wife, she fashions herself in her travelogue as a veritable member of the regiment and thus as actively shaping the history of the region. Vielé's narrative begins with the telling confession "No recruit ever entered the service with more enthusiasm than I did or felt more eager to prove himself a soldier" (Vielé 13). The narrator subsequently envisions herself as a "wonderful female . . . [who] could travel over hundreds of miles of prairie on horseback" and who had all the qualities of a frontierswoman: "Familiar intercourse with the most savage tribes of Indians was nothing to her! Human sympathy, food, or rest were mere frivolous weaknesses. . . . The allurements of dress, petty artifices, tears, or any other little feminine failings she scorned contemptuously!" (14–15). Although she does not picture herself as a combatant, the narrator transgresses the socially accepted boundaries of middle-class femininity as she embraces a life of physical hardships and the masculine-coded qualities that enabled her to endure them. She hastens to add that this was a young girl's romanticized view of army life. Yet unlike Sandra Myres ("Women" 99), I argue that this gesture was merely a strategic concession to the ideology of domesticity. Subsequently, the narrator not only complains about the "limited capacities" ascribed to her gender (Vielé 28) but also justifies her life at Ringgold Barracks and her writing about it: "Experience dimmed the roseate hue of my early day dreams, yet, they have been sufficiently realized to tempt a record of them" (16). At the end of her travelogue, she reiterates the view of herself as a soldier by calling her time in Texas "my brief campaign" (256). Presenting herself in this manner allows the narrator to claim social agency and a more public role in her story than the function of frontier homemaker and moral influence on her surroundings, the limiting positions that American society usually accorded white middle-class women at the time, especially in male-dominated domains like the armed forces.

Since Vielé spent most of her days in Texas at the barracks, it is no surprise that the army plays a key role in her journey narrative. The text calls the men under Egbert Vielé's command "gallant sons of Mars" (139), but this appears to be a mere platitude, recalling William Parker's using the same term to ridicule common soldiers in his expedition account *Through Unexplored Texas. Following the Drum* reveals prejudices toward enlisted men that were typical of many officers' wives. The travelogue expresses empathy for young recruits facing the hardships of frontier posts: "How soon their existence would probably terminate, on some march across the prairies, in the sickly swamps of Florida, or on the perilous Indian scout" (32). At the same time, the narrative characterizes a group of young soldiers as "a reckless set of men . . . a collection probably of black sheep." Their rascality was probably exacerbated by the fact that "some of them [were] well-educated, and undoubtedly of highly respectable parentage" (31). In contrast, *Following the Drum* acclaims the bravery, integrity, and "high toned spirit" of the usually middle- or upper-class officers. The text defends the army against its civilian critics by pointing out how the forces served the nation, particularly in the endeavor to extend and settle its territory: "Wherever the adventurous pioneer erects his cabin, [army units] . . . protect him in its possession" (173, 175).

The references to these pioneers tellingly illustrate how much "Vielé's observations [were] shaped by her sense of Anglos as a recently arrived, not a settled population" in Texas (Baym 16). Like many other middle-class easterners, the lieutenant's wife was appalled by the unkempt appearance, rough manners, and crude dwellings of many white Americans in Texas. For instance, at a Galveston hotel, she likens the attire of some female travelers to that of the mismatched clothing of "the baboon's sister in nursery tales" and notes house rules prohibiting spitting on walls or wearing boots in bed (Vielé 81–82). At the same time, *Following the Drum* is keen to counter the social prejudices many easterners had against westerners. In addition to demanding respect for the early Anglo pioneer achievements, the narrator claims that more recent settlers belonged to a "superior class" of migrants and that crime and violence in Texas were "isolated acts of a roving population" (153, 79, 152). A courageous, adventurous spirit, hospitality, courtesy, and male gallantry toward women appear as laudable traits of the Anglo Texans in the volume, along with the formation of a meritocratic social order (81, 110, 150, 153).

Like many Americans, Vielé supported Anglo-American Protestant missionaries' endeavors to evangelize and "civilize" unchurched Anglos and Catholic Mexicans in Texas (109, 163). Reminiscent of Rankin's and Fisher's accounts, *Following the Drum* evokes the biblical image of St. John the Baptist, living a frugal life of preaching in the desert, as a model for religious labor in the Lone Star State: "In Texas there are hundreds of intelligent human souls ripe for instruction. . . . There is a wilderness now as then to preach in, with the finest wild-cat skins, and wild honey like ambrosia" (163–164). Unlike the American missionaries, however, Vielé criticizes the social bias with which many Americans viewed the cultural and religious differences between the Northeast and the South and West of the country. Despite her background, she rejects the radicalism and hypocrisy of New England anti-Catholicism and abolitionism. She confesses to "conceive that the Pope *may* be an excellent good man [and] that those suffering and bleeding bondsmen *may have* an occasional ray of sunshine on their dreary path of life"

(31, original emphases). Moreover, revealing the long-standing entanglements of Christianization and European colonization, the narrator pays respect to the early Catholic missionaries of colonial New Spain: "Led on by visions as brilliant as those of Cortez, fired equally by religious zeal and ambition, these modern crusaders braving danger with more than military ardor, and meeting death with the martyr's enthusiasm . . . pressed on until they penetrated into the heart of the continent, where for centuries the wild idolater had offered sacrifice on the altar of an unknown God" (114). Moreover, while the "idolatry" of indigenous faiths appears here as the key target of the early colonial missionaries, later passages of the travelogue depict the friars' establishment of structured white settlements as their major achievement (110–111, 115–116, 236–237).

In contrast to the Spanish colonial missionaries, *Following the Drum* portrays contemporary Mexican priests as utterly wicked, "a dissolute, carnal, gambling jolly set of wine bibbers" who "rul[ed] . . . with the strong sway of superstition and dread," an accusation made even stronger because, as the book points out, many of the priests were educated and amiable (113). This view ties in with the volume's unabashed, typically Anglo-American ethnic and social-class bias against Latin American populations as compared with their colonial European ancestors (51–52, 63–68). Although Vielé admits to having friendships with Mexicans, acknowledges their kindness, and calls them "amiable . . . [and] innocent" (55–56), she reiterates the Black Legend–inspired stereotypes of them as hotheaded and uncontrolled. While the upper class retained at least a shadow of Spanish colonial grandeur, the lower class, in her account, was indolent, ignorant, dirty, and prone to vice (111, 148, 155, 183). Ethnocultural differences also manifest themselves in Vielé's portrayal of people's dwelling places. In several instances, her narrative treats Anglo and Mexican houses in the Lower Rio Grande Valley as indicators of their degrees of civilization. In Brownsville, the Americans' "red brick stores and white frame shops . . . bore the marks of inevitable progress . . . otherwise called 'manifest destiny,' while the [Mexicans'] rudely constructed huts . . . exhibited unmistakable evidence of a vanishing people, who in a few years will know no nationality" (104–105). In a similar vein, *Following the Drum* treats the decay of Spanish colonial architecture in the area as a sign of a Mexican lack of foresight and industry. The vicinity of Fort Brown "was once an exquisite garden, filled with plants and irrigated from the Rio Grande," the narrator states. But now "a ruined summer-house [remains], with luxuriant vines creeping wherever they can find a support to cling to, as the pillars . . . have probably long ere this lighted a fire, to cook some ranchero's meal" (107–108). This passage implies that the Mexicans not only failed to recognize the beauty of their cultural inheritance but also ignorantly destroyed it. In contrast, the US Army returned the region to grandeur and purpose. The fort's "well kept fences, and regularly placed barracks and buildings, with the vine-covered cottages . . . , add in no small degree to the beauty and importance of Brownsville; while the daily guard-mountings, parades, and drills . . . add greatly to the feelings of safety and importance of its citizens" (116–117).

Vielé's travelogue links Anglo and Mexican cultural differences to racial ones. From the vantage point of the "refined mind" and "cultivated taste" of the educated Anglo middle class, the book declares Mexican men to be "a diminutive race," displaying "something almost repulsive in their dark, swarthy, unintellec- tual beauty." *Following the Drum* acknowledges "a certain indescribable charm" belonging to upper-class Mexican women, yet declares that the "dark and coarse" complexion of peasant girls "destroyed that appearance of refinement so essential to . . . beauty" (111, 177–178). As Adrienne Caughfield observes, "Holding on to the racial beliefs then in vogue, Vielé not only considered blacks unable to reach white levels of civilization but also lumped blacks and Hispanics into one group" (108). Vielé notes with astonishment that Mexicans had internalized the very Anglo beauty standards according to which they were inferior. "The white complexion of an American and blue eyes are their ideal of beauty, in contrast to their own dark skins and black eyes," she states, and adds her dislike of the Mexi- cans' simultaneous emulation of African Americans (Vielé 156). She defends the American concept of the color line, which distinguished whites from all other, implicitly inferior, races and justified Anglos' domination over them. "I do not believe," the writer confesses, "that the colored and white races can ever by any possibility amalgamate to an equality!" (158).

In line with her racial prejudices and the prevailing gendered codes of conduct, Vielé minimizes her close interaction with and strong dependency on her African American manservant, Joseph Williams, in *Following the Drum*. At Ringgold Barracks, she writes, Williams "took the place of *femme de chambre*. . . . He was at once chambermaid, waiter, and housekeeper; and . . . prided himself on keeping up the *style* of the family!" (131, original emphasis). By pointing out his dedication to feminine-coded household duties and calling him a chamber*maid*, Vielé feminizes Williams. In this way, she not only asserts her power over her male household member but also tones down readers' potential anxieties about the close bond between a white woman and a Black man. This naturalized racial hierarchy also manifests itself in the way *Following the Drum* treats slavery. While the text does not explicitly advocate the peculiar institution, it never condemns it, either. Besides taking the bondage of slaves in Texas and peons in Mexico for granted, it cautions that short escape routes to Mexico rendered a plantation economy risky in the Texas-Mexico border region. Moreover, Vielé's narrator insists that Afri- can American slaves could have a "good life" in the United States. For instance, she describes the well-kept cabins and singing slaves she observed at work on a plantation as "present[ing] a picture of contented industry that would quite have amazed the Duchess of Sutherland, and other ... philanthropic ladies" (71–72). Explicitly targeting one of the most prominent British abolitionists of the time, this passage reiterates Vielé's earlier critique of New England abolitionists, which denounced their lack of firsthand knowledge of the peculiar institution and its "caring" side. Even more, twisting the abolitionist argument of Harriet Beecher Stowe's novel *Uncle Tom's Cabin* (1852), the narrator claims that life under white American rule elevated people of African descent to a degree of civilization otherwise beyond their reach. "If we could compare these brutal animal features, and lack of intellect" of the free Blacks of Cuba "to the 'Uncle Toms' and 'Aunt Chloes' of our land, we might be convinced that from one point of view at least, slavery might be regarded as a blessing instead of 'a curse'" (Vielé 56).

In contrast to her personal encounters with Mexicans and her African American servant, she had few contacts with Amerindians during her stay in Texas. Her travelogue nonetheless adopts the terms and views commonly found in American or Mexican writing about the region's indigenous populations. Usually calling them "Indians" or "tribes" as well by their names, *Following the Drum* vilifies nomadic societies as "wily savages of the plains" who were "untamable and rapacious" and "roamed at large over the wide prairies" (116, 114). In addition, the book invokes the specters of paganism and cannibalism to denounce the Amerindian rejection of Christianization and white colonization. While it calls Native converts "civilized," it labels resistant Amerindians "barbaric tribes who ... evince their gratitude for religious instruction by eating their instructors" (115, 163). As the most powerful and resistant nomadic nation in the region, and a key target of US military campaigns at the time, the Comanches appear in *Following the Drum* as a particular peril to white society. The Comanche warrior "enjoys the mere intelligence, or rather the instincts, of the brute," and is incorrigibly barbaric: "He is bloody, brutal, licentious, and an innate thief. Civilization will probably never reach him, as his feelings toward the white men are those of implacable hatred. Their blood he demands, and takes every occasion to obtain it" (121). Completely missing the socioeconomic functions of raids and warfare, especially for young men (Hämäläinen 245–247, 266–269), this description presents the Comanches as ferocious, animalistic creatures utterly incapable of becoming civilized. Other passages in the book reiterate this imagery, detailing the nation's "tiger-like ferocity" and "wild mode of life" (Vielé 124, 159). By emphasizing their danger and lack of humanness, this portrayal of the Comanches serves to justify their violent subjugation as natural and necessary. Even more, Vielé's travelogue explicitly promotes the tribe's "extermination" as the only viable means to "render many portions of the State of Texas a safe abode for white settlers" (121).

Like many other officers' wives, however, the narrator of *Following the Drum* also acknowledges the Amerindian point of view: "I cannot refrain from some feelings of sympathy for a people, who are driven from their rightful possessions, and can see, in their ignorance, many excuses for their tiger-like ferocity and bitter hatred of those who they feel have wronged them so sorely" (123–124). Even more, the book legitimizes the Natives' perspective by pointing out parallels in American society. "He who steals the greatest number of horses is regarded as the greatest man in the tribe," the narrator comments. "If for *horses* we read *dollars*, I fear we should have a peculiar fact in regard to more enlightened communities!" Given Anglo filibustering activities and Amerindian raids in northern Mexico, she asks her readers, "If we cannot control organized depredations on our neighbors, how can we blame the Indians for wishing to extend *their* 'area of freedom'?" (123, original emphases).

In contrast to the Comanches, the narrator praises the Carrizos as "a tribe once brave and famous" that had acquired "some of the rudiments of civilization" from friendly relations with Anglos and Mexicans. Her phrasing, however, shows how she attributes only a limited degree of civilization to even such a peaceful and sedentary nation. *Following the Drum* underlines this view by mentioning the Carrizos' wearing loincloths of animal skins, carrying traditional weapons, and offering help to Anglo filibusters in hope of sharing in the "plunder" (202–203, 197). Moreover, typical of white travelogues of the North American West, the book explains indigenous women's cultural and racial alterity and "inferiority" as deviance from Anglo-American gender roles. The text emphasizes Amerindian women's skills on horseback and in battle, their "unattractive" features, and their lack of "sensibility," which made them appear "more like men than women" (122, 233–234, 203–204). By masculinizing indigenous women, Vielé affirms their presumed racial-cultural inferiority to white women. The only exception to this homogenizing and derogatory depiction is a Carrizo chief's daughter whom Vielé frames as an Indian princess stereotype. The traveler assesses the young woman according to Eurocentric ideals of beauty as defined by classical Greek art and European physiognomy. "Her face was cut as if with the chisel of a Phidias, the nostril, mouth, and chin a study of beauty," Vielé remarks. "Her large, liquid, dreamy eyes, with their heavy lashes . . . bespoke the Anglo-Saxon blood which rendered her Indian beauty so peerless" (214–215). Thus, European civilization not only provides a legitimate standard of aesthetic judgment in *Following the Drum* but also, once again, of racial superiority.

Beauty and utility also provide the framework for Vielé's discussion of Texas nature. Like many other Anglo travelogues, her volume argues that large parts of the region featured fertile soil. "Under the hand of the husbandman," it promised "to yield abundant harvests" (240). Elsewhere, *Following the Drum* delights in appealing vistas of the South Texas landscape: "A beautiful chaparral . . . was thick with flowering shrubs and wild flowers. Each scraggy, ebony tree lodged in its branches myriads of brilliant tropical birds, whose sweet-toned melodies filled the soft air that floated around us with music" (99). In a similar vein, at a Tejano ranch "the picture of rural pursuits that here presented itself, was a study for an artist." Accordingly, the narrator goes on to sketch a clichéd pastoral idyll of slow-paced Mexican peasant life in an exoticized setting of simple huts where cooking was done "in real gypsy fashion" (124–126). But the predominant image of nature in Texas that her book conveys is that of an almost boundless and monotonous landscape that provides travelers with a sublime experience. "How meagre, how insignificant, do all the seaside scenes painted on memory seem, in comparison to this vast and apparently interminable extent of wave-beaten sand with its glorious breakers and their sad eternal moanings," the text muses about the coast near Galveston (85). Vielé further cautions readers against coming to the Lone Star State with exaggerated expectations. "To an eye unaccustomed to 'roughing it,'" she writes, South Texas "bore an aspect of misery and abject suffering." Like Eduard Ludecus's travelogue, hers characterizes the Lower Rio Grande Valley as particularly hostile to white settlement. It is "unfitted by nature to be the home of civilized man," even "seem[ing] to hate civilization" (97, 151). The coast similarly appears as a sublime, treacherous wasteland, for instance, in the region near Galveston: "Every imaginable vestige of wreck lay around, from the giant mast of some enormous ship to that of the smallest trading schooner. All this gave to the barren, sandy shores, an air of gloom and desolation that words cannot describe" (90–91).

As Adrienne Caughfield remarks, "By 1858, when Vielé's travelogue was published, Americans had become accustomed to the idea of filibusters working toward a Mexican republic" (123). Possibly with respect to the activities of the Knights of the Golden Circle, a secret society formed in 1854 and popular among Anglo-Texans, Vielé not only endorsed but also actively aided American filibustering activities in the Lower Rio Grande Valley, according to her narrative (Vielé 191–211). Besides promoting slavery, the Knights hoped to annex the West Indies and much of Central America into a slaveholding confederation with the US slave states (Caughfield 123). In *Following the Drum*, the officer's wife emphasizes the "true-souled honesty and genuine generosity" of the American filibusters and even presents one of them, the rancher Clay Davis, as a model Anglo-Texan, despite his known criminal record (Vielé 149, 142–147). In contrast to the filibusters, Vielé argues that Mexican soldiers were untrustworthy cowards. Tellingly, she exempts from this claim only the insurgent Tejano politician José María Carbajal, who fought for the independence of northern Mexico and collaborated with Anglos in the Merchants War, a tariff-driven conflict along the Texas-Mexico border in the early 1850s (192–193, 196, 200, 209–210). *Following the Drum* further presents US filibustering expeditions into northern Mexico as useful measures to improve the local population: "All the vitality that [the Mexicans] know is due to our influence, which . . . causes civilization to flow through these regions, like its river Rio Bravo del Norte, bringing with it the only blessing this barren country has ever known" (201). This view echoes Vielé's earlier characterization of Cuba in her travelogue as desiring both independence from Spain and integration into the United States but needing American intervention to realize these goals (60–61; see also Caughfield 130). She likewise discusses the possible annexation of Mexico to the United States as the only way to "improve" the neighboring nation (111).

Vielé was one of few army officers' wives who explicitly addressed current political affairs in her reminiscences of frontier life (Myres, "Army" 179–180n11). As Brigitte Georgi-Findlay points out, "The plural 'we' and the assumption of uncontested authority also predominates in . . . *Following the Drum*, which is exuberantly expansionist . . . , extolling the qualities of 'Anglo-Saxon endurance'" (305n55; see also Vielé 160–161, 105, 111, 144). This attitude becomes visible in Vielé's self-description as "a young pilgrim bound for the land of the Camanches" (Vielé 19). This image frames not only her sojourn in Texas but also the army's larger presence in the region, which followed in the steps of the Puritans' "sacred errand into the wilderness" of seventeenth-century New England. Vielé's travelogue thus validates the discourse of Manifest Destiny and the colonial policy of westward territorial expansion and Amerindian and Mexican subjugation, which were connected with it. *Following the Drum* similarly depicts the Texas Revolution as having naturally resulted from Anglo civilization taking hold in a region governed by a nation incapable of providing political stability and economic progress: "It was not in the nature of things that Texas, in which the Anglo-Saxon blood now predominated, should submit to the arbitrary laws and exactions of this fickle and miserable race [i.e., the Mexicans]. The dissolution of their connexion was the natural consequence of tyranny on the one hand and manly resistance on the other" (238). Like some of the American travelogues of Texas written to promote Anglo migration to the region or to caution against it, this passage frames the insurgency of the Anglo-Texans as a legitimate resistance to despotism, and it claims their right of revolution against an oppressive government. Since it calls the Anglos "manly" and pits them favorably against the feminized Tejanos, Vielé's book dresses the political conflict of the Texas Revolution in biologically essentialist terms of racial and gender hierarchies. In so doing, the narrative positions itself in the American colonial discourse of the time and naturalizes the proclaimed "superiority" of Anglo civilization to Mexican society, and the former's resulting political right to independence.

Unsurprisingly, *Following the Drum* characterizes the US-Mexican War as a heroic American struggle for a worthy cause. The text identifies battle sites connected with victories of the US Army and calls for erecting monuments to the fallen Americans at the battlefields of Palo Alto and Resaca de la Palma (92, 100–103, 110, 116). At the end of her travelogue, Vielé places this local history in a larger context. She argues that the annexation of Texas to the United States not only completed the process of political liberation and economic progress begun with the Texas Revolution but also made a crucial contribution to "a new and peculiar phase of civilization" (238–239, 241). In this line of reasoning, according to Adrienne Caughfield, "the absorption of Texas provided purpose to the Mexican War, allowed for the annexation of new territory into the United States, and made great strides for the cause of manifest destiny" (117). Moreover, Texas for Vielé was no mere beneficiary of Manifest Destiny but also a key site at which its principles were being preserved and carried on. Even if the Union disappeared one day, the writer claimed in her travelogue, Texas would still show "the elements of a magnificent empire" (Vielé 241).

ELIZA GRIFFIN JOHNSTON'S TEXAS DIARY

Three years after Teresa Vielé's Texan sojourn, another US Army officer's wife penned a travelogue about the region. In the fall and winter of 1855–1856, Eliza Griffin Johnston (1821–1896) accompanied her husband, Colonel Albert Sidney Johnston, and his newly formed regiment on a journey to the Lone Star State. Born in Virginia and raised in Kentucky, she married her husband in 1843. A month later, she joined him on her first of many journeys to the Lone Star State. When the army appointed Albert Johnston commander of the Second US Cavalry in 1855, he took his family and his regiment to the Lone Star State. On October 27 of that year, the party left Jefferson Barracks in Missouri, crossed the Red River into Texas in December, and reached their destination, Fort Mason, on the eastern ridge of the Texas Hill Country, on January 14, 1856. Two months later, Colonel Johnston was given command of the entire Military Department of Texas. In April, he relocated to San Antonio with his family (Mayhall xvii–xxviii; Roland 118–119, 168–169, 173–179).

While Eliza Johnston accompanied her husband to subsequent deployments to Texas, she memorialized only one of these trips in a travel journal. Although written almost daily from the fall of 1855 through the following spring, the text that became "The Diary of Eliza (Mrs. Albert Sidney) Johnston: The Second Cavalry Comes to Texas" (1957) was not published for more than a hundred years. The colonel's wife described her experiences and observations along the road, beginning with the regiment's departure from Jefferson Barracks on October 29, 1855, and ending with an entry on May 7, 1856, after her family had settled in San Antonio. She particularly comments on the topography, flora, and climate of the region; the resident populations; and her daily life and fellow travelers. As Robin

Doughty observes, she "vividly records her feelings of elation and despondence in trying circumstances" (58), and Mildred Mayhall adds that her narrative reveals Johnston's "perceptive observation and candid appraisal of persons, gossip, and experiences" (xxix).

Like Teresa Vielé, Johnston identified with the army. Throughout her journal, the narrator voices her willingness to face the privations of traveling and camp life, even though she simultaneously admits to struggling with them. For instance, her entry for Christmas Day reads: "I wonder if friends far away, with all their comforts now, can imagine us sleeping on the ground and shivring round a camp fire to keep life in us" (Johnston 484). At Fort Mason, she complains about a shortage of habitable buildings leading to cramped living conditions (490). Nonetheless, like Vielé, Johnston asserts the agency of soldiers' wives and children and their place in the military by fashioning her family as members of the regiment. "Well, here I am soldiering," her journal opens. In a later scene, she comments on her young daughter's bravery: "Maggie is . . . the best soldier of us all" (467, 470). In contrast to Vielé's narrative, Johnston's travel journal shows strong sympathy for the common soldiers. Besides expressing concern for their well-being, she admits missing them after leaving for San Antonio (470, 476, 485, 195). The deaths of two men particularly moved her to muse about the toll that army life in the Amerindian contact zone took on soldiers and on their loved ones left behind. "He was but 21 years old and an excellent soldier," she notes about one of the deceased. "It was a sad thing for his comrades to . . . leave him in that great solitude[.] I thought as we passed his lonely grave . . . that a poor mother & sisters and brothers perhaps were looking for his success in life and his return in 5 years with laurels" (487–488). In fellow feeling with the enlisted men, the diarist confesses her "disgust" with the harsh enforcement of military discipline. "I was shocked and distressed to hear that 6 of my husbands men had been whipped, and were to be drummed out," she writes. "Surely-surely some less degrading mode of punishment can be substituted" for these measures (467).

Despite her earlier plea for a humane execution of justice, Johnston endorses harsh punishments for officers and soldiers who commit slander, theft, and murder (474, 480, 482, 493). Similarly, although she accepts the class privilege that granted officers' families preferential treatment during the journey (468–469, 490), "The Diary of Eliza Johnston" criticizes the gendered and social-class-related license that governed the widespread acceptance of officers' misconduct toward women and disregard of their needs. "He had taken a woman from her good decent husband in Missouri and brought her here to Texas," the diarist writes about a lieutenant in the regiment. "I never can talk to the man with pleasure or patience again, & yet he is considered a gentleman and a fine officer" (493). She reproaches the same man for leaving his "poor woman . . . very sick in camp with a young baby

... and both neglected," and reprimands another officer for entertaining visitors in his quarters while his wife was in labor there (493). This concern for the female camp followers strongly contrasts with the lack of interest Johnston shows toward other civilians she met during her journey. Casual remarks about encountering "a party of emigrants to Kansas" and about the writer's Irish servant are the only hints in her journal at the massive American and European migration to the North American West taking place at that time (468, 472). Other white settlers residing along the journey route likewise appear in the text merely as trading partners who sold food to the regiment.

In one instance, the narrator records that "along the road the people told us that they had heard we were coming ... to whip the Mormons [or] the Comanches" (470). Indeed, the Second Cavalry had been formed and deployed to establish a new army post on the recently established Comanche reservation on the Clear Fork of the Brazos River. It was to complement a new line of garrisons on the Texas plains that would secure the permanent residence of the indigenous nations on allocated reservation lands and protect both them and white settlers in the region from indigenous raids (Mayhall xxx; Roland 172–173). Since it covers just the first weeks of the regiment's stay at its new post, Johnston's travel journal only briefly alludes to the ongoing conflicts—the risks of indigenous raids or Natives' resistance to the presence of the army in their territory (Johnston 486, 492, 494). Moreover, in contrast to Vielé, the diarist never mentions the term "Manifest Destiny" in her text. Yet she admits to having taken "two arrows stained with blood of the brave warrior" as a trophy from a skirmish that the regiment won against a band of Natives. (492). As she does not voice compassion over the warrior's death, she likely endorsed the American-Indian Wars the US Army waged against resistant Natives to safeguard US territorial expansion and white settlement in the West.

Apart from the Comanches, Johnston's travel journal largely addresses those indigenous nations whose lands the regiment passed through on their journey. The text calls these sedentary populations either "Indians" or "civilized Indians," or identifies them by their names. The diary supports the reservation system, praising the well-kept farms and towns of the Cherokees and Creeks in Indian Territory (477–478). Even though she depicts them as deceitful, the narrator simultaneously calls the Creeks "more civilized in appearance than any other Indians we have yet met with." She similarly notes with approval that the Choctaws clothed their Black slaves "as well as themselves" and allowed them to earn money (478–480). While the brevity and neutral tone of her comments do not indicate whether the writer supported the peculiar institution, the fact that the Johnstons owned slaves suggests that she did (Mayhall xxv–xxvi; Roland 166, 181, 241–242). Eliza Johnston's endorsement of slavery even seems to extend to the captivity of Mexicans.

The final entry of her journal comments on a Mexican who "was taken prisoner by the Indians ... when a very young child [and] raised by them as one of their warriors so that he is Indian in every essential except colour." Moreover, "he is fair with sandy hair & more like an Irishman than a Mexican" (Johnston 500). In contrast to Vielé's narrative and many other contemporary American travelogues of Texas, this passage does not express bewilderment about a Mexican acculturating to Amerindian life. On the contrary, paired with Johnston's astonishment about a Mexican's fair complexion, this scene reveals that the diarist subscribed to the widespread Anglo-American view of Mexicans as racially mixed—and thereby less distinguishable from indigenous peoples.

In line with some other officers' wives who spent time in the Mexican contact zones—but not Vielé—Johnston did not regard Anglo-American civilization as necessarily having an enlightening effect on Mexicans. Instead, her travel journal values her sons' Tejano classmates in San Antonio as a cultural resource to help the boys learn Spanish, a skill their mother considered an advantage for someone living in Texas (498). The text further deviates from many other American or German travelogues of the region in that it does not set up a hierarchical binary between a glorified Spanish colonial heritage in Texas and a deficient contemporary Mexican culture there. Whereas several other observers tended to interpret decaying Spanish colonial architecture as a sign of Mexicans' inferiority to their European ancestors, Johnston emphasizes continuity. For instance, she notes about the Mission Concepción, established by Spanish Franciscans near San Antonio in 1731: "The face of the building has been gorgeously painted in the style of the old illuminated manuscripts & books" (497). The references to "illuminated manuscripts & books" extend the period evoked here back to the European Middle Ages, the heyday of that type of text production. The account thereby presents Spanish colonial culture in Texas as a link between a more ancient European past and the North American present of the diarist.

More than anything else, Johnston had come to love the landscape of Texas during stays at her husband's plantation in Brazoria County in the 1840s (Mayhall xxii). In her diary of the 1855–1856 journey, she repeatedly observes the region's landscape and vegetation, particularly the wildflowers, which she would later make the subject of an illustrated botanical volume, published in 1972 as *Texas Wildflowers* (Johnston 471–472, 475, 489; see also Mayhall xxiv, xxxviii; Roland 142, 158–159). Like many other travelers, Johnston sought to make sense of novel experiences of nature through analogies. To convey the suffering of the regiment from the cold winter in North Texas, for example, she refers to the weather in northeastern Siberia, an area known to Americans for its long, bitter winters (Johnston 491, 475). Like other travelogues of Texas, "The Diary of Eliza Johnston" repeatedly points out beautiful landscapes, picturesque scenes such as the nocturnal camp of the regiment, or sublime experiences of nature. Most of these passages complement descriptions of the landscape with remarks on the fertility of the terrain and its suitability for farming (468, 481, 487–490, 496). Most striking is a scenic vista of the San Saba River region: "Today [we] passed through one of the most beautiful portions of Texas. We could see over a vast extent of Country covered with live-oaks & other growth dotted over the Prairie seemingly as ornaments to the landscape. The green trees & brown grass & bright sunshine gave the scene all the effect of a midsummer harvest, it was like a dream of August" (489). This intertwining of aesthetic and utilitarian discourses about the Texas landscape characterizes many works of travel writing about the region, especially texts seeking to lure prospective settlers to the Lone Star State. Johnston penned her journal solely for herself, yet this passage demonstrates her debt to the American political discourse that justified the nation's territorial expansion in the North American West by claiming that seemingly uncultivated lands in the region awaited white colonization and exploitation. Since the US Army played a key role in enforcing Native removal in order to facilitate white settlement in the West, the diarist was directly implicated in this development, although she never addresses this context in her journal.

In contrast to missionary travelogues, the interests of institutional sponsors play a less important role in the western journey accounts of US Army officers' wives. The antebellum Texas travelogues of Teresa Griffin Vielé and Eliza Griffin Johnston provide strikingly different examples of this type of text. The former fashions herself in her published narrative as a noncombatant member of her husband's regiment. To attract readers interested in the exploits of the army in the North American West, she romanticizes her life in the Texas-Mexico border region as a series of adventures. Johnston's private travel journal, in contrast, testifies to the hardships that traveling with the army held for the soldiers and their families. Although both authors present women as bravely and legitimately mastering privations on the frontier, Johnston's diary is largely devoid of the strong racial and class bias, as well as the agenda of Manifest Destiny informing Vielé's journey account, particularly when the lieutenant's wife negotiates the entangled hierarchies of rank, ethnicity, and gender in the Amerindian and Mexican contact zones. Nonetheless, both texts resulted from and legitimized the extended white settlement of the North American West after the war with Mexico and the ensuing Indian Wars and indigenous genocide.

EIGHT

Professional Pens

Anglo-American Travel Journalism of Texas

During the nineteenth century, print journalism developed into a distinct profession and became a major force shaping public opinion. This went hand in hand with the diversification of American media (Huntzicker 14, 163–164). Starting in the 1820s, the so-called penny press rivaled the established newspapers in sales and influence. While the latter were subscription-based and partisan in their sponsorship, distribution, and coverage, the penny papers enjoyed political and economic independence, since they were funded through advertisements and sold on the street for a low price. Moreover, their reporters used a simple writing style that frequently blended facts and opinions. The growing competition in American journalism triggered by the penny press forced all print media to differentiate themselves in a rapidly diversifying market. Partisan-press editors tapped into new audiences, and the penny papers often adopted the moralizing impulse, opinionated reporting, and stable political affiliations of the established media (Griffin 21–22; Huntzicker 1–49, 163–175). Most prominently, the *New York Sun*, the largest penny paper, increasingly tended to favor the Democrats, especially in its support of slavery, westward expansion, and the US-Mexican War. In contrast, the *New York Daily Times* (now the *New York Times*), which targeted a more learned readership than the other penny papers, was Whig leaning and critical of slavery (Huntzicker 1–12, 43, 163–164; Griffin 22, 53, 57).

As Megan Jenison Griffin observes, their steadily growing readership and professionalization gave both types of newspapers as well as other print media "an increasingly wider impact on nation-building and national identity" (56). The ongoing territorial expansion of the United States turned the North American West into a subject of journalism. On the one hand, Americans going west would establish media outlets in their new places of residence. On the other hand, facilitated by the invention of telegraphy in 1839, East Coast newspapers had been reporting more frequently on incidents in the region since the 1840s (Huntzicker 40, 93–110, 172). Their coverage of the West turned both old and new print media into "an integral part of the empire-building process" (Griffin 37) that was entailed by the extension of Anglo settlements and American influence. Many newspapers and periodicals promoted the paradigm of Manifest Destiny and its objective of extending the country's territory and sphere of influence as widely as possible in the hemisphere (Greenberg 57; Huntzicker 60, 97, 170–171). But the war with Mexico and the spread of slavery increasingly divided media outlets, separating them along Whig- or Democrat-leaning lines (Huntzicker 62–79, 171–173).

The growing professionalization of American journalism also brought new professional opportunities as well as challenges for women. The prevailing ideology of female domesticity did not consider journalism a suitable female profession, since it involved working outside the home and outside established female professions such as teachers or caretakers (Hudson 51). Nonetheless, in the 1830s, American women began working as newspaper and periodical publishers, editors, and reporters (Griffin; Huntzicker 13, 40, 82–88, 140). But like female missionaries and military wives, female journalists who traveled as part of their work had to reconcile what Susan Roberson calls the "twin ideologies of mobility and home"—the conflicting demands of US middle-class culture (4). This dynamic framed white women's social and spatial movement as progress but nevertheless declared women's "natural" place to be the home. Roberson adds that female journalists' travelogues "are complicated as well by the differing experiences of mobility they narrate and the roles they had in travel" (4). In their texts, female reporters claimed both traveling and writing to be part of their proper sphere in order to legitimize engaging in both areas. Since the journalists simultaneously emphasized their belonging to mainstream American culture and promoted its values through their writing, they "negotiated a place for themselves and their ideologies both against and within hegemonic institutions" (Roberson 11).

Although travel narratives from the West, including Texas, found an eager readership in newspapers and periodicals (Greenberg 5–6), only a few professional journalists also wrote books about sojourns in or journeys to Texas. Moreover, those who published such texts before the onset of the Civil War mostly depicted travels going beyond the Lone Star State, such as George Kendall's *Narrative of an Expedition* (1845), about his participation in the Texan Santa Fe Expedition. Alternatively, they composed volumes of historical scholarship, such as Henry Stuart Foote's 1841 *Texas and the Texans; or, Advance of the Anglo-Americans to the Southwest* (Bryan 64–66, 107; Sibley 17, 190). This leaves Jane McManus Cazneau's books *Texas and Her Presidents* and *Eagle Pass*, and Frederick Law Olmsted's account *A Journey through Texas*, as almost the only book-length works of travel journalism about the antebellum Lone Star State.

JANE MCMANUS CAZNEAU'S TEXAS WRITINGS

One of the most prominent female journalists of the mid-nineteenth century was the native New Yorker Jane McManus Cazneau (1807–1878). Inspired by the success of Stephen Austin's colony, she first came to Texas as a young divorcée in 1832 to settle German immigrants on a land grant she had purchased. Although this endeavor failed, she settled near Matagorda in 1838. Cazneau subsequently moved back and forth between Texas and the East Coast as well as abroad as she established a reputation in political journalism. Using several pseudonyms, she wrote for major American media outlets. The *New York Sun* deployed her as a war correspondent during the US-Mexican War. In 1849 she married the Texas congressional representative, trader, and army general William Leslie Cazneau. The couple founded the settlement of Eagle Pass on the Texas-Mexico border, where they resided for two years. Jane Cazneau was affiliated with the Young America movement (which advocated free trade, territorial expansion, and social reform); became an active land speculator in Texas, Mexico, and the Caribbean; and remained an ardent advocate of Manifest Destiny and American expansion into Texas and Mexico for the rest of her life (Griffin 24–25, 34–36, 50–55; Hudson; May 19–27).

In addition to her journalism, Cazneau published several books on the Caribbean and two volumes about Texas, usually under the pen name Cora (or Corinne) Montgomery. *Texas and Her Presidents, with a Glance at Her Climate and Agricultural Capacities* (1845) first appeared in the *United States Magazine and Democratic Review* (Hudson 56–57). "A history, geography, and guidebook for investors and settlers" (Hudson 21), the book recalls Mary Holley's travelogues from the early 1830s. It provides an Anglocentric history of Texas from the late colonial period to its annexation by the United States, followed by a geographic survey and a series of opinionated biographies of major Texas politicians. In 1852, Cazneau penned the travelogue-*cum*-settler narrative *Eagle Pass, or Life on the Border*. The book consists of a series of sketches told from the perspective of a fictionalized Anglo-American woman whom the text calls "Mrs. C." (Cazneau, *Eagle Pass* 32). *Eagle Pass* describes its narrator's journey from New York via Galveston, Indianola, and San Antonio to Eagle Pass on the Rio Grande in February and March 1850, and her life in the eponymous border settlement until June 1852 (Hudson 117–118; Kerrigan 275).

Both *Texas and Her Presidents* and *Eagle Pass* open with a classical gesture of modesty, no doubt a strategy to justify her, a woman, having written on controversial political topics (Hudson 118). In both volumes, the narrator argues that they were written either at the urging of friends and her publisher or because she was the only writer available for the task. She emphasizes social issues and downplays her texts' ambitions to shape American political discourse, which was considered a prerogative of men (Cazneau, *Texas* iii; Cazneau, *Eagle Pass* v). *Texas and Her Presidents* quotes from earlier writings on the Lone Star State by Mary Holley, William Kennedy, Alexander von Humboldt, and Juan Almonte to provide a "scientific, factual" basis for the narrator's arguments and thus bolster their authority (88, 90, 96–100). To familiarize their audiences with the nature and society of Texas, Cazneau's two volumes allude to American or European geographic locations, history, and literature, references likely to be known to an educated readership in the eastern and southern United States. For instance, the narrator captures the wine-growing potential of the El Paso region in an image of Rhenish merrymaking, and she compares the Rio Grande to the Hudson River (*Eagle Pass* 51; *Texas* 12). Similarly, an Anglo settler and a Mexican servant in Eagle Pass recall, respectively, the protagonist of James Fenimore Cooper's *Leatherstocking Tales* and the Roman orator Cicero (*Eagle Pass* 91, 49). *Texas and Her Presidents* and *Eagle Pass* further use images of domestic relations, a common trope in American expansionist discourse of the period (Kaplan 27), to articulate the claim of the United States to Texas. The books characterize the region as the child of a US "mother" and as a "sister" to the states of the Union (*Texas* 66, 9; *Eagle Pass* 11, 16). *Texas and Her Presidents* also takes up the popular view of Stephen Austin as the "Father of Texas . . . who guarded her cradle in the wilderness" (68).

Cazneau's two volumes seek to promote Anglo settlement in Texas by emphasizing the land's beauty and fertility and downplaying the privations of frontier life. They largely present the Texas countryside as a potential arcadia combining pleasant landscapes with the economic benefits of fertile soil, mineral resources, and a net of transportation routes. Their depiction of the Eagle Pass area contrasts with the pessimistic portraits that travelers such as Eduard Ludecus or Frederick Law Olmsted sketched of the Rio Grande region (Kerrigan 280–281, 287). Unlike them, Cazneau argues for the beauty and fertility of the area through the romanticist metaphor of a lively seascape. It was "one wide-rolling, ever-varying ocean of verdure, flashing back in golden smiles the radiant glance of the sun, while the fresh breeze tossed and waved the changeful tresses of bright flowers in frolic gaiety" (*Eagle Pass* 45). *Texas and Her Presidents* employs religious references of the same hyperbolic intensity to promote white settlement. It calls Central Texas "the Eden of the western world," whose prairie groves "seem planted by a gracious Providence to give beauty and shade to the cabin of the settler" (92–93).

Aligning with other Texas journey accounts promoting Anglo-Saxon immigration to the region, Cazneau's volumes assert that the settler's labor was needed to bring the natural advantages of Texas to fruition. Owing to the "hardihood" of Austin's colonists, *Texas and Her Presidents* states, "the broad prairie began to be dotted by the homes of the white race," and evidence of their excellent husbandry soon followed: "Herds of horses, and an abundance of cattle, swine, and poultry, had gathered round the settlers" (14–15). Their counterpart is the figure of the idle gentry seeking to live off the labor of others by profiting from land speculation. *Eagle Pass* uses the medical image of infectious disease to criticize land speculation in the Lone Star State: "Hundreds, too genteel to earn honest, independent bread ... swarmed into Texas and lived on speculation until the vigorous life of the young country outgrew the canker. The scar of this plague is still visible in the chaos of law suits and land monopolies" (13). To strengthen her point, Cazneau cites the Anglo-American cultural ideal of the independent yeoman farmer as the nucleus of republican virtues: "There is no country under the sun in which a sober, sensible, and industrious man can more certainly realize a quick independence and a delightful home. . . . If a healthy man is poor and homeless in Texas, it is because he is not manly enough to put his hands to useful labor" (*Eagle Pass* 12–13; see also *Texas* 93–94).

Like the Texas travelogues of Mary Holley, Melinda Rankin, or several German writers, Cazneau's volumes present garden cultivation as an indicator of a settler's diligence and refinement. Pointing out the easy husbandry and rich harvests that horticulture promised in large parts of the Lone Star State, Cazneau reproaches Anglo settlers: "So far, the Texians, in the abundance of their game, fish, and oysters, have been shamefully negligent of the luxuries of the garden and orchard" (*Texas* 102). Unlike them, the narrator of *Eagle Pass* claims, "I pined for shade, and fruit trees whose overarching arms should enfold me in a temple of tranquil repose ... with my thoughts, my books, and my birds. Gardening is with me an occupation and a delight" (79–80). Thus, in contrast to travelogues that view a garden only as a resource to enrich the pantry, Cazneau's text sketches it primarily as a space of private leisure. In line with other women's travelogues of the North American West, *Eagle Pass* praises this gendered and domesticated space in the wilderness as one that endows women gardeners with freedom and agency. In contrast to Holley's imagined female gardener, however, Cazneau's narrator does not mention that her leisurely use of her orchard was dependent on her wealth, which enabled her to prioritize the grove's shade over its fruits. Connecting her reading with her gardening recalls an earlier passage blending two lines of American political discourse that sought to establish the superiority of the United States over other countries, particularly European ones. Jeffersonian agrarianism emphasized America's socially egalitarian democracy, and the cult of domesticity established white women and the bourgeois home as carriers of its values (Kaplan 24). By contrast, Old World pastoral reveries of arcadian poetry, as well as biblical stories, Cazneau argues, present an image of country life that fails to acknowledge women's contributions: "It is only when society has shaped itself so as to expect service from all its members ... that women and civilization can be admitted to have found a position of value." Therefore, the line of reasoning continues, only a bourgeois, republican society like the United States could succeed in fulfilling the biblical command to "subdue the earth" (*Eagle Pass* 78).

The garden imagery also ties in with Cazneau's use of the Texas Creation

Myth, also employed in settlement-promoting American travelogues like Stephen Austin's and Mary Holley's writings, to naturalize the Anglo-Americanization of Texas. For instance, *Texas and Her Presidents* maintains that Mexico "never bought, conquered, settled, governed, or protected" the Lone Star State against warlike Amerindian nations. In response, "Divine Providence called forth [the Anglo colonists] ... to redeem Texas from the savage and create a new Anglo-American State" (11). *Eagle Pass* likewise frames West Texas as a "belt of uninhabited and Indian-haunted country that borders the Rio Bravo," in order to justify Anglo land taking in the area (32). The two volumes present Anglo-Texans as particularly suited to developing the region. "A mingled but rich debris of genius, enterprise, worth and crime, detached by an infinite variety of causes from the well-stratified society of the older States," they stood out for their bravery, loyalty, and entrepreneurship (*Texas* 65–66; see also *Eagle Pass* 26–27). *Texas and Her Presidents* legitimizes the Texas fight for independence by setting it in the tradition of the American Revolution. The book argues that restrictions on Anglo settlement naturally stirred resistance in a population imbued with a fundamental belief in civil liberties: "To submit to the capricious usurpations of martial law was impossible for the descendants of the Old Thirteen" (22). Cazneau's two volumes further treat the economic success of the Anglo-Texans as a sign of "the indomitable character of the Anglo-American race," which enabled the settlers to colonize new terrains (*Texas* 69). The "prosperous, well-stocked stores [and] intelligent society" of Eagle Pass thus exemplified "how the bold enterprise of our people knows to acquire territory, and to build up towns, and states" (*Eagle Pass* 10).

Believing in the benefits of US republicanism and a capitalist market economy for both Mexicans and Americans, Cazneau advocates annexing Mexico to the United States. Even though she dismisses José María Carbajal's uprising as being driven only by financial greed, she believed that the Republic of the Sierra Madre, which he envisioned, would follow in the footsteps of the Lone Star State (*Eagle Pass* 147, 179, 186–188; see also Kerrigan 285–286). With this prospect in sight, she saw even greater economic opportunities for the United States in the Southwest. In particular, the proposal to direct the planned transcontinental railroad line through Eagle Pass served not only the writer's expansionist beliefs but also her private interests. As the largest landholders in the area, the Cazneaus would have profited handsomely from the resulting economic boom (46–47, 179–183; see also Kerrigan 278). To realize these opportunities, *Eagle Pass* strongly seeks to tone down the widespread fear among political opponents of slavery in the United States that the annexation of Mexican territory would extend the reach of the peculiar institution and thus benefit the economy and political power of the slaveholding American South (97, 140–141). As Linda Hudson argues, Cazneau advocated gradual Black emancipation and supported the right of individual states to decide whether to maintain or abolish slavery (2, 119–120). Yet numerous passages of her writings endorse the institution. By pointing out the suitability of the Texas coastal area for cotton cultivation and sugar growing and by claiming that slavery was more lenient there than in other southern states, Cazneau's travelogues reach out simultaneously to both anti- and proslavery readers (*Texas* 15–16, 91, 100–101; *Eagle Pass* 12, 32), a strategy that Marilyn McAdams Sibley overlooks in her discussion of the topic (Sibley 133–134). *Eagle Pass* further reiterates the widespread racist evolutionary view that African Americans were at a lower stage of intellectual and cultural development than other races, which, therefore, destined them to serve "superior" civilizations. "A negro nation has never attained eminence since the birth of history," the volume maintains through the voice of a white Texan. None of them "ever made an important invention . . . , neither has mankind ever found among them a great teacher, whether as prophet, legislator, or poet" (19).

Other passages of Cazneau's writings explicitly target abolitionism. Drawing on a common defense of the peculiar institution, *Eagle Pass* presents slavery as a natural phenomenon of geography and climate as much as a social institution. It argues that a (possibly fictitious) Anglo traveler from Pennsylvania opposed the peculiar institution "by the accident of his birth rather than for any other reason," since "apples and anti-slavery are the natural growth of his latitude; oranges and negro servitude demand a warmer climate." Tellingly named Mr. Grey, the traveler's "northern anti-slavery morality . . . softened and expanded in the warm rays of the southern sun" in the course of his journey through the American South (20). Since it provides a "natural" explanation for the changing attitude of the traveler that neither criticizes his original position nor his subsequent views, *Eagle Pass* defends southern slavery while reaching out to northern readers who oppose it. This strategy becomes particularly obvious through the figure of Mr. Grey's British traveling companion, whom the narrator characterizes as a stubborn radical. "He will never change his point of view," she remarks. "At all costs and by whatever way he desires instant emancipation and the most perfect equality for the blacks in marriage relations, social influence, and political rights" (20). The narrator mocks the Englishman's reasoning as being "so profound, so logical, and so philanthropic that [William Ellery] Channing, had he heard it, would have hailed him as a disciple, and Frederick Douglass as a brother" (29). By placing him alongside a prominent British critic of slavery and an even more renowned African American abolitionist, Cazneau's volume discredits the foreign traveler as alien to American culture and hence unfit to judge it properly. By invoking the specters of interracial marriage and African American usurpation of power, the narrative not only denounces immediate Black emancipation as a threat to white America but also points to a blind spot of US opponents of slavery. Like their southern peers, many white northerners, fearing the loss of Anglo-Saxon superiority through miscegenation and African American voting, rejected the idea of Black equality in American society (Caughfield 112; Kerrigan 294).

To avoid this peril yet allow for eventual emancipation, *Eagle Pass* advocates settling free African Americans in Africa. The volume assures its white target readers of the beneficence of such a plan: "Colonization opens to [Black Americans] wealth, country, and distinction. . . . It is well to free one African slave; it is better to raise a hundred to the elevation of self-government, and make them a beacon-light before the race" (135, 138). With this line of reasoning, Cazneau's book contributes to the colonial political imaginaries circulating in American social discourses at the time. As Amy Kaplan points out, projects to plant African American colonies in Africa played a dual role in US political discourse in the 1850s: "to expel blacks to a separate national sphere, and to expand US power through the civilizing process" (36). Since settling African Americans in Africa promised to remove not only slavery but also the former slaves from the United States, "colonization offered a respectable, elitist solution to racial problems," William Huntzicker observes (62).

According to William Kerrigan, Cazneau sought to bolster her antiabolitionist argument, as she "quite unsuccessfully attempted to foster a new moral crusade . . . that would complement rather than stifle Southwestern expansion" (295). Published only a few months after the appearance of *Uncle Tom's Cabin*, in 1852, Eagle Pass sought to counter the popular impact of Stowe's novel by arousing a similar sympathy among American readers for the plight of Mexican peons (Hudson 117–118; Kerrigan 279, 295, 299). Characteristic of women's writings on political topics in the nineteenth century, Amy Greenberg observes, Cazneau used the rhetoric of female domesticity to make her case. "Focus[ing] on the horrors that debt peonage wrought on families" (226), Cazneau's narrative depicts this practice as resembling American slavery. Peonage appears here as an often-inherited condition of unfree labor in dire poverty, whose victims suffered whippings and being treated like "beasts of burden." Moreover, the travelogue employs the terms "slaves" and "slavery" to describe peons and their servitude (*Eagle Pass* 184, 38–39, 62–63). The text argues that this system of bondage was "more deadly and blighting than African slavery" and reproaches American politicians for ignoring it when praising Mexico's antislavery laws as a "bright model of pure liberty" (95, 62).

To establish Mexican peonage as a social scourge comparable to American slavery, *Eagle Pass* goes beyond deploring its presence in the neighboring republic. Though debt servitude is "new and alien to the sentiment of the United States," the book cautions that it "may take root, acclimate itself, and flourish on our soil, as is said of certain noxious insects with which the old world has gifted our grain fields" (32). By employing the analogy of a devouring pest introduced to the New World by European colonizers, the volume depicts peonage as jeopardizing the health of America and the wealth of its territory. The specific threat that Cazneau's travelogue sought to mobilize its American readers against was the abduction of escaped Mexican peons living in Texas and their repatriation into bondage in Mexico. Supported by several stories from the Eagle Pass area, the text claims that such kidnappings were frequent along the Rio Grande (37–39, 59–60, 80–86), a fact that other observers, such as Frederick Law Olmsted, did not verify (Olmsted 334). *Eagle Pass* reproaches President Fillmore and Congress for their failure to act to stop the practice and appeals to readers' patriotic urge to protect American sovereignty. "The interests of humanity and the honor of the country are utterly neglected on the Rio Bravo frontier," the preface states. A later passage calls these abductions "cowardly, cruel, and defiant of our laws," as well as "a daring insult to our flag" that represented acts of foreign "invasion" of the United States (*Eagle Pass* v, 80). To overcome readers' likely indifference to the fate of poor Mexicans and Natives, Cazneau highlights the impact of debt servitude on fair-skinned people. Drawing on Anglo-American anxieties about defenseless whites in "savage" bondage, she alerts her audiences that "the most delicate white lady, the fairest child of promise may be dragged down to [servitude] on the first cloud of misfortune" (131). As William Kerrigan observes, this passage seeks "to marshal sympathy by exploiting the whiteness of these victims, and thereby suggests that peonage was a more profound tragedy for whites than for mestizos and Indians" (298).

This view ties in with Cazneau's ambivalent portrayal of Mexicans. In line with hegemonic Anglo-American views, both *Texas and Her Presidents* and *Eagle Pass* identify sluggishness, fatalism, and improvidence as the key traits of the Mexican national character. The texts scorn the country's debased political and military elite and portray Mexican Catholicism as an "adulterous" union of church and state that exploited the devout poor (*Texas* 18, 21, 28, 57; *Eagle Pass* 96–97, 106–107, 150, 183–187; see also Myres, *Westering* 75). The two volumes moreover point out that miscegenation was common in Mexico (*Texas* 17; *Eagle Pass* 137–140), a claim that *Eagle Pass*, like other American or German travelogues, underlines by Orientalizing the Mexicans as "cousins" of the Arabs (53). Yet like many other members of the Young America movement, Cazneau based her US expansionist political agenda on the belief that in contrast to Blacks, Mexicans and Amerindians were able to assimilate to Anglo-American culture (Kerrigan 291, 299–300). *Eagle Pass* emphasizes the strong family ties, the "patience, endurance, and abstemiousness," and the loyalty to Anglo-Americans of the largely indigenous Mexicans on both sides of the Rio Grande (67). Echoing, among others, Mary Holley's travelogues, the volume frames the Mexicans as children who require

Anglo tutelage (56). It thus reiterates a popular discursive trope of infantilizing colonized populations, which served to justify the American policy of expanding its territory and political sphere of influence (Kaplan 32).

A similar ambivalence characterizes Cazneau's portrayal of the indigenous nations of Texas and the Mexican border region. Speaking of them in relatively benevolent terms as "Indians," "red men," "Native Americans," or "the Red Race," she follows the established distinction that travelers to Texas made between "friendly" and "hostile" tribes, depending on their way of life and relations with whites. Yet her view of them was equally informed by her conviction that the Amerindians had both the ambition and ability to uplift themselves from their "savage" state and acquire "civilization" by assimilating to American culture (*Eagle Pass* 42, 136–138, 169; see also Caughfield 29–30). Her Texas narratives prominently discuss the indigenous nations in order to counter abolitionist arguments and to criticize US policy toward Natives. The single Amerindian nation that Cazneau addresses at length in her narratives is the Seminoles, a band of whom resided on both sides of the Rio Grande near the settlement of Eagle Pass. Cazneau's *Eagle Pass* emphasizes, above all, their cultural differences from both Anglos and Mexicans, and it does this through images of ethnic mixing and eclectic clothing. The Seminole band included people of "all ages, sexes and sizes of negroes," who dressed in a "mixed array of army and barbaric gear" (73–74). The text's portrayal of their chief, Wild Cat, voices an ambivalent respect for this legendary indigenous leader. The chief and his African American and Arab interpreters appear as representatives of "plundered Asia, enslaved Africa, and martyred America." Cazneau's book depicts Wild Cat as a shrewd warrior with a penchant for colorful dress, as self-controlled but also restless, as desirous to show his loyalty yet not fully trustworthy (74–77, 143–145). At the same time, *Eagle Pass* never mentions that the Black Seminoles who formed part of the tribe were a maroon band descended from escaped American slaves and that Wild Cat's African American translator, John Horse, was their chief. Like many other Anglo-Americans, Cazneau likely opposed the presence of a maroon colony in the Texas-Mexico border region for fear that it could attract runaway slaves (Kerrigan 283, 291–292). Therefore, mentioning the Black Seminoles would have endangered her goal of luring prospective white settlers to Eagle Pass.

Although *Eagle Pass* recognizes the efforts of the Seminoles to gain the trust and esteem of the Anglo-Texans (143–145), both of Cazneau's travelogues express profound mistrust of all Amerindians. *Texas and Her Presidents* acknowledges the history of whites' mistreatment of Natives but nonetheless criticizes the lenience of Sam Houston's administration toward them. "The suspicious and blood-loving Indian mistrusts the white race," the narrator argues. "The traditions of three centuries of wrong and strife, are not washed away . . . The red men do not reciprocate, as yet, the loving kindness of the Texian government" (82). Like other journey narratives of Texas, *Eagle Pass* identifies the Comanches as the most hostile indigenous nation, whose ongoing raids threatened white settlement and economic development in the Texas-Mexico border region. To both make her case and assure readers that she was not transgressing her prescribed gender role through a political critique, the narrator uses an image of extreme violence that contains all ingredients of white anxiety about ethnic and cultural alterity: "The country is abandoned to the Indians, who press their depredations up to the very precincts of our [army] posts, leading their trains of stolen horses and captive women, and slaughtering the herds of our citizens within hearing of the drums of our posts, and those posts . . . are carelessly left without the means of repressing the savages. The citizens themselves are liable to be carried by violence from their homes and sold for debt in Mexico" (118). It is noteworthy that this passage and related ones do not linger on such raids primarily to convey the presumed "savagery" of the Comanches and thereby justify their elimination. Instead, they seek to display the inability of the understaffed US frontier army to protect settlers, in order to highlight the federal government's neglect of the southwestern periphery and to call for a policy change (45–46, 119, 151–153; see also Sibley 83–84).

In contrast to this scene, other passages in *Eagle Pass* rather downplay the Native threat so as to render the border region attractive to white settlers. They explain indigenous raids as a response to ongoing white encroachments on Amerindian ancestral lands. Strikingly echoing the crimes of the Comanches just cited, the narrator confesses, "We have slaughtered the red race, driven them from their groves, [and] buried their history and traditions in the graves of a hundred exterminated tribes" (32). But this admission did not imply a call for restricting white settlements. On the contrary, since Cazneau believed indigenous nations did not "improve" automatically through contact with whites, she maintains that Anglo-Americans had to take care of a population whose destruction they had brought about by their colonization of North America: "We owe something very different to the Indians on our borders from the mockery of gifts . . . of rum to destroy [and] treaties that covered their sure destruction with specious promises of peace and protection" (120).

Like several other Texas travelogues, Cazneau's narratives outline a model for this white tutelage of the Amerindians. *Eagle Pass* praises the Spanish colonial mission system for having subjugated and "civilized" the indigenous nations of the Americas through Christianization and education. The book undermines Anglo-Protestant readers' potential rejection of Catholicism by framing the indigenous belief systems of Texas Natives as if they were sixteenth-century Aztecs, in keeping with whites' negative perceptions of Mesoamerican traditions. For having put an end to the "cannibal" practice of making human sacrifices on the altars of "grim, monster idols," the Spanish friars appear in a positive light (41, 44). Following Randolph Marcy and Ferdinand Roemer, who criticized the United States for not missionizing its indigenous populations, the narrator of *Eagle Pass* takes up the call: "We, who send two or three hundred thousand dollars a year to enlighten the heathen of Asia should not refuse a tithe of this aid to our heathen at home. The less so . . . , as we have deprived them of all things else and so hemmed them up in little barren corners of what was once their heritage, that they must accept civilization or death" (41). This passage hints at the final point of Cazneau's critique of US Indian policy: her rejection of the enforced Amerindian removal to allocated reservations. *Texas and Her Presidents* praises Texas president Sam Houston's attempts to undo white injustice against the indigenous nations by permitting several of them to return to their ancestral lands (82). *Eagle Pass* labels the violent Amerindian relocations "a blot on the very name of Christianity" and an "inexorable system of despoilment and extermination" (v). By dressing her political argument in a moral-religious discourse considered compatible with female domesticity, Cazneau once again not only appeals to her readers' sense of civilizing mission but also elicits their support for a political cause.

Eagle Pass calls its titular settlement a "young island of civilization" (64), a budding utopia reminiscent of Mary Holley's framing of Austin's colony in the mold of Thomas More's fictional isle. Cazneau's travelogue points out a clear, race-based social stratification among the residents of Eagle Pass, yet paints an idyllic picture of a harmonious and thriving community (10, 94–95, 118–119, 167–168; see also Kerrigan 288–289). The book's depiction of the town is geared to attract Anglo-American settlers. In so doing, it strikingly deviates from the more critical—yet only partly more accurate—perceptions of this border settlement found in other journey accounts of the period, which describe a desolate and dangerous place. Whereas Frederick Law Olmsted's Texas travelogue counts only the small Anglo minority as "full" members of the settlement (Olmsted 315, 317–318), Cazneau's *Eagle Pass* encompasses a racially integrated community of the diligent and welcomes Anglos, Mexicans, and Amerindians as almost equal members. In so doing, it reaches beyond the agenda and discursive justification of Anglo colonization and the expansion of slavery in the indigenous and Mexican contact zones of the North American West articulated in *Texas and Her Presidents*. As William Kerrigan argues, "rather than dismiss Cazneau's pleasant description of Eagle Pass as a willful distortion of reality, it is perhaps more accurate to understand *Eagle Pass* as a reflection of her hopes and expectations for the community" (288), a place where she sought to put the agenda of her earlier book into practice.

FREDERICK LAW OLMSTED'S *A JOURNEY THROUGH TEXAS*

Frederick Olmsted (1822–1903) is best known today as a landscape designer, but before embarking on that career, he worked as a journalist. Born and raised in Connecticut, he studied engineering and science in New England. Beginning in the late 1840s, he wrote for agricultural and general-interest periodicals. His account of a trip through the British Isles in 1850, *Walks and Talks of an American Farmer in England* (1852), won him instant acclaim as well as a commission from the *New York Daily Times* to travel through the southern United States and report on the region's society and economy and the impact of slavery on them. From December 1852 through August 1854, Olmsted undertook two journeys through the South. He published his observations and experiences in sixty-three almost weekly letters to the *Times* and ten letters to the *New York Tribune*. After his return to New York, he collected them into a trilogy of travelogues: *A Journey in the Seaboard Slave States, with Remarks on Their Economy* (1856), *A Journey through Texas, Or: A Saddle-Trip on the South-Western Frontier* (1857), and *A Journey in the Back Country* (1860). Owing to their popular and critical recognition, he compiled the three books into an abridged, single-volume edition, *The Cotton Kingdom: A Traveller's Observation on Cotton and Slavery in the American Slave States* (Rybczynski; Beveridge 1–12, 19–35; Cox). These books also show how his experiences in the American South radicalized Olmsted's rejection of slavery. After his return to the East Coast, he actively supported the Free-Soil Movement in Kansas and the antislavery activism of German Texans (Beveridge and McLaughlin 314–321, 397–405, 431–451).

Accompanied by his brother John, Olmstead left New York for Texas on November 10, 1853, entered the Lone Star State at Gaines Ferry on the Sabine River a few days before Christmas, and reached Nacogdoches a week later. From January 9 through 14, 1854, the Olmsteds stayed in Austin before going to San Antonio. From there they undertook trips to the Gulf Coast, the Hill Country, and the Rio Grande region, with a brief excursion to Mexico. On April 24, the brothers began their return journey. While John sailed to New York from New Orleans, Frederick continued on horseback before boarding a ship in Virginia, which brought him home on August 2, 1854 (Beveridge and McLaughlin 471–482; Rybczynski 124–126, 131–132). Olmsted's original articles from Texas appeared as "A Tour in the Southwest" from March 6 through June 7, 1854, in the *New York Daily Times* (Beveridge 11; Beveridge and McLaughlin 460–461). Three years later, Olmsted published *A Journey through Texas*. Largely compiled by John Olmsted from his brother's notes and published articles, the volume consists of six chronological chapters charting the brothers' journey, along with an introduction and two systematic chapters (Beveridge 11–12, 17, 26; Rybczynski 146). The book informs readers about topography, flora and fauna, agriculture, weather and climate, infrastructure, settlements, and population groups.

As Witold Rybczynski remarks, Olmsted "was a perceptive observer" who cleverly made his point by blending descriptive passages with anecdotes, dialogues, and data. His recording of people's speech, including slang, dialect, and grammatical errors, "gives his reporting a lively, novelistic immediacy" (99, 123). References to nature and to works of literature or art from different continents that were likely to be known to educated New York readers familiarized the book's target audience with the alien landscapes, settlements, and population characteristics of Texas (Olmsted 69, 98, 131, 275). At times, the text recycles popular analogies such as Randolph Marcy's comparing the Llano Estacado to the Asian steppe, or a frontier town's main street to New York's Broadway (142, 448). To support his arguments, the narrator quotes from scholarly works on and travelogues of the Lone Star State, including writings by Jane Cazneau, William Parker, and US boundary commissioner John Russell Bartlett. The book further provides an appendix with historical and statistical tables and documents (315, 422–423, 442, 459–516). Although he presents himself in his journey account as an "impartial recorder of events and attitudes," John Cox argues that Olmsted was always a partisan commentator on the institution of Black slavery in the American South (146). Signing his articles for the *Times* with the pen name "Yeoman" indicates his identification with the American cultural-economic ideal of the family farmer who works his own land (Beveridge 7; Cox 144). Similarly, the introduction to *A Journey through Texas*, titled "A Letter to a Southern Friend" and addressed to an unidentified southerner, uses the format of seemingly private correspondence to articulate his views. According to Witold Rybczynski, "the literary device . . . underlin[es] Olmsted's sympathy for Southerners," which, in turn, endows his critique of slavery with greater weight (146).

Like almost all travelers, Olmsted assesses Texas with a combination of utilitarian discourse, focused on the state's agricultural and commercial potential, and an aesthetic outlook that applies categories of sensory perception in order to familiarize readers with an unknown landscape. Typical for migration-promoting journey accounts of the region such as Mary Holley's or Ferdinand Roemer's narratives, Olmsted's travelogue adheres to the English and American romanticist idea that human intervention improves nature. *A Journey through Texas* depicts vast "untouched" stretches of land, such as dense woods or treeless prairies, as hostile, intimidating environments. To convey their monotony or the peril of getting lost in such terrain, the text repeatedly returns to striking images of an open sea, as in the following passage: "The groundswells were long and equal in height and similar in form as to bring to mind a tedious sea voyage" (Olmsted 147). In contrast, a varied and "tamed" smaller-scale landscape provides pleasurable experiences for the narrator, who employs a discourse of the beautiful or picturesque to describe such scenery. For example, echoing Roemer's travelogue, Olmsted's volume compares the vicinity of San Antonio to an English landscape garden: "[Its] beauty is greatly increased by frequent groves of live-oak, elm, and hackberry.... In the elements of turf and foliage, and their disposition, no English park-scenery could surpass [it]" (278). Similarly, this time recalling Stephen Austin's or Mary Holley's accounts, *A Journey through Texas* captures the economic prospects of the region in an image of idyllic scenery: "With ... a gentle slope ... of soil matched in any known equal area, and a climate tempered for either work or balmy enjoyment, Texas has an Arcadian preeminence of position among our States, and an opulent future before her" (357, 412, 411).

In addition to agricultural utility and aesthetic impressions, Olmsted's narrative looks for indicators of "civilization," namely, well-kept dwellings and cultivated lands, in the Texas countryside. What rendered one landscape "more pleasing" than others was that "the houses were less rude, the negro-huts more comfortable, [and] the plantations altogether neater" (76). Above all, the text favorably views the well-kept gardens of German immigrants as a sign of a superior work ethic and domestic economy. Serving as evidence of what could be accomplished by yeoman farmers' diligence and free labor (140–143, 157, 281), they offered an economic alternative to the largely slavery-based Anglo agriculture. Labor and economic development were, indeed, the central lenses through which Olmsted looked at the peculiar institution. Although he shows awareness of its moral ills (92), the journalist sought to inspire social change via the economic transformation of the US South. Accordingly, his travelogues urge the ending of slavery for its inefficiency and corrupting force, which hindered the advancement of the South's society and economy (Beveridge 13–16, 33–35; Cox 141–164).

The texts do not blame slaves' lack of diligence and the poor agricultural production of plantations on the "natural indolence" of African Americans but on the institution of slavery itself (Cox 153–154, 162; Rybczynski 117). Slaves "were the laziest things in creation," a slaveholder exclaims in *A Journey through Texas*, because "their time isn't any value to themselves" (Olmsted 120–121). Elsewhere, the narrator criticizes the harsh regime imposed by many Texas slaveholders. He argues that, in contrast to the other southern states, where the peculiar institution had been entrenched for a long time, "in Texas ... there seemed to be the consciousness of a wrong relation and a determination to face conscience down, and continue it; to work up the [slaves], with a sole eye to selfish profit" (123). Moreover, he repeatedly mentions slave escapes across the Rio Grande in order to show the limits of coercion in a southwestern border state (257, 323–327, 331). The geographic proximity to Mexico, the text concludes, successfully prevented West Texas from becoming "a great enslaving planting country" akin to other parts of the region (136).

Although Olmsted's Texas journey account characterizes runaway slaves as "lawless and . . . very mischievous and desperate" (328), it pays respect to their courage and desire for freedom:

> The impulse must be a strong one, the tyranny extremely cruel, the irksomeness of slavery keenly irritating, or the longing for liberty much greater than is usually attributed to the African race, which induces a slave to attempt an escape to Mexico. . . . He faces all that is terrible to man for the chance of liberty. . . . I pity the man whose sympathies would not warm to a dog under these odds. How can they be held back from the slave who is driven to assert his claim to manhood? (326–327)

The passage validates the Black struggle for liberty by framing it as a fight against despotism, on the one hand, and as a striving for manhood—in the sense of humanness and agency, although the masculine gender connotation of the two is present here as well—on the other. Since the American Revolution, the act of fighting for freedom from tyranny had been constitutive of US national identity. Through the voices of a group of slave catchers, *A Journey through Texas* presents the common proslavery argument that African Americans could not survive without white guardianship and that they thus fared better in bondage than in freedom. "How much happier that fellow'd 'a' been, if he'd just stayed and done his duty," one of the men says about a fugitive slave. "His master'd 'a' taken care of him. . . . Now, very likely, he'll starve to death, or get shot" (257). Another passage counters this line of reasoning by pointing out the intellectual capacities of slaves, intelligence being widely considered a prerequisite for liberty. "That which makes slavery possible at all [is] the want of sufficient intelligence and manliness: Enlighten the slave and slavery will end." The narrator further argues that true freedom entailed social agency in addition to physical liberty: "Even the miserable sort of liberty possessed by a laboring man in Mexico is, probably, more favorable to the development of manliness, than that nominal liberty meanly doled in most of our northern states to the African race" (335, 339).

Despite his critique of slavery, Olmsted, like most northerners and foreign visitors to the southern United States (Lockard xviii), did not advocate the equality of Blacks and whites. Although African American individuals thrived in freedom, he argues, Blacks as a whole required white guidance in order to adapt to life in liberty (Olmsted 339; see also Honeck 59–60). According to Joe Lockard, acknowledging the human equality of African Americans would have necessitated questioning US society, which had been based on Black bondage and exploitation since the early colonial period (xxiii–xxv). This critical failure becomes manifest in Olmsted's principal concern about slavery, namely, its negative impact on the development of white civilization (Olmsted 517, 529; see also Cox 154; Honeck 47, 59–60). As John Cox points out, like the writers of American and European travelogues seeking to bring white settlement and trade to Texas, Olmsted belonged to the "capitalist vanguard" of visitors who promoted a rationalized free-market economy across the Americas on behalf of European or US capital (17, 161, 164). Mary Louise Pratt adds, "Ideologically, the vanguard's task [was] to reinvent America [i.e., the Americas] as backward and neglected, to encode its non-capitalist landscape and societies as manifest in need of ... rationalized exploitation" (148–149). For Olmsted, the US South was this "America" in need of reinvention, and his area of reference was New England. *A Journey through Texas* frequently laments the rough manners of Anglo-Texans, their rugged individualism, unwillingness to work, and disregard for education. Farmers were "too lazy to milk" their cows, inns were badly kept, and children grew up "silly, rude, illiterate, and stupid" (Olmsted 118, 111, 369). Above all, slave owners used their entire surplus to "buy *more negroes* and enlarge their plantations" (51, original emphasis). The text attributes the condition of white society in Texas to the corrupting impact of the peculiar institution. Since it stimulated egotism instead of community spirit and "degrade[d] labor" by associating manual work with slaves, "an active intellectual life, and desire for knowledge and improvements among the masses of the people, like that which distinguishes the New-Englanders, ... is unknown" where slavery prevails (179; see also Cox 154).

Since New England served as the antithesis of the slaveholding American South, it is no surprise that *A Journey through Texas* especially criticizes the white northern or European settlers who moved from abolitionism to a defense of slavery after relocating to Texas. Following popular thought of the time (Sibley 148), a passage of the text implies that integrating into a society based on slavery debased these migrants: "Northern people, when they come to the South, have less feeling for the negroes than Southerners themselves usually have" (Olmsted 119). Besides expressing disdain for people who "gave away" the antislavery cause, this critique articulates a typically northern white uneasiness with close contacts between the races in the southern United States (Cox 160; Sibley 146–147). *A Journey through Texas* particularly exposes the hypocrisy entailed in moral justifications of slavery based on the extended kinship of slave owners' families, whose white tutelage aided the slaves. Even "many cultivated, agreeable, and talented persons," the narrator complains, "honestly and confidently believe the institution to be a beneficial one[,] gradually and surely making the negroes a civilized and a Christian people, and . . . that all the cruelty, or most of it, is a necessary part of the process (Olmsted 112–113).

Olmsted's journey narrative seeks to tone down northern readers' anxieties about a possible US annexation of Mexican territories as slave states by pointing out the unsuitability of the terrain for a slave-based plantation economy as well as the likely Mexican resistance to such enterprises (454–457). Nonetheless, *A Journey through Texas* contributes to the US colonial discourse of expansion into Mexican territory, since it justifies the Anglo-American colonization and annexation of Texas. Resorting to elements of the Texas Creation Myth, the narrator characterizes the region while it was under Mexican rule as "idle lands" to which the Anglo settlers brought "wonderful progress." As they "subdued the lands, the savages, and . . . the impertinent Spaniards," they "asserted[ed] their natural rights as the smartest [population] to the highest and fairest inheritance." Moreover, the travelogue draws on the political ideology of Manifest Destiny to defend the Anglo colonists' only superficial conversion to Catholicism and their circumventing of Mexico's antislavery laws as "stratagems likely to occur in the progress of any nation before its destiny has become sufficiently manifest to warrant the blunt use of force" (408–409).

Particularly in the passages on Anglo settlers' westward movement in the Lone Star State, the narrator sketches a distinctly western frontier culture, which was removed even further from his ideal of New England civic society than from the American South: "In the rapid settlement of the country, many an adventurer crossed the border, spurred by a love of liberty, forfeited at home, rather than drawn by the love of adventure or of rich soil." *A Journey through Texas* thus affirms the widely purported lawlessness of early Anglo-Texans (124). More recently established settlements such as Eagle Pass, the budding utopia of Jane Cazneau's travelogue, similarly thrived primarily on the vicious triad of gambling, drinking, and smuggling contraband, according to Olmsted (317–318). He exempts only the army officers stationed in Texas from his critique. "We found our hosts gentlemen of spirit and education, preserving on the rough and lazy border the cultivation belonging to a more brilliant position," he remarks about a visit to an army post (286). Yet, the positive role of the army was marred, in his eyes, by its inability to protect white settlements in Texas against Native raids (285, 298–299).

Indeed, the ongoing conflicts between settlers and Amerindians in the Lone Star State were another matter of the journalist's concern. *A Journey through Texas* always refers to the indigenous people as "Indians" or by their names, and it distinguishes between "semi-civilized" and "wandering tribes" (296). The text mentions the friendly relations between Natives and German immigrants, and admits that Anglo Americans' violent removal of indigenous nations from their ancestral lands had justifiably aroused Native hatred (176, 202, 296–297, 353). More prominently, however, the book resorts to stereotypes of the indigenous nations as postcontact "degenerate Indians"—notorious thieves, drunkards, and beggars whose coarse features "revealed" their vices (273, 290–295, 345). The narrator poignantly articulates their presumed "animalistic" character as he calls the Natives "red wolves" whose "young, like those of other animals, can be caught and tamed." He similarly conveys the violence of their conflicts with white settlers when he states, "A swarm of these vagabonds . . . [was] loose again upon the settlements, scalping, kidnapping, and throat-cutting" (297–298, 289–290). By framing the indigenous nations as wild beasts and dangerous predators, he belittles and naturalizes their enforced removal and genocide at the hands of white settlers and soldiers.

Other passages of Olmsted's volume take up this view. The writer aligns himself with his fellow journalist Jane Cazneau in proposing the Spanish colonial missions of Latin America as a suitable model for pacifying the indigenous nations of the region. "The Jesuit mission-farms are an example for us," he remarks. "Our neighborly responsibility for these Lipans is certainly closer than those for [the Fijians], and if the glory of converting them to decency be less, the expense would certainly be in proportion" (298). Like the travelogues by Cazneau, Randolph Marcy, and Ferdinand Roemer, *Journey through Texas* appeals to readers who endorsed missionary labor among foreign nations to elicit their support for similar "civilizing missions" among the indigenous population of the United States. The volume, also echoing the journey accounts of Mexican military explorers as well as the Anglo writer Teresa Vielé, especially praises the labor of Spanish colonial missionaries among the Texas Natives: "The old Spanish fathers . . . pushed off alone into the heart of a savage and unknown country, converted the cruel brutes that occupied it, not only to nominal Christianity, but to actual hard labor, and persuaded and compelled them to construct these ponderous but rudely splendid edifices, serving, at the same time, for the glory of the faith, and for the defense of the faithful" (154). This scene strikingly echoes the narrator's depiction of the Anglo colonization of Texas, emphasizing the act of subjugating a wild terrain and its equally ferocious indigenous inhabitants. This passage thus frames the Spanish missionary efforts in the mold of the colonizing work of (subsequent) Anglo settlers, and as a model for future US Indian policy. In so doing, it validates the discourse and practice of American westward territorial expansion, including mandatory Native subjugation, removal, or assimilation.

As David Montejano observes, Olmsted's travelogue "touched on the significance of the Mexican War and annexation for the Mexican settlements" (11). *A Journey through Texas* recognizes the kindness, hospitality, faith, and strong family ties of the Tejanos and criticizes Anglo settlers for taking unfair advantage of them (Olmsted 161–163, 264–266, 455). Yet the volume reiterates the Black Legend–inspired Anglo cliché of Mexicans as ignorant and unambitious, yet simultaneously cruel, "bigoted, childish, and passionate" (456), and details their purported inclination to vice in a manner that casts doubt on their capacity for reason and self-governance (126–127, 159, 265, 268). Similarly, the narrator sums up the prospects of the Mexican Texans in an equally patronizing manner, which unmasks his ethnocultural bias. Most prominently, he concludes, "they make . . . docile and patient laborers, and, by dint of education and suitable management, are not incapable of being elevated into a class that shall occupy a valuable position in the development of the resources of the region" (162, 427). *A Journey through Texas* further downplays the historical continuity of Spanish and Mexican culture in Texas. The book asserts that the Spanish missions were "beyond any connection with the present—weird remains of the silent past," and while it sketches the Spanish Catholic colonial missionaries as heroic, it deplores the fact that the Mexicans of Olmsted's time were "under control of their Church" (155, 427).

As was common in the racialist discourse of the time, the travelogue indigenizes the Tejanos in their physical appearance, dress, and behavior in order to convey their ethnocultural alterity and presumed inferiority to Anglo-Americans. For instance, in Nacogdoches the narrator watches "two or three [Mexicans], wrapped in blankets and *serapes* . . . leaning against posts, and looking on in grand decay" (78). Tejano families in San Antonio were "made up of black-eyed, olive girls, full of animation of tongue and glance, but sunk in a soft embonpoint"; by contrast, "the matrons [were] dark and wrinkled" (151–152). Another passage frames the Mexican Texans as a "naturally" debased mixture of Spanish, Amerindian, and African origins to justify their increasing marginalization in postannexation Texas: "The Mexican masses are vaguely considered as degenerate and degraded Spaniards; it is, at least, equally correct to think of them as improved and Christianized Indians. In their tastes and social instincts, they approximate the African. . . . There are many Mexicans of mixed negro blood" (454–455).

The less constrained interracial interactions and the intertwined race- and class-based hierarchies in Mexican society raised special anxieties among the supporters of African American slavery. Through the voice of another white traveler, *A Journey through Texas* captures their concern about "the danger to slavery in the West by the fraternizing of the blacks with the Mexicans," since the former "helped [the latter] in all their bad habits, married them, stole a living from them, and ran off every day to Mexico" (65). The volume confirms these fears by providing examples of unbiased Mexican behavior toward Blacks (163, 230, 323–325, 427). In Mexico "there are thousands in respectable social positions whose color and physiognomy would subject them, in Texas, to be sold by the sheriff as negro-astrays who cannot be allowed at large without detriment to the commonwealth" (455). Elsewhere Olmsted's journey account points out how the Texas Anglos used the entangled categories of race and nation to take unfair advantage of Mexican Texans in business matters and to repudiate Tejano rights (265, 272). "White folks and Mexicans were never made to live together . . . , and the Mexicans had no business here," a planter's wife exclaims in the text (245). By categorizing Tejanos as Mexicans and as people of color, Anglo-Texans disavowed the Mexican Texans' US citizenship and historical presence in the region. In so doing, they justified denying Tejano land rights.

The traveler notes how German immigrants in San Antonio resisted Anglo efforts to expel large parts of the town's Mexican residents (Olmsted 164; see also Montejano 28–29). In writing about this population, Mischa Honeck observes, Olmsted "repeatedly crossed the line between ethnography and political journalism, helping to disseminate the myth of a German Texan population unanimously opposed to slavery" (42; see also Struve 76). The journalist was impressed particularly by a community of Forty-Eighters (supporters of the revolutions in Europe in 1848) he encountered near Sisterdale in Central Texas. In *A Journey through Texas*, he romanticizes these German intellectual farmers and exiles and presents them as a foil to the Anglo-Texan planters. The latter abused their freedom to cultivate "aristocratic" idleness yet often lacked cultural refinement. The former, in contrast, gave up their country rather than their freedom and happily upheld German high culture in the Texas wilderness (Olmsted 191–200, 202, 429–430). *A Journey through Texas* frames not only the Forty-Eighters but also the region's entire German community in striking contrast to the Anglo-Texans to demonstrate how free-labor capitalism and communitarianism enabled a slavery-free economy in the Lone Star State. In depicting thriving German yeoman farmers, the text seeks to demonstrate the profitability of free white labor in the region and particularly renounces the proslavery theory of climate, according to which only people of African descent could perform heavy physical work in the Texas summer heat (182, 198–199, 359; see also Sibley 141–142). Drawing on writings of the German political émigrés Friedrich Kapp and August Siemering, the volume critically reviews the activities of the Society for the Protection of German Emigrants to Texas, whose naïveté in business matters "carried many emigrants only to beggary and miserable death" (174; see also Honeck 52, 195n34).

Olmsted's travelogue further points to the economic success of German immigrants to prove the superiority of their ethic of hard work, enterprising spirit, democratic and antislavery persuasion, communitarianism, and regard for education (139–147, 177–190, 202–203, 429–433). A crucial way in which the Germans' civilization manifested itself to the Anglo traveler was their thriving towns and well-kept homes. For example, a description of New Braunfels indulges in clichés of German industry and homeliness: "The main street of the town . . .

was . . . three times as wide . . . as Broadway in New York. The houses . . . were small, low cottages of no pretensions, yet generally looking neat and comfortable. Many were furnished with verandas and gardens, and the greater part were either stuccoed or painted. There were many workshops of mechanics and small stores, . . . and . . . women and men . . . were seen everywhere at work" (142–143). Like Olmsted's model population, the New Englanders, the Germans brought a degree of "civic improvement" to the Lone Star State, which *A Journey through Texas* found lacking in the slavery-based Anglo civilization in the region.

But Olmsted's overwhelmingly positive impression of the Texas Germans is marred by their lack of politicization (except for the Forty-Eighters) and by his prejudices against their Jewish members. Although he admits to "know of no other spot in a Southern state . . . where the relative advantages of slave labor can be even discussed in peace," he voices his disappointment with the indifference of many Germans to the presence of slavery around them: "Few of them concern themselves with the theoretical right or wrong of the institution, and while it does not interfere with their own liberty or progress, are careless of its existence" (202, 432). With even greater disdain, he claims that German Jewish immigrants endorsed slavery. Rather than explaining his assumptions or attempting to identify a rational cause for their attitude, he resorts to the anti-Semitic stereotype of the ruthlessly money-driven Jew: "In Texas, the Jews, as everywhere else, speculate in everything—in popular sympathies, prejudices, and bigotries, in politics, in slavery" (329). Although his references to the Jews are brief, they demonstrate how the writer's ethnocultural biases informed his judgment. Just as he rejects both the equality of African Americans and their enslavement, Olmsted ignores the motives of Jewish migration to Texas while acknowledging the desire of their Christian peers to obtain economic improvement or political freedom through migration. Although he criticizes the project of extending Anglo-American culture to the indigenous and Mexican periphery of the nation-state, such instances reveal how much the journalist's travelogue is indebted to the idea of Anglo-Saxon superiority. The volume thus contributed to legitimizing an American colonial discourse about Texas that was soon to lead to the Lone Star State becoming a theater of the Civil War.

Like the officer's wife Teresa Vielé, Jane Cazneau was fundamentally concerned with mid-nineteenth-century American territorial expansion. According to Susan Roberson, "In Cazneau's hands, Manifest Destiny means liberation from oppression and poverty and not the imperialistic domination often associated with it" (159). Understanding herself as "a kind of missionary for American civilization" (Kerrigan 279), Cazneau envisioned the future of the US slave population as lying in the colonization of Africa. Such massive forced relocation would "solve" the problem of Black liberation and integration in the United States and would contribute to the country's increasingly imperial policy of extending its economic and political influence, in this case beyond the Western Hemisphere. In contrast to Cazneau, Frederick Law Olmsted in his travelogue unmasked the popular myth of a benign plantation regime in Texas, propaganda that was used to justify the extension of the peculiar institution to the Amerindian and Mexican contact zones. According to Broadus Mitchell, "No one understood better than Olmsted . . . that slavery was not only a system for the government of slaves under individual masters, but a system of colonization as well" (qtd. in Cox 151–152). Yet while his Texas travelogue wholeheartedly criticizes the colonial discourse and regime of African American slavery in the United States, the text never recognizes its structural parallels to the project of the country's westward territorial expansion, with its attendant agendas of Mexican and Amerindian subjugation, displacement, or coerced assimilation to Anglo culture.

Conclusion

This study analyzes narrative constructions of Texas as a geographic and social space from the de facto independence of Mexico, in 1821, to the beginning of the American Civil War, in 1861, in selected works of Mexican, Anglo-American, and German travel writing. Based on the premise that journey narratives about a given space actively contribute to the discursive construction of its landscapes and cultures, these case studies represent travel accounts written by members of three major nonindigenous ethnic groups that resided in Texas and undertook journeys through the region. This approach admittedly excludes the numerous indigenous nations of Texas as well as the largely enslaved Black population, whose living conditions hindered their contributing to this body of writing. Nonetheless, I argue that the trinational perspective provides a more complex picture than most previous scholarship on the cultural history of the region during the period in question. The present volume identifies some of the mechanisms of narrative constructions of ideas, places, and peoples. Examining accounts penned by a broad range of writers for distinct purposes and audiences, this study explores different subcategories of journey narratives to formulate a poetics of the travel genre and to render these texts and text types more readily amenable to further analysis.

The American, Mexican, and German travelogues about Texas written between 1821 and 1861 strongly vary in quantity, thematic scope, and purpose, depending on the author's ethnonational background and on the purpose of the journey depicted in each text. The few existing Mexican works are either official reports or private journals written by officers and civilians participating in two military-scientific expeditions deployed to the Mexican province of Texas during the late 1820s and early 1830s. In line with their authors' objective to assess the potential of the land for economic development, the state of Mexican and Anglo-American settlement, and the behavior of resident Native nations, the texts often view scientific and political matters through the lens of their writers' official missions. They participate in Mexico's ultimately failed colonial policy of settling Texas with Europeans and Anglo-Americans willing to integrate into Mexican society, subdue the Amerindians, and thwart US territorial claims to the province.

In contrast to the Mexicans, Germans wrote a large number of journey accounts about Texas. These texts first appeared in the 1830s, boomed in the following decade, and somewhat declined during the 1850s. They closely interacted with and contributed to the period's German migration wave to the region as well as the larger context of the national public debate about German overseas migration and colonization efforts. This body of writings thus was primarily concerned with the conditions and opportunities that Texas offered settlers from German-speaking lands. It evaluates not only the terrain but also the challenges of life in a foreign country and in the face of indigenous resistance to white settlement.

The Anglo-American corpus of travelogues about Texas differs from both the Mexican and the German journey accounts by covering a larger time frame as well as by encompassing a greater variety of text types, subject matters, and sociopolitical agendas. The texts cover the entire period of Mexican, independent, and antebellum American Texas. They represent all three subgenres of the travel genre analyzed here—scientific exploration accounts, migration-related travelogues, and journey narratives of itinerant professionals—and they share specific yet regularly interconnected concerns about exploring the land, settling it with white immigrants, and assimilating or displacing resident Mexican and indigenous populations. Accordingly, the opportunities that Texas offered to white settlers play a key role in most Anglo-authored travelogues. The texts hence contribute to the US colonial policy of westward territorial expansion and often seek to legitimize it by drawing on the ideology of Manifest Destiny. As part of this line of reasoning, most of the analyzed travelogues also endorse the coerced removal of Amerindian nations and the marginalization of Mexicans in Texas as a natural consequence of Anglo racial-cultural superiority and socioeconomic development. In contrast, the subject of Black slavery divided the writers, just as it would soon split the nation at large. While some texts reject the peculiar institution on either moral or economic grounds, others defend it in the name of progress.

This body of American journey accounts about Texas includes several texts by women too. According to Nina Baym, this group's western writings tend not only to emphasize the suitability of the region for colonization and to outline the personal and professional skills required for settlement but also to address the particular conditions and opportunities awaiting female colonists (12). Female travelers' mobility often put them at odds with the hegemonic social ideology of women's domesticity. To assert both their entitlement to travel and their authority as writers, these women commonly emphasized their adherence to the ideology of "Manifest Domesticity," their commitment to social (rather than economic or political) issues, and their humble calling to their causes by a higher power. As the missionary and educator Melinda Rankin aptly put it, "I feel sometimes like a wanderer and an exile, yet I console myself that I did not come to Texas for my own benefit, and the hope that I may do some little good, makes me bear my privations with fortitude."[1]

The hardships that Rankin alludes to here resulted largely from the difficulties of life and travel in a vast, sparsely settled territory with little infrastructure and an often-harsh climate. In their depiction of Texas as geographic space, almost all travelogues analyzed in the present study intertwine an aesthetic discourse with a utilitarian one and thus link a rational argument with an emotional appeal to their target audiences. They seek to convey to their readers the experience of the alien Texas landscape and to familiarize them with it by describing the terrain according to the romanticist aesthetic categories of the beautiful, the picturesque, and the sublime. The texts particularly evoke scenes of idyllic country life to present Texas as a desirable destination. At the same time, they assess the economic potential of the region for agriculture, manufacturing, and trade. Except for those travelogues that warn readers against migrating to Texas, the narratives aim to show the economic use that white settlers and capital investors can make of the land. Anglo-American journey accounts further argue that neither the indigenous nor the Mexican population of Texas had developed more than a mere subsistence economy, and this weakness justified the American colonial policy of appropriating land for Anglo-Saxon settlement, subjugating or removing Natives and Mexicans, and culturally assimilating other white residents and immigrants.

The travelogues' depictions of the population groups residing in Texas strongly depend on the ethnonational identity of the travelers and their target readers as well as on the purpose of the journeys. The texts largely reiterate their authors' individual and collective cultural self-perceptions and views of other societies, ethnicities and races, religious denominations, and social classes. Simultaneously, the writers' encounters with other cultures led, at best, to only minor corrections to popular stereotypes and preconceived opinions. Each writer tends to view his or her ethnic group more positively than others and to paint an ambivalent picture of those groups that they felt in competition with for political power, social status, or economic resources. Moreover, most of the travelogues ignore Black slavery in Texas, downplay its cruelty, or criticize it for economic rather than moral reasons. A strict ethnocultural hierarchy further marks their portrayals of the Amerindians of Texas. While their narratives ascribe some degree of civilization to those sedentary indigenous nations that were willing to assimilate to hegemonic Mexican or American culture, the writers present the resistance of nomadic nations to white land taking as a severe threat that, in their eyes, legitimized violent Native subjugation, removal, and genocide.

Formally, the travelogues of Texas examined here can be divided into three categories on the grounds of their thematic foci, intended readership, and language use. The military-scientific exploration reports were overwhelmingly penned on behalf of institutions sponsoring the expeditions depicted therein. The texts' views of Texas articulate the travelers' distinctive political, scholarly, economic, and strategic concerns. Accordingly, the language is largely scientific and based on careful observation of the natural and social phenomena they address. Unlike this body of writing, the Texas travelogues that either promoted or warned against migration to the region were strongly informed by their writers' economic involvement in colonization projects in the Lone Star State. The texts focusing on settlement in Texas targeted an audience of potential migrants from the authors' native countries or regions who were looking for information about suitable places of settlement. In contrast, the journey accounts written by itinerant professionals vary more widely in their key concerns and target audiences than the other types of travel narratives examined here. In addition, this body of texts provided white middle-class women with a public forum for voicing their observations, experiences, and concerns. In so doing, this text corpus legitimized, in tension with the prevailing ideology of female domesticity and submission, women's authority to address broad audiences on issues within the "male prerogative" of politics or the economy.

My study of American, Mexican, and German travelogues of Texas from 1821 to 1861 is situated at the intersection of transational US-American, Inter-American, and US-Mexico border studies, and takes a literary-critical approach to the study of colonialism and postcolonialism. Long before they formally became colonial powers in the late nineteenth century, Germany and the United States debated—and the United States carried out—the extension of their territories or the establishment of settler colonies abroad. Mexico similarly sought to strengthen its position toward the expanding United States by settling its northern border provinces with white colonists and by Mexicanizing the region's indigenous population. Arguing for the active role of narrative texts in acts of social and cultural meaning making, I analyzed how selected works of travel writing constructed Texas as a postcolonial colonial space. I showed how they contributed to colonial discourses and practices by documenting the Anglo-American, Mexican, and German involvement in colonization efforts in the Lone Star State and beyond.

The texts discussed here illuminate how individuals, institutions, and societies viewed scientific exploration, white migration and settlement, military intervention, religious mission, and the circulation of information. Many of the travelogues hint at the harshest consequences of their authors' activities, namely, the violent subjugation or removal of Native nations, the Anglo-Americanization of Texas, and the marginalization of Blacks, Mexicans, and—to a lower degree—European immigrants. In so doing, the travelogues provide a springboard for a critical reflection on colonial discourses and policies, and particularly on current tendencies. These include the ongoing structural discrimination against populations of color or "unwanted" immigrants in both North America and Europe, a coloniality of power informing political and economic relations between these regions and the Global South, and the often-ambivalent role of religious denominations, the military, and the media in spreading and securing ideas and ideologies. A comparison of the Texas travelogues with other political discourses and media representations of the time reveals the longevity and stability of stereotypical depictions of ethnoracial and cultural alterity, especially of those populations considered inferior to the travel writers. The analyzed journey accounts can thus teach us the need for a differentiated treatment of our cultures and vantage points as well as those of others as we strive to understand the way either position interacts with the causes, processes, and effects of exploration, migration, and knowledge formation.

Acknowledgments

Writing a monograph is a journey of its own. Pursuing the itinerary that has resulted in the present volume would not have been possible without the generous support I received from the individuals and institutions that I acknowledge here with gratitude. Primarily, I am indebted to my colleagues and friends at the Department of British and American Studies and the Center for Inter-American Studies at Bielefeld University, Germany. Wilfried Raussert in particular gave good advice and brought steady commitment to my work. A research grant from the German Research Foundation (project number 195040265) provided the financial resources for carrying out this project in Bielefeld. During two research stays, Mexico City and Austin, Texas, became temporary homes. In Mexico, Ana Rosa Suárez Argüello at the Instituto Mora and Graciela Martínez-Zalce at the Universidad Nacional Autónoma de México provided me with individual and institutional support. In Austin, the staff at the Dolph Briscoe Center for American History and those at other research libraries at the University of Texas helped me access materials, and Melissa Tothero was a more-than-generous host. Most recently, the Institute for Black Atlantic Research at the University of Central Lancashire, UK, has become a new and welcoming academic home. Collaborating with my editor at the University of Texas Press, Robert Devens, and his team has been a productive and gratifying experience. Apart from scholarly matters, the Inter-American soccer team at Bielefeld University gave me the chance—more than happily taken—to put the mobility paradigm into regular physical practice. Finally, family and friends offered true inspiration, helpful feedback, and encouragement, which allowed me to travel more than one road not taken and to continue doing so.

Earlier versions of parts of chapters 1, 4, and 5 have been published elsewhere, and I gratefully acknowledge the publishers' granting me republication rights. Parts of the section on the Mexican Comisión de Límites appeared in my essay "Mexican Travelers and the 'Texas Question,' 1821–1836," in *Hemispheric Encounters: The Early United States in a Transnational Perspective*, edited by Gabriele Pisarz-Ramírez and Markus Heide (Frankfurt/Main: Peter Lang, 2016), 117–132. Passages on the German travelogues were included in my "From Göttingen to Galveston: Travel Writing and German Migration to Texas, 1830–1848," in *Migration in Context: Literature, Culture, and Language*, edited by Marcus Hartner and Marion Schulte (Bielefeld: Aisthesis, 2016), 135–151, and in my "Prairie Promises, Lone Star Limits: Depictions of Texas in German Travelogues from 1830–1860," in *Deutschland und die USA im Vor- und Nachmärz: Politik—Literatur—Wissenschaft*, edited by Birgit Bublies-Godau and Anne Meyer-Eisenhut (Bielefeld: Aisthesis, 2018), 235–253.

I dedicated my first book to my parents. This one is for my sister, Kirsten.

Notes

Introduction
1. The epigraphs to the introduction are from Humboldt, *Briefe*, 307–308, and Humboldt, *Political Essay*, 2:231.

Chapter 1. Assessing El Norte
1. All references to texts originally written in another language are cited and referred to here in the published English versions, except for passages or texts for which no English edition exists. All English translations from these passages or texts are by the author.

2. This is the only publication of Berlandier's original French manuscript, "Voyage au Mexique par Louis Berlandier pendant les années 1826 à 1834" (Muller xii–xiv). The text also covers the writer's abandoned trip to Nacogdoches (April–June 1828) and his excursions from San Antonio to Goliad and the coast, which are not included in the *Diario* (February–May 1829).

3. The Spanish-language version of the published diary covers only the journey from the Rio Trinidad to Nacogdoches (late May to early June 1828).

4. The English translation of Sánchez's text lacks the passages describing the boundary commission's journey from Mexico City to Laredo, which are not relevant for the present study (*Viaje* 4–17).

5. The use of "which" to refer to the slaves in the English-language edition conveys their chattel status, which the Spanish original formulation, "lo más de ellos" (*Viaje* 49), does not.

6. Interestingly, the English translation omits the most neutral of these passages ("Statistical" 67–68; *Noticia* 68).

Chapter 2. Charting the Land
1. The *Congressional Record* and first book editions of the Red River report also contain several scientific appendices—not relevant to the present study—that are not included in *Adventure on Red River* (Foreman xiv–xvi). Moreover, the map in the book does not fit with Marcy's text (Marcy, *Adventure* 94n4; Morris 277).

Chapter 3. A Place for Southerners
1. Ramón Musquiz to the governor of Coahuila y Texas, November 7, 1828, Nacogdoches Archives 45:147, Dolph Briscoe Center for American History, University of Texas at Austin.

Chapter 4. America's Italy
1. The organization is also known as "Adelsverein" ("Society of Nobles"), "Mainzer Verein" ("Mainz Society"), "Texasverein" ("Texas Society"), or simply as the "Verein."

2. To avoid confusion, the English edition of the book will be cited as *Texas*, the German as *Handbuch*.

3. The words in square brackets are missing in the English edition and have been added from the German original (*Handbuch* 32).

4. The English edition of his book bends Solms's attitude to the Texas Revolution toward an American viewpoint by translating the phrase that Texas had "broken away from the mother country" (*Handbuch* 1) as having "shaken off the Mexican yoke" (*Texas* 13).

5. Solms to Count Carl of Castell, May 18, June 4, and June 19, 1844, and to William Kennedy, December 3, 1844, Solms-Braunfels Archives, Dolph Briscoe Center for American History, University of Texas, at Austin, box 2Q 380, vol. 49: 112–113, 118–119, 121–123, 127, and box 2Q 358, vol. 1: 226–231.

6. Solms to Count Carl of Castell, July 4 and 15, 1844, Solms-Braunfels Archives, box 2Q 380, vol. 49: 150, 153.

7. The English translation of Roemer's book does not contain the appendix, and none of the reprint editions contains the map. Neither document is relevant to the present study.

8. Interestingly, Roemer's German text speaks of African Americans as "Negroes," thus downplaying their slave status, whereas the English edition uses "(black) slaves," relying on reader's familiarity with the racialization of American slavery (Roemer, *Texas* 40; Roemer, *Roemer's Texas* 31).

Chapter 5. Newcomers' Plight

1. The poetic quality of the passage is even stronger in the German text's onomatopoetic alliteration of "schnell schmarotzende, schleichende Schlingpflanzen" (Thran 52).

Conclusion

1. Melinda Rankin, unidentified article in the *Texas Presbyterian*, January 15, 1848, cited in "Melinda Rankin," Dolph Briscoe Center for American History, University of Texas at Austin, Melinda Rankin Vertical Files, 4.

Works Cited

Adelman, Jeremy, and Stephen Aron. "From Borderlands to Borders: Empires, Nation-States, and the Peoples in Between in North American History." *American Historical Review* 104, no. 3 (June 1999): 814–841.

Allen, Martha Mitten. *Traveling West: 19th Century Women on the Overland Routes*. El Paso: Texas Western, 1987.

Almonte, Juan Nepomuceno. "Informe secreto sobre la presente situación de Texas, 1834." Appendix B in *Como México perdió Texas: Análisis y transcripción del informe secreto (1834) de Juan Nepomuceno Almonte*, edited by Celia Gutiérrez Ibarra, 5–37. Mexico City: INAH, 1987.

———. *Noticia estadística sobre Tejas*. 1835. In *Northern Mexico on the Eve of the United States Invasion: Rare Imprints Concerning California, Arizona, New Mexico, and Texas, 1821–1846*, edited by David J. Weber, 2–96. New York: Arno, 1976.

———. "Secret Report on the Present Situation in Texas 1834." Translated by John Wheat. In *Almonte's Texas: Juan N. Almonte's 1834 Inspection, Secret Report and Role in the 1836 Campaign*, edited by Jack Jackson, 210–262. Austin: Texas State Historical Association and Center for Studies in Texas History, University of Texas at Austin, 2003.

———. "Statistical Report of Texas." Translated by Carlos E. Castañeda. *Southwestern Historical Quarterly* 28, no. 3 (January 1925): 177–222.

Austin, Stephen F. "Descriptions of Texas by Stephen F. Austin." 1828–1833. Edited by Eugene C. Barker. *Southwestern Historical Quarterly* 28, no. 2 (October 1924): 98–121.

———. "Journal of Stephen F. Austin on His First Trip to Texas, 1821." *Quarterly of the Texas State Historical Association* 7, no. 4 (April 1904): 286–307.

Baker, T. Lindsay, and Julie P. Baker, eds. *Till Freedom Cried Out: Memories of Texas Slave Life*. College Station: Texas A&M University Press, 1997.

Banker, Mark T. *Presbyterian Missions and Cultural Interaction in the Far Southwest, 1850–1950*. Urbana: University of Illinois Press, 1993.

Barton, Paul. *Hispanic Methodists, Presbyterians, and Baptists in Texas*. Austin: University of Texas Press, 2006.

Bauer, Ralph. "Hemispheric Studies." *PMLA* 124, no. 1 (2009): 234–250.

Baym, Nina. *Women Writers of the American West, 1833–1927*. Urbana: University of Illinois Press, 2011.

Benson, Nettie Lee. "Texas as Viewed from Mexico, 1820–1834." *Southwestern Historical Quarterly* 90, no. 3 (January 1987): 219–291.

Berkhofer, Robert F. *The White Man's Indian: Images of the American Indian from Columbus to the Present*. New York: Vintage, 1979.

Berlandier, Jean Louis. *Journey to Mexico during the Years 1826 to 1834*. Edited by C. H. Muller. Translated by Sheila M. Ohlendorf, Josette M. Bigelow, and Mary M. Standifer. 2 vols. Austin: Texas State Historical Association and Center for Studies in Texas History, University of Texas at Austin, 1980.

Berlandier, Luis [Jean Louis], with Rafael Chovell. *Diario de viaje de la Comisión de Límites*.

1850. Edited by David Eduardo Vázquez Salguero. San Luis Potosí: El Colegio de San Luis and Universidad Autónoma de San Luis, 2010.

Beveridge, Charles E. Introduction to *The Papers of Frederick Law Olmsted*. Vol. 2: *Slavery and the South, 1852–1857*, 1–39 Baltimore: Johns Hopkins University Press, 1981.

Beveridge, Charles E., and Charles Capen McLaughlin, eds. *The Papers of Frederick Law Olmsted*. Vol. 2: *Slavery and the South, 1852–1857*. Baltimore: Johns Hopkins University Press, 1981.

Birk, Johanna. *Mexiko in Berichten deutscher Reisender: Die kulturelle Wahrnehmung um 1830*. Halle/Saale, Germany: GILCAL, 2008.

Birkle, Carmen. "Travelogues of Independence: Margaret Fuller and Henry David Thoreau." *Amerikastudien / American Studies* 48, no. 4 (2003): 497–512.

Blanton, Casey. *Travel Writing: The Self and the World*. New York: Routledge, 2002.

Brenner, Peter J. *Reisen in die "Neue Welt": Die Erfahrung Nordamerikas in deutschen Reise- und Auswandererberichten des 19. Jahrhunderts*. Tübingen: Niemeyer, 1991.

Brister, Louis E. "Eduard Ludecus's Journey to the Texas Frontier: A Critical Account of Beales's Rio Grande Colony." *Southwestern Historical Quarterly* 108, no. 3 (January 2005): 369–385.

———. Introduction to *John Charles Beales's Rio Grande Colony: Letters by Eduard Ludecus, a German Colonist, to Friends in Germany in 1833–1834, Recounting His Journey, Trials, and Observations in Early Texas*, by Eduard Ludecus, ix–xvii. Austin: Texas State Historical Association, 2008.

Brose, Eric Dorn. *German History, 1789–1871: From the Holy Roman Empire to the Bismarckian Reich*. Providence, RI: Berghahn, 1997.

Brown, Sharon Rogers. *American Travel Narratives as a Literary Genre from 1542 to 1832: The Art of a Perpetual Journey*. Lewiston, NY: Mellen, 1993.

Bryan, Jimmy L., Jr. *The American Elsewhere: Adventure and Manliness in the Age of Expansion*. Lawrence: University Press of Kansas, 2017.

Callahan, Generosa. "The Literature of Travel in Texas, 1803–1846: An Analysis of Ideas and Attitudes." PhD diss., University of Texas at Austin, 1945.

Campbell, Randolph B. *An Empire for Slavery: The Peculiar Institution in Texas*. Baton Rouge: Louisiana State University Press, 2013.

———. *Gone to Texas: A History of the Lone Star State*. New York: Oxford University Press, 2003.

Campbell, Robin Dell. *Mistresses of the Transient Hearth: American Army Officers' Wives and Material Culture, 1840–1880*. New York: Routledge, 2005.

Campos-Farfán, César. *General Juan N. Almonte: Insurgente, liberal y conservador—Ensayo biográfico*. Morelia, Mexico: Casa Natal de Morelos, 2001.

Cañizares-Esguerra, Jorge, and Benjamin Breen. "Hybrid Atlantics: Future Directions for the History of the Atlantic World." *History Compass* 11, no. 8 (2013): 597–609.

Cantrell, Greg. *Stephen F. Austin: Empresario of Texas*. New Haven, CT: Yale University Press, 1999.

Carballo, Emmanuel. Prologue to *¿Qué país es este? Los Estados Unidos y los gringos vistos por escritores mexicanos de los siglos XIX y XX*. Edited by Emmanuel Carballo. Mexico City: CONACULTA, 1996.

Castañeda, Carlos Eduardo. "Review of *Viaje a Texas en 1828–1829* by José María Sánchez." *Hispanic American Historical Review* 23, no. 1 (February 1943): 111–112.

Caughfield, Adrienne. *True Women and Westward Expansion*. College Station: Texas A&M University Press, 2005.

Cazneau, Jane McManus [Cora Montgomery]. *Eagle Pass; or, Life on the Border*. 1852. Edited by Robert Crawford Cotner. Austin: Pemberton, 1966.

———. [Cora Montgomery]. *Texas and Her Presidents: With a Glance at Her Climate and Agricultural Capabilities*. 1845. Charleston, SC: Nabu Press, 2012.

Chavez, Thomas, Jr. *Texas American Presbyterians*. Midland, TX: First Presbyterian Church Press, 1980.

Clifford, James. *Routes: Travel and Translation in the Late Twentieth Century*. Cambridge, MA: Harvard University Press, 1997.

Cox, John D. *Traveling South: Travel Narratives and the Construction of American Identity*. Athens: University of Georgia Press, 2005.

Crang, Mike. *Cultural Geography*. London: Routledge, 1998.

Davis, Graham. *Land! Irish Pioneers in Mexican and Revolutionary Texas*. College Station: Texas A&M University Press, 2002.

DeLay, Brian. *War of a Thousand Deserts: Indian Raids and the U.S.-Mexican War*. New Haven, CT: Yale University Press, 2008.

Doolen, Andy. *Territories of Empire: U.S. Writing from the Louisiana Purchase to Mexican Independence*. New York: Oxford University Press, 2014.

Doughty, Robin W. *At Home in Texas: Early Views of the Land*. College Station: Texas A&M University Press, 1987.

Dunt, Detlef. *Journey to Texas, 1833*. Translated by Anders Saustrup. Edited by James C. Kearney and Geir Bentzen. Austin: University of Texas Press, 2015.

———. *Reise nach Texas, nebst Nachrichten von diesem Lande für Deutsche, welche nach Amerika zu gehen beabsichtigen*. Bremen: Wiehe, 1834.

Ette, Ottmar. *Literature on the Move*. Translated by Katharina Vester. Amsterdam: Rodopi, 2003.

Fehr, Kregg. "Red Traces: Randolph B. Marcy's Explorations of a Hostile Land." In *Tales of Texoma: Episodes in the History of the Red River Border*, edited by Michael L. Collins, 1–25. Wichita Falls, TX: Midwestern State University Press, 2005.

Fenske, Hans. "Ungeduldige Zuschauer: Die Deutschen und die europäische Expansion 1815–1880." In *Imperialistische Kontinuität und nationale Ungeduld im 19. Jahrhundert*, edited by Wolfgang Reinhard, 87–123. Frankfurt/Main: Fischer, 1991.

Finke, Roger, and Rodney Stark. *The Churching of America, 1776–1990: Winners and Losers in Our Religious Economy*. 2nd ed. New Brunswick, NJ: Rutgers University Press, 2005.

Finney, Gail. *The Counterfeit Idyll: The Garden Ideal and Social Reality in Nineteenth-Century Fiction*. Tübingen: Niemeyer, 1984.

Fisher, Orceneth. *Sketches of Texas in 1840, Designed to Answer, in a Brief Way, the Numerous Enquiries Respecting the New Republic, as to Situation, Extent, Climate, Soil, Productions, Water, Government, Society, Religion, etc.* 1840. Edited by James M. Day. Waco, TX: Texian, 1964.

Foreman, Grant. Introduction to *Adventure on Red River: Report on the Exploration of the Headwaters of the Red River*, by Randolph Barnes Marcy and George Brinton McClellan, v–xxii. Edited by Grant Foreman. Norman: University of Oklahoma Press, 1968.

Fox, Claire, and Claudia Sadowski-Smith. "Theorizing the Hemisphere: Inter-Americas Work at the Intersection of American, Canadian, and Latin American Studies." *Comparative American Studies* 2, no. 1 (March 2004): 5–38.

Francaviglia, Richard V. *The Cast Iron Forest: A Natural and Cultural History of the Cross Timbers*. Austin: University of Texas Press, 2000.

———. *Go East, Young Man: Imagining the American West as the Orient*. Logan: Utah State University Press, 2011.

Fritz, Christian G. *American Sovereigns: The People and America's Constitutional Tradition before the Civil War*. New York: Cambridge University Press, 2008.

Gabbaccia, Donna. "A Long Atlantic in a Wider World." *Atlantic Studies* 1, no. 1 (2004): 1–27.

Geiser, Samuel Wood. *Naturalists of the Frontier.* 2nd ed. Dallas: Southern Methodist University Press, 1948.

Georgi-Findlay, Brigitte. *The Frontiers of Women's Writing: Women's Narratives and the Rhetoric of Westward Expansion.* Tucson: University of Arizona Press, 1996.

Geue, Chester William, and Ethel Hander Geue. *A New Land Beckoned: German Immigration to Texas, 1844–1847.* 2nd ed. Baltimore: Clearfield, 2002.

Gibson, Charles. Introduction to *The Black Legend: Anti-Spanish Attitudes in the Old World and the New,* 3–27. Edited by Charles Gibson. New York: Knopf, 1971.

Göbel, Volker W., and Helga Stein. "Ferdinand Roemers Reise nach Nordamerika 1845–1847." In *Gesammelte Welten: Das Erbe der Brüder Roemer und die Museumskultur in Hildesheim, 1844–1994,* 337–392. Festschrift zum 150jährigen Bestehen des Hildesheimer Museumsvereins. Edited by Rudolf W. Keck. Hildesheim, Germany: Gerstenberg, 1998.

Goetzmann, William H. *Army Exploration in the American West, 1803–1863.* Rev. ed. Austin: Texas State Historical Association, 1991.

———. *Exploration and Empire: The Explorer and the Scientist in the Winning of the American West.* 1966. New York: History Book Club, 2003.

———. *New Lands, New Men: America and the Second Great Age of Discovery.* 1986. Austin: Texas State Historical Association, 1995.

Gonzales, Manuel G. *Mexicanos: A History of Mexicans in the United States.* 2nd ed. Bloomington: Indiana University Press, 2009.

González Navarro, Moisés. *Los extranjeros en México y los mexicanos en el extranjero, 1821–1970.* Vol. 1: *1821–1867.* Mexico City: El Colegio de México, 1993.

González-Quiroga, Miguel Ángel, and Timothy Paul Bowman. Introduction to *Twenty Years among the Mexicans: A Narrative of Missionary Labor,* by Melinda Rankin, ix–xxxi. 1875. Edited by Miguel Ángel González-Quiroga and Timothy Paul Bowman. Dallas: DeGolyer Library and William P. Clements Center for Southwest Studies, Southern Methodist University, 2008.

Görisch, Stephan W. *Information zwischen Werbung und Warnung: Die Rolle der Amerikaliteratur in der Auswanderung des 18. und 19. Jahrhunderts.* Darmstadt, Germany: Hessische Historische Kommission, 1991.

Greenberg, Amy. *Manifest Manhood and the Antebellum American Empire.* Cambridge: Cambridge University Press, 2005.

Greenblatt, Stephen. *Marvelous Possessions: The Wonder of the New World.* 2nd ed. Chicago: University of Chicago Press, 2017.

Greenfield, Bruce Robert. *Narrating Discovery: The Romantic Explorer in American Literature, 1790–1855.* New York: Columbia University Press, 1992.

Griffin, Megan Jenison. "Partisan Rhetorics: American Women's Responses to the U.S.-Mexico War, 1846–1848." PhD diss., Texas Christian University Press, 2010. https://repository.tcu.edu/handle/116099117/4234.

Gründer, Horst. *Christliche Heilsbotschaft und weltliche Macht: Studien zum Verhältnis von Mission und Kolonialismus.* Edited by Franz-Joseph Post, Thomas Küster, and Clemens Sorgenfrei. Münster: Lit, 2004.

Gutiérrez Ibarra, Celia. *Como México perdió Texas: Análisis y transcripción del informe secreto (1834) de Juan Nepomuceno Almonte.* Mexico City: INAH, 1987.

Haas, Astrid. "Between Monroe Doctrine and Manifest Destiny: Spanish American Travel Narratives of Jacksonian America." In *Mobile Narratives: Travel, Migration, and Transculturation,* edited by Eleftheria Arapoglou, Mónika Fodor, and Jopi Nyman, 30–42. New York: Routledge, 2014.

———. "Mexican Travelers and the 'Texas Question,' 1821–1836." In *Hemispheric Encounters: The Early United States in a Transnational Perspective*, edited by Gabriele Pisarz-Ramírez and Markus Heide, 117–132. Frankfurt/Main: Peter Lang, 2016.

———. "Nature, Natives, and Nativism in Gideon Lincecum's Travelogues of Texas." In *Traveling, Narrating, Comparing: Travel Narratives of the Americas from the 18th to the 20th Century*, edited by Julian Gärtner and Marius Littschwager. Göttingen: Vandenhoeck & Ruprecht, 2021.

———. "Prairie Promises, Lone Star Limits: Depictions of Texas in German Travelogues from 1830–1860." In *Deutschland und die USA im Vor- und Nachmärz: Politik—Literatur—Wissenschaft*, edited by Birgit Bublies-Godau and Anne Meyer-Eisenhut, 235–253. Bielefeld: Aisthesis, 2018.

Hämäläinen, Pekka. *The Comanche Empire*. New Haven, CT: Yale University Press; Dallas: William P. Clements Center for Southwest Studies, Southern Methodist University, 2008.

Hämäläinen, Pekka, and Samuel Truett. "On Borderlands." *Journal of American History* 98, no. 2 (September 2011): 338–361.

Helbich, Wolfgang: "Land der unbegrenzten Möglichkeiten? Das Amerika-Bild der deutschen Auswanderer im 19. Jahrhundert." In *Deutschland und der Westen im 19. und 20. Jahrhundert*, vol. 1, *Transatlantische Beziehungen*, edited by Jürgen Elvert, 295–321. Stuttgart: Steiner, 1993.

Hernández, José Angel. "From Conquest to Colonization: *Indios* and Colonization Policies after Mexican Independence." *Mexican Studies / Estudios Mexicanos* 26, no. 2 (Summer 2010): 291–322.

Hoerig, Karl A. "The Relationship between German Immigrants and the Native Peoples in Western Texas." *Southwestern Historical Quarterly* 97, no. 3 (January 1994): 423–451.

Holley, Mary Austin. *Letters of an Early American Traveller: Mary Austin Holley, Her Life and Her Works, 1784–1846*. Edited by Mattie Austin Hatcher. Dallas: Southwest Press, 1933.

———. *Texas*. 1836. Edited by Marilyn McAdams Sibley. Austin: Texas State Historical Association, 1990.

———. *The Texas Diary, 1835–1838*. Edited by J. P. Bryan. Austin: Humanities Research Center, University of Texas at Austin, 1965.

———. *Texas: Observations, Historical, Geographical and Descriptive, in a Series of Letters, Written During a Visit to Austin's Colony, with a View to a Permanent Settlement in That Country, in the Autumn of 1831*. 1833. London: British Library, 2010.

Hollon, W. Eugene. *Beyond the Cross Timbers: The Travels of Randolph B. Marcy, 1812–1887*. Norman: University of Oklahoma Press, 1955.

Honeck, Mischa. *We Are the Revolutionists: German-Speaking Immigrants and American Abolitionists after 1848*. Athens: University of Georgia Press, 2011.

Hudson, Linda S. *Mistress of Manifest Destiny: A Biography of Jane McManus Storms Cazneau, 1807–1878*. Austin: Texas State Historical Association, 2001.

Humboldt, Alexander von. *Briefe aus Amerika, 1799–1804*, edited by Ulrike Noheit. Berlin: Akademie-Verlag, 1993.

———. *Political Essay on the Kingdom of New Spain*. 1811. Vol. 2. Translated from the French by John Black. Edited by Mary Maples Dunn. New York: Knopf, 1972.

Hume, Brad D. "The Romantic and the Technical in Early Nineteenth-Century American Exploration." In *Surveying the Record: North American Scientific Exploration to 1930*, edited by Edward G. Carter III, 301–316. Philadelphia: American Philosophical Society, 1999.

Huntzicker, William E. *The Popular Press, 1833–1865*. Westport, CT: Greenwood, 1999.

Hyde, Anne Farrar. *An American Vision: Far Western Landscapes and National Culture, 1820–1920*. New York: New York University Press, 1990.

Jackson, Jack, ed. *Almonte's Texas: Juan N. Almonte's 1834 Inspection, Secret Report and Role in the 1836 Campaign*. Translated by John Wheat. Austin: Texas State Historical Association and Center for Studies in Texas History, University of Texas at Austin, 2003.

———. Introduction to *Texas by Terán: The Diary Kept by General Manuel de Mier y Terán on His 1828 Inspection of Texas*, edited by Jack Jackson, 1–39, 201–209. Austin: University of Texas Press, 2000.

James, Joshua, and Alexander MacRae. *A Journal of a Tour in Texas with Observations on the Laws, Government, State of Society, Soil, etc. by the Agents of the Wilmington Emigrating Society*. Wilmington, NC: Loring, 1835.

Johnston, Eliza. "The Diary of Eliza (Mrs. Albert Sidney) Johnston: The Second Cavalry Comes to Texas." Edited by Charles P. Roland and Richard C. Robbins. *Southwestern Historical Quarterly* 60, no. 4 (April 1957): 463–500.

Kaplan, Amy. *The Anarchy of Empire in the Making of U.S. Culture*. Cambridge, MA: Harvard University Press, 2002.

Kearney, James C. *Nassau Plantation: The Evolution of a Texas-German Slave Plantation*. Denton: University of North Texas Press, 2010.

Kearney, James C., and Geir Bentzen. Introduction to *Journey to Texas, 1833*, by Detlef Dunt. Translated by Anders Saustrup. Edited by James C. Kearney and Geir Bentzen, 1–23. Austin: University of Texas Press, 2015.

Kerrigan, William T. "Race, Expansion, and Slavery in Eagle Pass, Texas, 1852." *Southwestern Historical Quarterly* 101, no. 3 (January 1998): 275–301.

Kökény, Andrea. "Travellers and Settlers in Mexican Texas." In *Acta Universitatis Szegediensis: Acta Hispanica*, vol. 7, edited by Ádám Anderle, 97–108. Szeged, Hungary: Department of Hispanic Studies, University of Szeged, 2002.

Kolodny, Annette. *The Land before Her: Fantasy and Experience of the American Frontiers, 1630–1860*. Chapel Hill: University of North Carolina Press, 1984.

Kraut, Alan M. *Silent Travelers: Germs, Genes, and the "Immigrant Menace."* New York: Basic Books, 1994.

Kunow, Rüdiger. "Going Native with God on the Side: Mission as Traveling Culture." *FIAR: Forum for Inter-American Research* 6, no. 1 (May 2013). http://interamerica.de/current-issue/kunow.

Lagarde, François. *The French in Texas: History, Migration, Culture*. Austin: University of Texas Press, 2003.

LaVere, David. *The Texas Indians*. College Station: Texas A&M University Press, 2004.

Lawson, Russell M. *Frontier Naturalist: Jean Louis Berlandier and the Exploration of Northern Mexico and Texas*. Albuquerque: University of New Mexico Press, 2012.

Ledbetter, Robert Edgar, Jr. "Orceneth Fisher, Pioneer Methodist Preacher of Texas and the Pacific Coast." Master's thesis, University of Texas at Austin, 1938.

Lee, Rebecca Smith. *Mary Austin Holley: A Biography*. Austin: University of Texas Press, 1962.

LeMenager, Stephanie. *Manifest and Other Destinies: Territorial Fictions of the Nineteenth-Century United States*. Lincoln: University of Nebraska Press, 2004.

Lockard, Joe. *Watching Slavery: Witness Texts and Travel Reports*. New York: Peter Lang, 2008.

López, Marissa. "The Sentimental Politics of Language: Ralph Waldo Emerson and José

María Sánchez's Texas Diaries." *Western American Literature* 45 (Winter 2011): 384–409.

Ludecus, Eduard. *John Charles Beales's Rio Grande Colony: Letters by Eduard Ludecus, a German Colonist, to Friends in Germany in 1833–1834, Recounting His Journey, Trials, and Observations in Early Texas.* Translated and edited by Louis E. Brister. Austin: Texas State Historical Association, 2008.

———. *Reise durch die mexikanischen Provinzen Tumalipas, Cohahuila und Texas im Jahre 1834: In Briefen an seine Freunde.* 1837. Charleston, SC: Nabu, 2012.

Machann, Clinton, and James W. Mendl. *Krásná Amerika: A Study of the Texas Czechs, 1851–1939.* Austin: Eakin, 1983.

Mackenthun, Gesa. "Encountering Colonialism: A Transnational View of 'Colonial America.'" In *Colonial Encounters: Essays in Early American History and Culture,* edited by Hans-Jürgen Grabbe, 1–27. Heidelberg: Winter, 2003.

Marcy, Randolph B. *Report of an Expedition to the Sources of the Brazos and Big Witchita Rivers, During the Summer of 1854.* US Sen. Exec. Doc. 60, 34th Cong., 1st sess., 1856. Available at Readex Archive of Americana: U.S. Congressional Serial Set, 1817–1994, http://infoweb.newsbank.com (subscription required).

Marcy, Randolph B., and George Brinton McClellan. *Adventure on Red River: Report on the Exploration of the Headwaters of the Red River.* 1854. Edited by Grant Foreman. Norman: University of Oklahoma Press, 1968.

Marx, Leo. *The Machine in the Garden: Technology and the Pastoral Ideal in America.* 1964. New York: Oxford University Press, 2000.

Mauch, Christof. "Zwischen Edelmut und Rohheit: Indianer und Schwarze aus deutscher Perspektive: Sichtweisen des 19. Jahrhunderts." *Amerikastudien / American Studies* 40, no. 4 (1995): 619–636.

May, Robert E. "'Plenipotentiary in Petticoats': Jane M. Cazneau and American Foreign Policy in the Mid-Nineteenth Century." In *Women and American Foreign Policy: Lobbyists, Critics, and Insiders,* edited by Edward P. Crapol, 19–44. Wilmington, DE: Scholarly Resources, 1992.

Mayhall, Mildred Pickle. "Eliza Griffin Johnston." In *Texas Wildflowers,* by Eliza Griffin Johnston, xvii–xl. Austin: Shoal Creek, 1972.

McDougall, Walter A. *Promised Land, Crusader State: The American Encounter with the World since 1776.* Boston: Houghton Mifflin, 1997.

Mier y Terán, Manuel de. "Fragmento del diario de Manuel de Mier y Terán." In *Crónica de Tejas: Diario de viaje de la Comisión de Límites,* edited by Mauricio Molina, 119–128. Mexico City: Gobierno del Estado de Tamaulipas et al., 1988.

———. *Reflexiones a la ley del 6 de abril de 1830: Transcripción de los documentos sobre Texas del general Manuel de Mier y Terán, y del informe realizado por Constantino de Tarnava.* Edited by Celia Gutiérrez Ibarra. Mexico City: BNAH-INAH, 1991.

———. "Texas by Terán, His Journey, 1828." In *Texas by Terán: The Diary Kept by General Manuel de Mier y Terán on His 1828 Inspection of Texas,* edited by Jack Jackson, 41–174. Translated by John Wheat. Austin: University of Texas Press, 2000.

Mignolo, Walter D. *Local Histories, Global Designs: Coloniality, Subaltern Knowledges, and Border Thinking.* Princeton, NJ: Princeton University Press, 2000.

Millett, Nathaniel. "Borderlands in the Atlantic World." *Atlantic Studies* 10, no. 2 (2013): 268–295.

Molina, Mauricio, ed. *Crónica de Tejas: Diario de viaje de la Comisión de Límites.* Mexico City: Gobierno del Estado de Tamaulipas et al., 1988.

Montejano, David. *Anglos and Mexicans in the Making of Texas, 1836–1986*. Austin: University of Texas Press, 1987.

Morgenthaler, Jefferson. *Promised Land: Solms, Castro, and Sam Houston's Colonization Contracts*. College Station: Texas A&M University Press, 2009.

Mörner, Magnus. "European Travelogues as Sources to Latin American History from the Late Eighteenth Century to 1870." *Revista de Historia de América* 93 (January–June 1982): 91–149.

Morris, John Miller. *El Llano Estacado: Exploration and Imagination on the High Plains of Texas and New Mexico, 1536–1860*. Austin: Texas State Historical Association, 1997.

Morton, Ohland. "The Life of Don Manuel de Mier y Terán." PhD. diss., University of Texas, 1939. Reprint, *Southwestern Historical Quarterly* 46–48 (July 1942–April 1945). Reprint, Whitefish, MT: Kessinger, 2010.

Moyano Pahissa, Angela. *La pérdida de Texas: Historia no oficial*. 2nd ed. Mexico City: Planeta, 1999.

Muller, C. H. Introduction to *Journey to Mexico during the Years 1826 to 1834*, by Jean Louis Berlandier, xi–xxxvi. Translated by Sheila M. Ohlendorf, Josette M. Bigelow, and Mary M. Standifer. Vol. 1. Austin: Texas State Historical Association and Center for Studies in Texas History, University of Texas at Austin, 1980.

Myres, Sandra L. "Army Women's Narratives as Documents of Social History: Some Examples from the Western Frontier." *New Mexico Historical Review* 65, no. 2 (April 1990): 175–198.

———. *Westering Women and the Frontier Experience, 1800–1915*. Rev. ed. Albuquerque: University of New Mexico Press, 1993.

———. "Women and the Texas Military Experience: The Nineteenth Century." In *The Texas Military Experience: From the Texas Revolution through World War II*, edited by Joseph G. Dawson III, 97–112. College Station: Texas A&M University Press, 1995.

Nielssen, Hilde, Inger Marie Okkenhaug, and Karina Hestad Skeie. Introduction to *Protestant Missions and Local Encounters in the Nineteenth and Twentieth Centuries: Unto the Ends of the World*, edited by Hilde Nielssen, Inger Marie Okkenhaug, and Karina Hestad Skeie, 1–22. Leiden: Brill, 2011.

Nünning, Ansgar. "Zur Präfiguration/Prämediation der Wirklichkeitsdarstellung im Reisebericht: Grundzüge einer narratologischen Theorie, Typologie und Poetik der Reiseliteratur." In *Points of Arrival: Travels in Time, Space, and Self / Zielpunkte: Unterwegs in Zeit, Raum und Selbst*, edited by Marion Gymnich et al., 11–32. Tübingen: Francke, 2008.

Olmsted, Frederick Law. *A Journey through Texas; or, A Saddle-Trip on the South-Western Frontier*. 1857. Lincoln: University of Nebraska Press, 2004.

Oo-Chee-Ah. "The Story of Sequoyah's Last Days." Edited by Grant Foreman. *Chronicle of Oklahoma* 12 (March 1934): 25–41.

Padget, Martin. "The Southwest and Travel Writing." In *The Cambridge Companion to American Travel Writing*, edited by Alfred Bendixen and Judith Hamera, 78–99. Cambridge: Cambridge University Press, 2009.

Paredes, Raymund A. "The Mexican Image in American Travel Literature, 1831–1869." *New Mexico Historical Review* 52, no. 1 (January 1977): 5–29.

Parker, William B. *Through Unexplored Texas: Notes Taken during the Expedition Commanded by Capt. R.B. Marcy, U.S.A., in the Summer and Fall of 1854*. 1856. Austin: Texas State Historical Association and Center for Studies in Texas History, University of Texas at Austin, 1990.

Paul, Heike. *Kulturkontakt und 'Racial Presence': Afro-Amerikaner und die deutsche Amerika-Literatur, 1815–1914*. Heidelberg: Winter, 2005.

Pawel, Robert. "Getreide und Hülsenfrüchte kamen aus Rußland." *Preußische Allgemeine Zeitung*, May 1, 1982, 12. http://archiv.preussische-allgemeine.de/1982/1982_05 _01_18.pdf.

Ponko, Vincent, Jr. "The Military Explorers of the American West, 1838–1860." In *North American Exploration*. Vol. 3, *A Continent Comprehended*, ed. John Logan Allen, 332–411. Lincoln: University of Nebraska Press, 1997.

Pratt, Mary Louise. *Imperial Eyes: Travel Writing and Transculturation.* 2nd ed. London: Routledge, 2008.

Quijano, Aníbal. "Coloniality and Modernity/Rationality." *Cultural Studies* 21, nos. 2–3 (March–May 2007): 168–178.

Rajchenberg S., Enrique, and Catherine Héau-Lambert. "La frontera en la comunidad imaginada del siglo XIX." *Frontera Norte* 19, no. 38 (July–December 2007): 37–61.

———. "¿*Wilderness* vs. desierto? Representaciones del septentrión mexicano en el siglo XIX." *Norteamérica* 4, no. 2 (July–December 2009): 15–36.

Rankin, Melinda. *Texas in 1850.* 1850. Edited by John C. Rayburn. Waco, TX: Texian, 1966.

———. *Twenty Years among the Mexicans: A Narrative of Missionary Labor.* 1875. Edited by Miguel Ángel González-Quiroga and Timothy Paul Bowman. Dallas: DeGolyer Library and William P. Clements Center for Southwest Studies, Southern Methodist University, 2008.

Renda, Mary A. "Conclusion: Religion, Race, and Empire in U.S. Protestant Women's Missionary Enterprise, 1812–1960." In *Competing Kingdoms: Women, Mission, Nation, and the American Protestant Empire, 1812–1960,* edited by Barbara Rees-Ellington, Kathryn Kish Sklar, and Connie A. Shemo, 367–389. Durham, NC: Duke University Press, 2010.

Rese, Beate. *Texas—Ziel deutscher Auswanderung im 19. Jahrhundert.* Pfaffenweiler, Germany: Centaurus, 1996.

Reséndez, Andrés. *Changing National Identities at the Frontier: Texas and New Mexico, 1800–1850.* Cambridge: Cambridge University Press, 2004.

Rifkin, Mark. *Manifesting America: The Imperial Construction of U.S. National Space.* New York: Oxford University Press, 2009.

Ritzenhofen, Ute. *Amerikas Italien: Deutsche Texasbilder des 19. Jahrhunderts.* Frankfurt am Main: Peter Lang, 1997.

Roberson, Susan L. *Antebellum American Women Writers and the Road: American Mobilities.* New York: Routledge, 2010.

Roemer, Ferdinand. *Roemer's Texas: With Particular Reference to German Immigration and the Physical Appearance of the Country.* Translated by Oswald Mueller. San Marcos: German-Texan Heritage Society and Department of Modern Languages, Southwest Texas State University, 1983.

———. *Texas: Mit besonderer Rücksicht auf deutsche Auswanderung und die physischen Verhältnisse des Landes nach eigener Betrachtung geschildert.* 1849. London: British Library, 2010.

———. "Dr. Ferdinand Roemer's Account of the Llano–San Saba County." Translated and edited by Rudolph L. Biesele. *Southwestern Historical Quarterly* 62, no. 1 (July 1958): 71–77.

Roland, Charles Pierce. *Albert Sidney Johnston: Soldier of Three Republics.* Lexington: University Press of Kentucky, 2001.

Rybczynski, Witold. *A Clearing in the Distance: Frederick Law Olmsted and America in the Nineteenth Century.* New York: Scribner, 1999.

Said, Edward W. *Culture and Imperialism*. New York: Vintage, 1994.

———. *Orientalism*. Harmondsworth, UK: Penguin, 2003.

Sánchez, José María. "A Trip to Texas in 1828." Translated by Carlos E. Castañeda. *Southwestern Historical Quarterly* 29, no. 4 (April 1926): 249–295.

———. *Viaje a Texas en 1828–1829: Diario del teniente don José María Sánchez, miembro de la Comisión de Límites*. Edited by Jorge Flores D. Mexico City: Papeles Históricos Mexicanos, 1939.

Saustrup, Anders. Appendix 3: Wolters-Achenbach. In *Journey to Texas, 1833*, by Detlef Dunt, translated by Anders Saustrup, edited by James C. Kearney and Geir Bentzen, 141–148. Austin: University of Texas Press, 2015.

Sayre, Gordon M. Introduction to *American Captivity Narratives: Olaudah Equiano, Mary Rowlandson, and Others; Selected Narratives with Introduction*, edited by Gordon M. Sayre, 1–17. Boston: Wadsworth, 2000.

Schloeman, Sophia Brown. *A Foundation Is Laid*. Gatesville, TX: Schloeman, 1968.

Scott, Larry E. *The Swedish Texans*. San Antonio: University of Texas Institute of Texan Cultures, 1990.

Sibley, Marilyn McAdams. *Travelers in Texas, 1761–1860*. Austin: University of Texas Press, 1967.

Smith, Henry Nash. *Virgin Land: The American West as Symbol and Myth*. 1950. Cambridge, MA: Harvard University Press, 1981.

Smith, Sherry Lynn. *The View from Officers' Row: Army Perceptions of Western Indians*. Tucson: University of Arizona Press, 1990.

Solms-Braunfels, Carl. *Texas, 1844–45*. Anonymous translation. Houston: Anson Jones Press, 1936.

———. *Texas, geschildert in Beziehung auf seine geographischen, socialen und übrigen Verhältnisse mit besonderer Rücksicht auf die deutsche Colonisation: Ein Handbuch für Auswanderer nach Texas*. 1846. Available at The Portal to Texas History, University of North Texas Libraries, http://texashistory.unt.edu/ark:/67531/metapth29393.

———. *Voyage to North America, 1844–45: Prince Carl of Solms's Texas Diary of People, Places, and Events*. Translated and edited by Wolfram M. Von-Maszewski. Denton: German-Texan Heritage Society and University of North Texas Press, 2000.

Spurr, David. *The Rhetoric of Empire: Colonial Discourse in Journalism, Travel Writing, and Colonial Administration*. Durham, NC: Duke University Press, 1993.

Struve, Walter. *Germans and Texans: Commerce, Migration, and Culture in the Days of the Lone Star Republic*. Austin: University of Texas Press, 1996.

Sundquist, Eric J. "Exploration and Empire." In *The Cambridge History of American Literature*, vol. 2, *1820–1865*, 127–174. Cambridge: Cambridge University Press, 1995.

Tate, Michael L. *The Frontier Army in the Settlement of the West*. Norman: University of Oklahoma Press, 1999.

Thran, Jakob. *Meine Auswanderung nach Texas unter dem Schutz des Mainzer Vereins: Ein Warnungsbeispiel für Auswanderungslustige*. Preface by August Theodor Woeniger. 1848. Staatsbibliothek zu Berlin, Preußischer Kulturbesitz, 2012. Available at http://digital.staatsbibliothek-berlin.de/dms/werkansicht/?PPN=PPN68768997X.

Torget, Andrew Jonathan. *Seeds of Empire: Cotton Slavery and the Transformation of the Texas Borderlands, 1800–1850*. Chapel Hill: University of North Carolina Press, 2015.

Torget, Andrew Jonathan, and Debbie Liles, eds. *The Digital Austin Papers*. Denton: University of North Texas, 2015–2020. http://digitalaustinpapers.org.

Trott, Nicola. "The Picturesque, the Beautiful and the Sublime." In *A Companion to Romanticism*, edited by Duncan Wu, 72–90. Malden, MA: Blackwell, 1999.

Tyler, Ron, and Lawrence R. Murphy, eds. *The Slave Narratives of Texas*. Austin: State House Press, 1997.

Vázquez Salguero, David Eduardo. "Un naturalista francés en México." In *Diario de viaje de la Comisión de Límites*, by Luis Berlandier and Rafael Chovell, edited by David Eduardo Vázquez Salguero, 9–48. San Luis Potosí: El Colegio de San Luis and Universidad Autónoma de San Luis, 2010.

Vázquez y Vera, Josefina Zoraida. *México y el expansionismo norteamericano*. Mexico City: El Colegio de México, 2010.

Velasco Ávila, Cuauhtémoc. "'Nuestros obstinados enemigos': Ideas e imágenes de los indios nómadas en la frontera noreste mexicana, 1821–1840." In *Nómadas y sedentarios en el norte de México: Homenaje a Beatriz Braniff*, edited by Marie-Areti Hers et al., 441–459. Mexico City: UNAM, 2000.

Vielé, Teresa Griffin. *Following the Drum: A Glimpse of Frontier Life*. 1858. Lincoln: University of Nebraska Press, 1984.

Ward, George B. Introduction to *Through Unexplored Texas, in the Summer and Fall of 1854*, by William B. Parker, xi–xiv. Austin: Texas State Historical Association and Center for Studies in Texas History, University of Texas at Austin, 1990.

Watson, Alan D. *Wilmington, North Carolina, to 1861*. Jefferson, NC: McFarland, 2003.

Weber, David J. *The Mexican Frontier, 1821–1846: The American Southwest under Mexico*. 4th ed. Albuquerque: University of New Mexico Press, 2001.

Weniger, Del. *The Explorers' Texas*. 2 vols. Austin: Eakin, 1984, 1997.

Index

abolitionism: Cazneau on, 167–168, 170;
Fisher on, 135; German migrants and,
81; Olmstead on, 177–178; Vielé on,
149, 152
Adventure on Red River (Marcy), 33–41
aesthetic discourse: Austin, 61–62; Johnston, 160; migration propaganda and,
53; Olmstead, 174–175; Rankin, 137;
Roemer and, 96–97; Sánchez on arcadia,
19–20. *See also* landscape aesthetics;
pastoral landscape ideal; romanticist
aesthetics
Africa, African American colonies in, 168
African Americans, enslaved. *See* slavery and
enslaved African Americans
agriculture: Berlandier on, 12; Fisher on,
134; Marcy on, 35, 39; Olmstead on,
174; Rankin on, 137; Roemer on, 96;
Solms-Braunfels on, 92–93; Thran on,
117. *See also* garden trope
Alabamas, 16
Almonte, Juan Nepomuceno, 23–30, 163
American colonists. *See* Anglo-Texans
Amerindian assimilation: Almonte on, 29;
assistance, military calls for, 5, 38; Berlandier on, 14–15, 18; Cazneau on, 169;
labels based on degrees of, 55, 98, 169;
Marcy on, 38; Mexican government and,
9; Olmstead on, 179; Romer on, 98
Amerindians: Almonte on, 28–29; associated with nature, 39, 42, 45, 114; Austin
on, 63–64; Berlandier on, 14–16; captivity narratives, xvii, 37, 43, 100–101,
171; Cazneau on, 170–172; Fisher on,
133; guides and scouts, 35; hierarchical
classification of, 5, 14, 22, 43; Holley
on, 72–73; Indian princess stereotype,
153; Johnston on, 158; Ludecus on,
108, 113–114; MacRae on, 76; Marcy
exploration for reservation land, 33–41;

Marcy on, 34–39; military-scientific
portrayals of, 4–6; Olmstead on, 178–
179; Parker on, 42–45; protection of,
38; Rankin on, 138, 141–142; removal,
relocation, and migration of, 18, 23, 28,
98–99, 158, 172; reservation law, Texas
(1854), 33; reservations, 33–41, 45, 48,
158, 172; Roemer on, 98–99; Sánchez
on, 22–23; Solms-Braunfels on, 88–89;
Terán on, 17–18; territorial claims of,
18; Thran on, 117–118; unequal exchange and, 89; vanishing Indian trope,
44; Vielé on, 152–153. *See also* raids,
Amerindian
Anglo-Texans: Almonte on, 26; Amerindians as barrier against, 29; Anglo-Tejano
relations, 31, 72; Berlandier on, 13–14;
Cazneau on, 172; Dunt on, 84; Fisher
on, 133; James on, 75–76; Johnston on,
159; Ludecus on, 110–111; MacRae
on, 77; numbers under Mexican rule, 9;
Olmstead on, 177, 181; Parker on, 45;
Rankin on, 137–138, 142; resistance
to Mexicanization, 26; Roemer on,
99–100; Sánchez on, 20–21; Solms-
Braunfels on, 89–90, 92; Texas Republic
and, 31; Thran on, 118; Vielé on, 148,
150–151, 155. *See also* migration/
colonization propaganda
anti-conquest discourse, 4, 6, 68
anti-Semitism, 182
Apaches. *See* Lipan Apaches
architecture: Anglo vs. Mexican houses,
150; Spanish colonial, 97, 150, 159
army officers' wives' accounts (US): about,
145–146; Johnston, 156–160; Vielé,
147–156. *See also* military, US
Audubon, John James, 3
Austin, Henry, 65, 66
Austin, Stephen: about, 60; Berlandier on,